THE MADNESS OF CROWDS

THE MADNESS OF CROWDS

Gender, Race and Identity

DOUGLAS MURRAY

BLOOMSBURY CONTINUUM
LONDON · OXFORD · NEW YORK · NEW DELHI · SYDNEY

BLOOMSBURY CONTINUUM
Bloomsbury Publishing Plc
50 Bedford Square, London, WC1B 3DP, UK

BLOOMSBURY, BLOOMSBURY CONTINUUM and the Diana logo are trademarks of
Bloomsbury Publishing Plc

First published in Great Britain 2019

Douglas Murray has asserted his right under the Copyright, Designs and
Patents Act, 1988, to be identified as Author of this work

Library of Congress Cataloguing-in-Publication data has been applied for

ISBN: HB: 978-1-63557-998-7; eBook: 978-1-63557-999-4

10 9

Typeset by Deanta Global Publishing Services, Chennai, India
Printed and bound in USA by Berryville Graphics Inc., Berryville, Virginia

Bloomsbury Publishing Plc makes every effort to ensure that the papers used in the
manufacture of our books are natural, recyclable products made from wood grown
in well-managed forests. Our manufacturing processes conform to the
environmental regulations of the country of origin.

To find out more about our authors and books visit www.bloomsbury.com and
sign up for our newsletters

CONTENTS

'The special mark of the modern world is not that it is sceptical, but that it is dogmatic without knowing it.'

G. K. Chesterton

'Oh my gosh, look at her butt
Oh my gosh, look at her butt
Oh my gosh, look at her butt
(Look at her butt)
Look at, look at, look at
Look, at her butt'

N. Minaj

INTRODUCTION

We are going through a great crowd derangement. In public and in private, both online and off, people are behaving in ways that are increasingly irrational, feverish, herd-like and simply unpleasant. The daily news cycle is filled with the consequences. Yet while we see the symptoms everywhere, we do not see the causes.

Various explanations have been given. These tend to suggest that any and all madnesses are the consequence of a Presidential election, or a referendum. But none of these explanations gets to the root of what is happening. For far beneath these day-to-day events are much greater movements and much bigger events. It is time we began to confront the true causes of what is going wrong.

Even the origin of this condition is rarely acknowledged. This is the simple fact that we have been living through a period of more than a quarter of a century in which all our grand narratives have collapsed. One by one the narratives we had were refuted, became unpopular to defend or impossible to sustain. The explanations for our existence that used to be provided by religion went first, falling away from the nineteenth century onwards. Then over the last century the secular hopes held out by all political ideologies began to follow in religion's wake. In the latter part of the twentieth century we entered the postmodern era. An era which defined itself, and was defined, by its suspicion towards all grand narratives.[1] However, as all schoolchildren learn, nature abhors a vacuum, and into the postmodern vacuum new ideas began to creep, with the intention of providing explanations and meanings of their own.

It was inevitable that some pitch would be made for the deserted ground. People in wealthy Western democracies today could not simply remain the first people in recorded history to have absolutely no explanation for what we are doing here, and no story to give life purpose.

1

Whatever else they lacked, the grand narratives of the past at least gave life meaning. The question of what exactly we are meant to do now – other than get rich where we can and have whatever fun is on offer – was going to have to be answered by something.

The answer that has presented itself in recent years is to engage in new battles, ever fiercer campaigns and ever more niche demands. To find meaning by waging a constant war against anybody who seems to be on the wrong side of a question which may itself have just been reframed and the answer to which has only just been altered. The unbelievable speed of this process has been principally caused by the fact that a handful of businesses in Silicon Valley (notably Google, Twitter and Facebook) now have the power not just to direct what most people in the world know, think and say, but have a business model which has accurately been described as relying on finding 'customers ready to pay to modify someone else's behaviour'.[2] Yet although we are being aggravated by a tech world which is running faster than our legs are able to carry us to keep up with it, these wars are not being fought aimlessly. They are consistently being fought in a particular direction. And that direction has a purpose that is vast. The purpose – unknowing in some people, deliberate in others – is to embed a new metaphysics into our societies: a new religion, if you will.

Although the foundations had been laid for several decades, it is only since the financial crash of 2008 that there has been a march into the mainstream of ideas that were previously known solely on the obscurest fringes of academia. The attractions of this new set of beliefs are obvious enough. It is not clear why a generation which can't accumulate capital should have any great love of capitalism. And it isn't hard to work out why a generation who believe they may never own a home could be attracted to an ideological world view which promises to sort out every inequity not just in their own lives but every inequity on earth. The interpretation of the world through the lens of 'social justice', 'identity group politics' and 'intersectionalism' is probably the most audacious and comprehensive effort since the end of the Cold War at creating a new ideology.

To date 'social justice' has run the furthest because it sounds – and in some versions is – attractive. Even the term itself is set up to be

2

anti-oppositional. 'You're opposed to social justice? What do you want, social *in*justice?'

'Identity politics', meanwhile, has become the place where social justice finds its caucuses. It atomizes society into different interest groups according to sex (or gender), race, sexual preference and more. It presumes that such characteristics are the main, or only, relevant attributes of their holders and that they bring with them some added bonus. For example (as the American writer Coleman Hughes has put it), the assumption that there is 'a heightened moral knowledge' that comes with being black or female or gay.[3] It is the cause of the propensity of people to start questions or statements with 'Speaking as a . . .'. And it is something that people both living and dead need to be on the right side of. It is why there are calls to pull down the statues of historical figures viewed as being on the wrong side and it is why the past needs to be rewritten for anyone you wish to save. It is why it has become perfectly normal for a Sinn Fein senator to claim that the IRA hunger strikers in 1981 were striking for gay rights.[4] Identity politics is where minority groups are encouraged to simultaneously atomize, organize and pronounce.

The least attractive-sounding of this trinity is the concept of 'intersectionality'. This is the invitation to spend the rest of our lives attempting to work out each and every identity and vulnerability claim in ourselves and others and then organize along whichever system of justice emerges from the perpetually moving hierarchy which we uncover. It is a system that is not just unworkable but dementing, making demands that are impossible towards ends that are unachievable. But today intersectionality has broken out from the social science departments of the liberal arts colleges from which it originated. It is now taken seriously by a generation of young people and – as we shall see – has become embedded via employment law (specifically through a 'commitment to diversity') in all the major corporations and governments.

New heuristics have been required to force people to ingest the new presumptions. The speed at which they have been mainstreamed is staggering. As the mathematician and writer Eric Weinstein has pointed out (and as a Google Books search shows), phrases like 'LGBTQ', 'white privilege' and 'transphobia' went from not being used at all to becoming mainstream. As he wrote about the graph that results from this, the 'woke stuff' that Millennials and others are presently using 'to tear apart millennia of oppression and /or civilization . . . was all made up about 20 minutes ago'. As he went on, while there is nothing wrong with trying out new ideas and phrases, 'you have to be pretty damn reckless to be leaning this hard on so many untested heuristics your parents came up with in untested fields that aren't even 50 years old'.[5] Similarly, Greg Lukianoff and Jonathan Haidt have pointed out (in their 2018 book *The Coddling of the American Mind*) how new the means of policing and enforcing these new heuristics have become. Phrases like 'triggered' and 'feeling unsafe' and claims that words that do not fit the new religion cause 'harm' only really started to spike in usage from 2013 onwards.[6] It is as though, having worked out what it wanted, the new metaphysics took a further half-decade to work out how to intimidate its followers into the mainstream. But it has done so, with huge success.

The results can be seen in every day's news. It is behind the news that the American Psychological Association feels the need to advise its members on how to train harmful 'traditional masculinity' out of boys and men.[7] It is why a previously completely unknown programmer at Google – James Damore – can be sacked for writing a memo suggesting that some jobs in tech appeal more to men than they do to women. And it is why the number of Americans who view racism as a 'big problem' doubled between 2011 and 2017.[8]

Having begun to view everything through the new lenses we have been provided with, everything is then weaponized, with consequences which are deranged as well as dementing. It is why *The New York Times* decides to run a piece by a black author with the title: 'Can my Children be Friends with White People?'[9] And why even a piece about cycling deaths in London written by a woman can be framed through the headline: 'Roads Designed by Men are Killing Women'.[10] Such rhetoric exacerbates any existing divisions and each time creates a number of new ones. And for what purpose? Rather than showing how we can all get along better, the lessons of the last decade appear to be exacerbating a sense that in fact we aren't very good at living with each other.

For most people some awareness of this new system of values has become clear not so much by trial as by very public error. Because one thing that everybody has begun to at least sense in recent years is that a set of tripwires have been laid across the culture. Whether placed by individuals, collectives or some divine satirist, there they have been waiting for one person after another to walk into them. Sometimes a person's foot has unwittingly nicked the tripwire and they have been immediately blown up. On other occasions people have watched some brave madman walking straight into the no man's land, fully aware of what they were doing. After each resulting detonation there is some disputation (including the occasional 'coo' of admiration) and then the world moves on, accepting that another victim has been notched up to the odd, apparently improvisatory value system of our time.

It took a little while for the delineation of these tripwires to become clear, but they are clear now. Among the first was anything to do with homosexuality. In the latter half of the twentieth century there was a fight for gay equality which was tremendously successful, reversing terrible historic injustice. Then, the war having been won, it became clear that it wasn't stopping. Indeed it was morphing. GLB (Gay, Lesbian, Bi) became LGB so as not to diminish the visibility of lesbians. Then a T got added (of which much more anon). Then a Q and then some stars and asterisks. And as the gay alphabet grew, so something changed within the movement. It began to behave – in victory – as its opponents once did. When the boot was on the other foot something ugly happened. A decade ago almost nobody was supportive of gay marriage. Even gay rights groups like Stonewall weren't in favour of it. A few years down the road and it has been made into a foundational value of modern liberalism. To fail the gay marriage issue – only years after almost everybody failed it (including gay rights groups) – was to put yourself beyond the pale. People may agree with that rights claim, or disagree, but to shift mores so fast needs to be done with extraordinary sensitivity and some deep thought. Yet we seem content to steam past, engaging in neither.

Instead, other issues followed a similar pattern. Women's rights had – like gay rights – been steadily accumulated throughout the twentieth century. They too appeared to be arriving at some sort of settlement.

Then just as the train appeared to be reaching its desired destination it suddenly picked up steam and went crashing off down the tracks and into the distance. What had been barely disputed until yesterday became a cause to destroy someone's life today. Whole careers were scattered and strewn as the train careered along its path.

Careers like that of the 72-year-old Nobel Prize-winning Professor Tim Hunt were destroyed after one lame joke, at a conference in South Korea, about men and women falling in love in the lab.[11] Phrases such as 'toxic masculinity' entered into common use. What was the virtue of making relations between the sexes so fraught that the male half of the species could be treated as though it was cancerous? Or the development of the idea that men had no right to talk about the female sex? Why, when women had broken through more glass ceilings than at any time in history, did talk of 'the patriarchy' and 'mansplaining' seep out of the feminist fringes and into the heart of places like the Australian Senate?[12]

In a similar fashion the civil rights movement in America, which had started in order to right the most appalling of all historic wrongs, looked like it was moving towards some hoped-for resolution. But yet again, near the point of victory everything seemed to sour. Just as things appeared better than ever before, the rhetoric began to suggest that things had never been worse. Suddenly – after most of us had hoped it had become a non-issue – everything seemed to have become about race. As with all the other tripwire issues, only a fool or a madman would think of even speculating – let alone disputing – this turnaround of events.

Then finally we all stumbled, baffled, into the most unchartered territory of all. This was the claim that there lived among us a considerable number of people who were in the wrong bodies and that as a consequence what certainties remained in our societies (including certainties rooted in science and language) needed to be utterly reframed. In some ways the debate around the trans question is the most suggestive of all. Although the newest of the rights questions also affects by far the fewest number of people, it is nevertheless fought over with an almost unequalled ferocity and rage. Women who have got on the wrong side of the issue have been hounded by people who used to be men. Parents who voice what was common belief until yesterday have their fitness to be parents questioned. In the UK and elsewhere the police make calls on people who will not concede that men can be women (and vice versa).[13]

Among the things these issues all have in common is that they have started as legitimate human rights campaigns. This is why they have come so far. But at some point all went through the crash barrier. Not content with being equal, they have started to settle on unsustainable positions such as 'better'. Some might counter that the aim is simply to spend a certain amount of time on 'better' in order to level the historical playing field. In the wake of the #MeToo movement it became common to hear such sentiments. As one CNN presenter said, 'There might be an over-correction, but that's OK. We're due for a correction.'[14] To date nobody has suggested when over-correction might have been achieved or who might be trusted to announce it.

What everyone does know are the things that people will be called if their foot even nicks against these freshly laid tripwires. 'Bigot', 'homophobe', 'sexist', 'misogynist', 'racist' and 'transphobe' are just for starters. The rights fights of our time have centred around these toxic and explosive issues. But in the process these rights issues have moved from being a product of a system to being the foundations of a new one. To demonstrate affiliation with the system people must prove their credentials and their commitment. How might somebody demonstrate virtue in this new world? By being 'anti-racist', clearly. By being an 'ally' to LGBT people, obviously. By stressing how ardent your desire is – whether you are a man or a woman – to bring down the patriarchy.

And this creates an auditioning problem, where public avowals of loyalty to the system must be volubly made whether there is a need for them or not. It is an extension of a well-known problem in liberalism which has been recognized even among those who did once fight a noble fight. It is a tendency identified by the late Australian political philosopher Kenneth Minogue as 'St George in retirement' syndrome. After slaying the dragon the brave warrior finds himself stalking the land looking for still more glorious fights. He needs his dragons. Eventually, after tiring himself out in pursuit of ever-smaller dragons he may eventually even be found swinging his sword at thin air, imagining it to contain dragons.[15]

If that is a temptation for an actual St George, imagine what a person might do who is no saint, owns no horse or lance and is being noticed by nobody. How might they try to persuade people that, given the historic chance, they too would without question have slain that dragon?

In the claims and supporting rhetoric quoted throughout this book there is a good deal of this in evidence. Our public life is now dense with people desperate to man the barricades long after the revolution is over. Either because they mistake the barricades for home, or because they have no other home to go to. In each case a demonstration of virtue demands an overstating of the problem, which then causes an amplification of the problem.

But there is more trouble in all of this, and it is the reason why I take each of the bases of these new metaphysics not just seriously but one by one. With each of these issues an increasing number of people, having the law on their side, pretend that both their issue and indeed all these issues are shut down and agreed upon. The case is very much otherwise. The nature of what is meant to be agreed upon cannot in fact be agreed upon. Each of these issues is infinitely more complex and unstable than our societies are currently willing to admit. Which is why, put together as the foundation blocks of a new morality and metaphysics, they form the basis for a general madness. Indeed a more unstable basis for social harmony could hardly be imagined.

For while racial equality, minority rights and women's rights are among the best products of liberalism, they make the most destabilizing foundations. Attempting to make them the foundation is like turning a bar stool upside down and then trying to balance on top of it. The products of the system cannot reproduce the stability of the system that produced them. If for no other reason than that each of these issues is a deeply unstable component in itself. We present each as agreed upon and settled. Yet while the endless contradictions, fabrications and fantasies within each are visible to all, identifying them is not just discouraged but literally policed. And so we are asked to agree to things which we cannot believe.

It is the central cause of the ugliness of both online and real-life discussion. For we are being asked to perform a set of leaps and jumps which we cannot, and are perhaps ill-advised to make. We are asked to believe things that are unbelievable and being told not to object to things (such as giving children drugs to stop them going through puberty) which most people feel a strong objection to. The pain that comes from being expected to remain silent on some important matters and perform impossible leaps on others is tremendous, not least because the problems (including the internal contradictions) are so evident. As anyone who has lived under totalitarianism can attest, there is something demeaning and eventually soul-destroying about being expected to go along with claims you do not believe to be true and cannot hold to be true. If the belief is that all people should be regarded as having equal value and be accorded equal dignity, then that may be all well and good. If you are asked to believe that there are no differences between homosexuality and heterosexuality, men and women, racism and anti-racism, then this will in time drive you to distraction. That distraction – or crowd madness – is something we are in the middle of and something we need to try to find our way out from.

If we fail, then the direction of travel is already clear. We face not just a future of ever-greater atomization, rage and violence, but a future in which the possibility of a backlash against all rights advances – including the good ones – grows more likely. A future in which racism is responded to with racism, denigration based on gender is responded to with denigration based on gender. At some stage of humiliation there is simply no reason for majority groups not to play games back that have worked so well on themselves.

This book suggests a number of ways out of this. But the best way to start is not just to understand the basis of what is going on at the moment but to be free to discuss it. While writing this book, I discovered that the British Army has a mine-clearing device now named 'The Python', but in an earlier design it was known as 'The Giant Viper'. When this trailer-mounted system is fired at a minefield it unleashes a rocket, behind which unfurls a hose-like trail hundreds of metres long and all packed with explosives. Once the whole thing is lying across the minefield (and like everything else you can see videos of this online), it causes what is called 'sympathetic detonation'. That is, the whole thing explodes, setting off the mines within a significant radius of the rocket and its tail. Although it cannot clear the entire minefield, it can clear a path across the minefield, allowing other people, trucks and even tanks to travel safely across what was previously impassable terrain.

In my own modest way I think of this book as my Viper system. I do not aim to clear the whole minefield and could not, even if I wished to. But I hope that this book will help clear some terrain across which afterwards other people may more safely pass.

1

Gay

It is a chill February day in London in 2018 and a small demonstration is taking place outside a cinema just off Piccadilly Circus. Wrapped-up warm, the quiet protestors are holding up posters that say 'Silenced' in capital letters. Most Londoners trying to get to their bus stops or across to the bars of Soho barely notice them. A passing couple clock that the group is mainly middle-aged and elderly. One says to the other, 'Some kind of UKIP protest I guess.' But it is not. The assembled dozens came here to watch a film called *Voices of the Silenced*. But as their placards point out, *Voices of the Silenced* has itself been silenced.

The organizers booked the cinema three months earlier, and say they had complied with all the cinema's rules for private screenings, including sending them the film in advance. But a day before the screening *Pink News* – an online remnant of Britain's gay press – found out about the screening and called for its immediate cancellation. The call was successful. The Vue cinema swerved around any negative publicity by swiftly announcing that it had the right not to honour private hires if the film to be shown was 'in direct contradiction' of its 'values'. The cinema also warned the group who had hired the venue that there might be a 'public order' and even 'security' threat if the screening was to go ahead.

So on the big night, with exactly 126 people apparently travelling to attend the screening from as far away as the Netherlands, the organizers are scrambling to try to find another venue at which their assembled punters might view the film. Chief among the evening's organizers is

Dr Michael Davidson of the Core Issues Trust. Davidson is not a doctor of medicine. He has a doctorate in education, but like some other public figures who use the prefix you feel that Davidson would not be displeased if someone laboured under a misapprehension about the precise nature of his qualifications.

Davidson had come to national attention in Britain six months earlier when he had been invited as a guest on ITV's *Good Morning Britain*, co-hosted by Piers Morgan, to discuss homosexuality and so-called 'conversion therapies'. Davidson has admitted that he used to be gay himself – or at least had 'homosexual experiences'. But at some point he decided that it was not for him. He has been married to his wife for 35 years and has two children. He believes that where he has gone other people can follow, and so through his group he offers counselling on a voluntary basis to other people who would like to move from being gay to becoming a heterosexual like himself who admits that he still gets – though doesn't act on – certain 'urges'.

When challenged about all this on national television, Davidson calmly and politely makes it clear that he thinks homosexuality is an 'aberration' and specifically that it is a learned behaviour. Asked whether it can be unlearned, he claims that it 'in some cases is reversible for people who want to make that the trajectory of their lives'. Dr Davidson managed to get this out before his main interviewer denounced him to the others present in the studio. 'Do you know what we call these people, Dr Michael?' Piers Morgan asked. 'We call them horrible little bigots, in the modern world. Just bigoted people who actually talk complete claptrap and are in my view a malevolent and dangerous part of our society. What's the matter with you? How can you think that nobody's born gay and they all get corrupted and they can all be cured? Who are you to say such garbage?'

A relatively unflustered Davidson asked Morgan for evidence that people are born gay, pointing out that neither the American Psychological Association nor the Royal College of Psychiatrists believe that homosexuality is innate and unchangeable. At which point his interviewer ordered him to 'stop talking for a moment' and 'stop banging on about whacky-backy scientists in America'. Morgan then continued to shout at his guest, 'Shut up you old bigot', before he brought the whole interview to a close with the words 'I've had enough of him. Dr Michael, shut up.'[1] And so it finished. ITV had sent a car to a guest's home in the early morning to bring him to a national television studio only for him to be told during his interview to shut up.

Six months after that event and Davidson remains clearly unmoved by that high-profile brouhaha. Talking on his mobile phone outside the cancelled venue in Piccadilly, he is relieved to be able to tell his audience that he has finally found a venue which would allow him to screen his film. So the assembled men and women head to Westminster's Emmanuel Centre, just around the corner from the Houses of Parliament.

The doors to that venue are tightly shut, but at one side door, if you mention your name and your name is checked off the list, then the entire evening opens up. Indeed, once inside it becomes a rather jolly affair. We are all given a glass of prosecco and a bag of popcorn to take into the screening. One elderly woman comes over and thanks me for coming. 'Obviously I know your own background,' she adds, and I realize she is not talking about where I was brought up, 'as you talk about it often,' she adds gnomically. But she explains that this only means she is even more pleased to see me here. It is true that I may be the only out person at this gay-cure film-screening. But I suspect that I am not the only gay in the room.

The film *Voices of the Silenced* itself is less coherent than might have been hoped. The main point (as explained by Davidson himself in the film's opening) is that 'Ancient ideologies and modern ideologies are coming together.' It is never quite clear how, and the whole thing feels like two different films awkwardly melded together at a late stage in the editing process. The first film is about the ancient world, with very scary apocalyptic images. The second film consists of some very specific testimony from doctors and patients talking about being gay and then not being gay any more. As well as Dr Davidson there is a Dr Stephen Baskerville and an expert from Texas named (I cannot stifle an audible laugh) David Pickup.

So each time there is something in the film on the loss of the Temple in AD 70 and the Arch of Titus, then it cuts to the gays again. Or the ex-gays. We are told that 'the new state orthodoxy celebrates homosexuality'. Then, along with a range of 'experts' – mainly from the

United States – we get the testimonies. What any of these have to do with the Arch of Titus is never fully made clear. Perhaps homosexuality is causing the collapse of this civilization? If so the accusation is never quite made. There is an 'ex-lesbian' now married with five children who says that her 'vulnerability' resurfaced ten years ago but that she got help from a ministry. Several witnesses talk of suicidal thoughts, alcohol abuse and 'self-centredness'. One (called John) mentions that his mother was 'a Jewess', which is a word you don't often hear these days. There is a lot of testimony from a handsome 29-year-old German called Marcel. He describes his own tribulations. He says that as a child his mother beat him, naked, in front of his sister and this – it is suggested – may be one of the reasons why he has in the past found himself attracted to men. Some of the interviewees were from families where their parents divorced. Others were not. Several of the interviewees seem to have been very close to their mothers. Others not.

Dr Joseph Nicolosi – one of the stars of the film – offers up the idea that many of his 'patients' actually hate their mothers, don't know how to deal with men and thus develop certain fantasies as a result. He suggests that one cure for anyone troubled by homoerotic temptations is that they might consider taking up a healthy pursuit such as 'going to a gym'. Suggesting, perhaps, that Dr Nicolosi has never been to a gym.

Of course it is easy to snigger at all this, and for some people it would be easy to be outraged too. Yet the human stories are there. John and Lindsay say that they have both suffered from SSA (Same-Sex Attraction) but have been able to tackle it together and are now working together as a very successful heterosexual couple with five children. 'It's not just us,' Lindsay reassures the viewer. 'We know several people [who have also had SSA] who are happily married. It is hard work,' she continues, with John sitting slightly awkwardly beside her. 'It's not for the faint-hearted. And I think you have to just push through. Particularly in the present era: all the media and all the cultural pressures to do something else.'

Sadder than this couple are the several interviewees who were gay once but now appear here with their faces blacked out. Perhaps it is too charitable to reflect that it wasn't so long ago that this need for blackened-out faces and back-of-head shots would have applied the other way around.

Towards the film's end an Irish pastor sums up a part of the film's point. He explains that he doesn't mind people holding out the view that homosexuality is inherent and unchangeable. He just wants to be allowed to be able to hold his view. As Dr Baskerville reiterates, only one position on this matter appears to be able to be held in academia and the media, and that is 'promotion' of homosexuality. 'Sexuality is being politicized,' we are told in the final moments. And then, after another inexplicable reference to the Ancient Jews, the film ends with the dramatic yet careful line: 'It is time to accept difference.'

Unsurprisingly this audience gives the film a very warm reception. And then something mortifying happens. Several of the film's interviewees are in the audience and are invited up onstage to receive more applause. Among them is a young British man from the film called Michael. He seems slightly twitchy and nervous and filled with suffering. His forehead is more than usually wrinkled for someone of his age. For various reasons he has already expounded on in the film he doesn't want to live as a gay man and so has put himself on an obviously internally wracking path to try to live as a heterosexual and to become (as Dr Davidson himself has) an ex-gay – perhaps also, in time, with the same pleasures of having a wife and children of his own. The evening finishes with a prayer.

On the way home and in the days that followed I wondered about my evening with the voluntary conversion therapists. And I wondered in particular why I was not more bothered by it.

First, it must be said that I do not fear these people – and certainly could not kick up that level of outrage which the gay press has decided to trade in as it loses its purpose. If there is a reason it is because I cannot see that events are going in the direction of the people in the Emmanuel Centre that night. Today, and for the foreseeable future, they are on the losing side.

When they appear on television they are treated with scorn – perhaps too much scorn. They find it hard to make watchable documentaries, and find it even harder to screen them. They are forced to hide away in secret venues, and seem unlikely to be taking anywhere by storm any time soon.

Of course if I was a young gay man growing up in parts of rural America or Britain – even today – I might think differently. Certainly if I had grown up in parts of the American Bible Belt, or had ever lived through (or been threatened with) the forced conversion therapies that went on there – and still go on in parts of the world today – I might look at Michael (Dr) Davidson and his friends in a very different light.

But here, this evening, they are the losers. And aware of the thrill that can occur when the boot is on the other foot, I feel a reluctance to treat them in victory as some of their ideological confrères might have treated me if we had met before, in different circumstances. The manner in which people and movements behave at the point of victory can be the most revealing thing about them. Do you allow arguments that worked for you to work for others? Are reciprocity and tolerance principles or fig-leaves? Do those who have been censored go on to censor others when the ability is in their own hands? Today the Vue cinema is on one side. A few decades ago they might have been on the other. And *Pink News* and others who celebrate their victory in chasing *Voices of the Silenced* a mile down the road one February night seem very ready to wield such power over a private event. In doing so they contradict the claims made by gay rights activists from the start of the battle for gay equality, which is that it should be no business of anyone else what consenting adults get up to in private. If that goes for the rights of gay groups then surely it ought to apply to the rights of Christian fundamentalists and other groups too.

There are two other things. The first is that in order to fear what was happening that evening you would have to extrapolate from it. You would have to suspect that, when Davidson says he only wants to deal with people who come to him seeking help, this is a mere cover-story. You would have to believe that this is in fact just a front – the first part of a wider plan to turn something voluntary into something compulsory and from something compulsory for some people into something compulsory for all. And that would be to trample all over one of the bases of political tolerance. It would be to award yourself the right not just to come to your own conclusions about people, but to attribute motives to others that you cannot see but which you suspect. Which leads to a question that everybody in genuinely diverse and pluralistic societies must at some point ask: 'Do we take other people at face value, or do we try to read behind their words and actions, claim to see into their hearts and there divine the true motives which their speech and actions have not yet revealed?'

If we were to do this in cases like these, then how would we do it? Do we insist that the other party has the darkest possible motives unless they fully satisfy us that their motivations are otherwise? Or do we have to learn some degree of forbearance and taking on trust? Even the responses to that question aren't fixed. They fluctuate depending on date, location, circumstance and luck. Someone now in their seventies who was put through forced conversion therapy (especially if put through 'aversion' therapy) will have more cause to be suspicious than anyone from each of the successively luckier generations that have followed. Warning sirens go off earlier if they were set earlier, or in harsher times.

Perhaps these generational and geographical differences will diminish over time and the flattening effects of social media will make everyone equally sanguine. Or perhaps these tools have the opposite effect, persuading a gay in 2019 Amsterdam that they are permanently at risk of living in 1950s Alabama. Nobody knows. We live in a world in which every fear, threat and hope imaginable is always available to us.

Yet one prerequisite for avoiding perpetual confrontation is an ability to listen to people's words and hold some trust in them. True, in borderline cases, when alerted that something strange may be going on, it may be necessary to dig behind the words to ensure that nothing else is happening. But if that has been done and nothing found then the words must be trusted. None of the press which had sought to silence *Voices of the Silenced* had shown that Davidson or his colleagues were forcing unwilling participants to submit to a regime of heterosexual conversion. None had even enquired into what details the film included or how his 'counselling' was being done. And so a set of assumptions had been made about his group and words assigned different interpretations because of their speaker. In this calibration 'voluntary' meant 'forced', 'counselling' meant 'persecution' and everybody who went to him was irrevocably and unalterably gay.

It is this last assumption which provokes the only big challenge that Davidson and his colleagues present. In *On Liberty*, first published in 1859, John Stuart Mill famously laid out four reasons for why free speech was a necessity in a free society: the first and second being that a contrary opinion may be true, or true in part, and therefore may require to be heard in order to correct your own erroneous views; the third and fourth being that even if the contrary opinion is in error, the airing of it may help to remind people of a truth and prevent its slippage into an ignorant dogma which may in time – if unchallenged – itself become lost.[2]

Abiding by Mill's principles would appear to be hard for many people today. Harder, indeed, than simply changing dogmas. In recent years the accepted opinion on gay rights in America, Britain and most other Western democracies has shifted unimaginably, and for the better. But it has moved so swiftly that it has also seen the replacement of one dogma with another. A move from a position of moral opprobrium to a position of expressing opprobrium to anyone whose views fall even narrowly outside the remit of the newly adopted position. The problem with this is not just that we are at risk of being unable to hear positions that are wrong, but that we may be preventing ourselves from listening to arguments that may be partially true.

As it happens, confused as their film-making was, and disagreeable though much of their world view might be, Davidson and his colleagues are onto something around the nature of sexual attraction. These are deep and toxic waters. But there is no point in identifying such waters and not plunging into them.

When it comes to matters around sexuality a set of presumptions have been adopted which are proving quite as dogmatic as the notions they replaced. In June 2015 the then Conservative Education Secretary declared that homophobic views were evidence of potential 'extremism' in school pupils in Britain. Indeed as the BBC reported, Nicky Morgan said that 'attacking core British values or being extremely intolerant of homosexuality were examples of behaviour that could raise the alarm'. They were evidence that a pupil might have been being 'groomed' by 'extremists', and a pupil who said they thought homosexuality 'evil' might need to be reported to the police.[3] Of some interest is the fact that in May 2013 Morgan had voted against the law introducing gay marriage into the UK. One year later, in 2014, she said that she now supported gay marriage and would vote for it if it had not already become law. Another year later, in 2015, she was declaring views such as those she herself had held two years earlier as not merely evidence of 'extremism' but fundamentally un-British.

In the 1990s Hillary Clinton supported her husband's 'defence of marriage act' which sought to prevent gay marriage from becoming possible in the United States. She watched as he backed the policy of 'Don't Ask, Don't Tell' for gays in the US military, meaning that any gay soldier who told even one other person about their sexuality could immediately be dismissed from the armed forces. As Robert Samuels wrote in the *Washington Post*, 'Hillary Clinton had the chance to make gay rights history. She refused.'[4] Yet in 2016 when she was campaigning for the Presidency for the second time and the views of wider society had shifted markedly, the LGBT community (as gays had now become) were one of the specific sections of the country whom Clinton claimed to be campaigning especially hard for. It is not unusual for politicians to shift positions. But the speed with which the times changed made for some remarkably sharp changes of position in the political class.

Other people and countries have instituted even swifter and noisier U-turns. Almost immediately after gay marriage became legal in Germany, acceptance of it was made a condition of citizenship in the state of Baden-Württemberg. Yesterday there was one dogma. Now there is another.

It is not just some politicians who must have suffered whiplash in recent years. Newspapers that were until recently decidedly unpleasant about homosexuals now cover same-sex weddings like any other society news. Columnists who were damning about equal ages of consent only a few years ago now berate people not fully onboard with gay marriage. In 2018 the MSNBC host Joy Reid was publicly shamed and made to apologize after historic comments from a decade earlier were found in which she had been critical of gay marriage – at a time when almost everybody else was unsupportive of gay marriage as well. When change happens so swiftly, there is much making up for lost time to be done, and little pity for those found dragging behind.

MAKING EVERYTHING GAY

And so some individuals, governments and corporations appear to believe that their job is to make up for lost time. They are forcing discussion of gay issues in a manner slightly beyond acceptance and more in the realms of 'This will be good for you.'

By 2018 the BBC seemed to have decided that items of specifically gay news needed to be not just reported but headlined as major news. One of its top stories of the day on the corporation's website in September that year was that the diver Tom Daley had felt 'inferior' about his sexuality but that this had given him the motivation to become a success.[5] This story was published five years after Daley had come out. He had not been silent about his private life in the interim period. And yet this human interest story was a lead item on the BBC's website just beneath news of an earthquake and tsunami in Indonesia which had killed more than 800 people. One day later and the BBC website had as one of its lead stories the news that a minor reality television star called Ollie Locke had announced that he and his fiancé (Gareth Locke) were going to join their surnames to make themselves the Locke-Lockes after their forthcoming marriage.[6] In other headline news, the death toll from the Indonesian earthquake had risen significantly overnight.

Perhaps it requires someone who is gay to say this, but there are times when such 'news' reporting doesn't feel like news reporting at all. Rather it seems that some type of message is being sent out either to the public or to people whom the media believe to be in positions of power. This goes beyond 'This will be good for you' and nearer to the realm of 'See how you like this, bigot.' There are days when you wonder how heterosexuals feel about the growing insistence with which gay stories are crow-barred into any and all areas of news.

Take a fairly average day at *The New York Times*. On 16 October 2017 a reader of the International Edition of the paper might decide to take a break from the opinion pages and turn to some richer fare. They might turn to the business pages. There they would find the lead story in the 'Business' section to be 'Gay in Japan and No Longer Invisible.' Perhaps the average reader of the business pages of *The New York Times* had never thought much about the visibility or otherwise of gay people in Japan. So here was their opportunity to learn about something they didn't know. Specifically, about the story of Shunsuke Nakamura who recently used a morning meeting with fellow employees at his insurance company to come out as gay. This in a country where attitudes towards homosexuality have tended to be (as one professor at a Tokyo university is quoted as saying in the piece) 'indifference rather than hate'. So *The New York Times* had chosen to splash a story over two pages, as their lead Business feature, about how a man had come out in a company with no negative consequences in a country that had no special problem with gays. Ordinarily it would have to be an exceptionally quiet day in the markets for such a story to be the most important story of the day in 'Business'.

Turn one page and the story continues, this time under the headline 'Companies in Japan More Welcoming to Gays'. By which point the casual reader may well have satisfied their interest in the position of gay men in Japanese companies and begun casting their eye guiltily to the opposite page and the 'Culture' section. And what is the lead story and main headline there? 'A Broader Stage for Love'.

The subject matter of this article could be guessed from the half-page accompanying photo of two male ballerinas, their arms and bodies entwined. 'Ballet is slower to change than most art forms', the paper informed its readers, continuing excitedly, 'but in the span of just two recent weeks, New York City Ballet, one of the world's premier companies, showed two ballets featuring significant same-sex duets'.

The cause for this vast splash is a ballet called *The Times Are Racing*, the latest production of which – at New York City Ballet – includes the casting of a man in a role originally created for a woman. *The New York Times* goes on to explain how the hitherto overwhelmingly heterosexual world of ballet was finally 'responding to the contemporary world and putting it on the ballet stage'. A male choreographer who was involved promised an 'exploration of gender-neutrality' in his work in an Instagram post hash-tagged 'loveislove', 'genderneutral', 'equality', 'diversity', 'beauty', 'pride' and 'proud'. A sole heretical outside choreographer was singled out for criticism for his stated belief that 'there are gender roles in traditional ballet' and that while 'men and women are of equal value' they have 'different tasks'. The New York City Ballet's stars – and *The New York Times* – did not agree.

To the amazement of nobody it turned out that several of the male leads in the New York City Ballet are themselves gay, and one of them explained to *The New York Times* how early in rehearsals his dance partner had turned to him and said, 'It's so nice to get to step into a role where I feel I could actually potentially fall in love with the person I'm dancing with, as opposed to pretending to be a prince falling in love with a princess.' To which one might say that anyone who feels any tedium enacting scenes in which princes fall in love with princesses may find ballet isn't their medium. But in case this outburst of diversity on the ballet stage is not enough, the story adds more of the five-a-day moral nutrition to the story with the news that this production 'explores not only a same-sex relationship but also issues of race.' Describing the overall effect of two men dancing together, the choreographer declared that it just 'blew her away'. 'Suddenly, they could just be themselves', the story concludes. At which point the reader of *The New York Times* has the opportunity to read the other main story about 'Culture': a story about how female comics joking about pregnancy and motherhood are finally becoming big.[7]

There is nothing wrong with a newspaper of record deciding to devote its Business and Culture pages as well as much of its opinion and news pages to stories about being gay. But it sometimes feels as though there is something else going on in all this. The use of gay special interest stories for purposes other than those of actual news: perhaps making up for lost time, or perhaps just rubbing things in the faces of those not yet up to speed with the changed mores of the age. Either way something strange and vaguely retributive is in the air.

Of course people change, learn and often shift their positions. Most do so quietly, generally after others have done the heavy lifting. But one problem of changing societal positions so swiftly is that unexplored, even unexploded, issues and arguments are left behind in the wake. When Piers Morgan demanded of his guest, 'How can you think that nobody's born gay?' he displays too great a certainty over a question that is still uncertain. And whether or not anyone is born gay, or whether everyone who is gay is born gay, it does not follow at all that being gay is a one-way street.

A ONE-WAY STREET?

That idea is just one curious place that our culture has arrived at. In society at large, when people come out as gay they are celebrated for having arrived at their natural end-point. For most people this is a decent recognition by society that there is no problem with them being who they are: they have arrived at the place that is natural and right for them. But one oddity of this position is that anybody who is gay and then subsequently decides they are straight will be the subject not just of a degree of ostracism and suspicion, but widespread doubt that they are being honest about their true selves. A straight who becomes gay has settled. A gay who has become straight has rendered himself an object of permanent suspicion. From being strongly inclined towards straight the culture has settled with a mild inclination towards gay.

After writing the watershed gay drama *Queer as Folk* in the late 1990s, the screenwriter Russell T. Davies followed this up with another television series called *Bob and Rose* (2001). It told the story of a gay man who falls in love with a woman. It was provoked, as Davies told the press at the time, by the recognition that gay men who went straight often received more resentment from their circle of friends than a straight man who came out as gay.[8]

Perhaps that is one reason why the whole direction of traffic is so little addressed. For many gay men and women the idea that sexuality is fluid and that what goes one way may go another (what goes up must come down) is an attack on their person. And this isn't a fear without basis. Plenty of gay people will hear in the suggestion some echo of those dread words 'It's only a phase.' People who are gay find this suggestion enormously offensive, as well as destabilizing in their relationships with parents, family and others. So since the phrase 'It's only a phase' is offensive for some people, the idea that it might actually be true for some people is unsayable.

For their part, Millennials and 'Generation Z' have attempted to provide their own ways around this by stressing sexual fluidity. Opinion surveys suggest that these people now in their late teens are moving away from the idea of there being fixed points in sexuality, with one 2018 study showing that only two-thirds of Generation Z claim to be 'exclusively heterosexual.'[9] While that is still a majority it suggests a distinct shift from the attitudes of the generations before them.

For those generations older than Millennials the issue of 'fluidity' remains a complex and often painful one. For many of them, people who join the club and then leave it are far more likely to be reviled than those who never joined at all. They may not show up on surveys, and they certainly don't have national spokespeople or 'community leaders', but a lot of gay people know cases like this. Friends who didn't quite fit in the gay world, who disliked the scene and couldn't find another. People who dipped into it and then jumped out. Or people who had other things they sought in life. People, for instance, who wanted children and the security of marriage and who stopped or sidelined being gay to pursue being something else. Or (and nobody knows what proportion of people this might comprise) people who, having had relationships with members of the same sex for most of their lives, suddenly – like the title character in *Bob & Rose* – met a member of the opposite sex with whom they fell in love.

Will these sorts of behaviour diminish now that there are civil partnerships and gay marriage, not to mention gay adoption and even the possibility of gay parenting? Will people increasingly adopt the looser sexual identities of Generation Z? Perhaps. Or perhaps not. Because everybody also knows people who that wasn't meant for. People who had the odd gay kiss or more, but who went back to being straight afterwards. And yet where the culture in the recent past would have seen the gay kiss as the aberration – the falling away from the norm – today the culture suggests that the gay kiss is the moment of revelatory truth.

Today the person who once did anything gay is the one believed to be living a lie. Because in some way the perception has developed that to once be gay is to have fallen into your true state of nature, whereas to be forever afterwards straight is not. This is different from a claim of bisexuality. It is a presumption that the see-saw of sexuality is not evenly balanced but in fact inclines towards gay. And that whereas a previous era might have tilted the see-saw towards straight, this one has decided to tilt it in the other direction. Perhaps in order to right a wrong (in the hope that the see-saw will at some point arrive at an even position). But how people are to work out when the see-saw has arrived at the right position is impossible to tell. Because like everything else, we are making all this up as we go along.

For the time being, the generations above Millennials – as well as an ongoing majority among them – retain the idea of at least some fixed points of sexual identity. Perhaps not least because knowing where other people stand imposes at least some clarity on relationships and potential relationships. But the fact that all this can change from one fixed identity to another, and from there to fluidity, points to more than a leap around from one dogma to another. It suggests a deep uncertainty about one underlying and rarely mentioned fact, which is that we still don't have much or any idea as to why some people are gay. After decades of research this is a huge – and potentially destabilizing – question to remain unresolved on an identity question which has arrived at the very forefront of our purported values.

Some sensitivity over this whole subject is naturally understandable. After all, it was only in 1973 that the American Psychiatric Association decided that there was no scientific evidence for continuing to treat homosexuality as a disorder. That year they removed it from the APA's glossary of mental disorders (a rare example for that ever-growing tome of something being taken out). The World Health Organization performed the same task in 1992. None of which is very long ago, and a good reason why there is some remaining suspicion of the language or practice of medicalization or psychiatry making its way into any discussion of homosexuality.

Yet from an acceptance that being gay is not a mental disorder it does not follow that it is a wholly inbuilt and immovable state of being. In 2014 the Royal College of Psychiatrists (RCP) in London issued a fascinating 'statement on sexual orientation'. They were commendably adamant in their condemnation of anything that seeks to stigmatize people who say they are gay. And they explained that in any case the RCP does not believe that therapies to alter anyone's sexual orientation could work in either direction. The RCP could no more make a homosexual straight than they could make a heterosexual gay. And yet they do make a fairly important acknowledgement, which is that 'The Royal College of Psychiatrists considers that sexual orientation is determined by a combination of biological and postnatal environment factors.' They cite a set of sources to back up this statement,[10] and they follow it up again with the reassertion that 'There is no evidence to go beyond this and impute any kind of choice into the origins of sexual orientation.'[11]

But while being concerned about putative 'conversion therapies', which create an environment in which 'prejudice and discrimination flourish', as 'wholly unethical' and purporting to address something which is 'not a disorder', the RCP does say this:

> It is not the case that sexual orientation is immutable or might not vary to some extent in a person's life. Nevertheless, sexual orientation for most people seems to be set around a point that is largely heterosexual or homosexual. Bisexual people may have a degree of choice in terms of sexual expression in which they can focus on their heterosexual or homosexual side.
>
> It is also the case that for people who are unhappy about their sexual orientation – whether heterosexual, homosexual or bisexual – there may be grounds for exploring therapeutic options to help them live more comfortably with it, reduce their distress and reach a greater degree of acceptance of their sexual orientation.[12]

The American Psychological Association is in agreement on this. Its most up-to-date advice on the matter says:

> There is no consensus among scientists about the exact reasons that an individual develops a heterosexual, bisexual, gay or lesbian orientation. Although much research has examined the possible genetic, hormonal, developmental, social and cultural influences on sexual orientation, no findings have emerged that permit scientists to conclude that sexual orientation is determined by any particular factor or factors. Many think that nature and nurture both play complex roles; most people experience little or no sense of choice about their sexual orientation.[13]

This is all very admirable from the point of view of attempting to reduce discrimination or tortuous and unsuccessful attitudes to 'straighten people out'. But it highlights the fact that the whole question of what makes someone gay remains unanswered. The law may have changed. But there is almost no more knowledge now than there was beforehand about why and whether someone is or chooses to be homosexual.

Not that there haven't been some useful discoveries. In the 1940s the sexologist Alfred Kinsey performed what was up to that point the most sophisticated and wide-ranging fieldwork into human sexual preferences. Despite plenty of methodological quibbles, his findings were for years assumed to be roughly accurate. In the works that were the products of that research (*Sexual Behaviour in the Human Male*, 1948, and *Sexual Behaviour in the Human Female*, 1953) Kinsey and his colleagues declared that they had found that 13 per cent of men were 'predominantly homosexual' for at least a three-year period between the age of 16 and 55 and that around 20 per cent of women had had some same-sex experience. Kinsey's famous 'scale' of human sexual experience would produce the headline claim that around 10 per cent of the general population was homosexual. In the years since Kinsey these figures have been – like everything else in the area – a battleground. Religious groups have welcomed any and all surveys which suggest the number of homosexuals is lower than that. For instance they leapt on the 1991 US National Survey of Men, which claimed that only 1.1 per cent of men were 'exclusively homosexual', and Britain's Office for National Statistics (ONS), which arrived at the same figure two decades later. In 1993 a face-to-face interviews-based survey conducted by the Alan Guttmacher Institute in America came up with the headline figure of just 1 per cent of the population being gay. This figure – the lowest such figure arrived at to date – was embraced by the same religious groups. So the chairman of the Traditional Values Coalition hurrahed 'Finally, the truth has surfaced.' And one right-wing radio host declared 'We've been vindicated.'[14]

But just as there are those who welcome all statistics which minimize the number of gays in the general population, so there are obviously also those who wish to maximize the numbers. The gay rights group Stonewall has described the statistic of 5–7 per cent of the general population being gay as a 'reasonable estimate', but this is a considerable way south from Kinsey. New technology allows some of the debate around all of this to be concluded, or at least clarified. It has its own methodological problems, just as the ONS's questions to households does (in that case caused by difficulties such as how to factor in closeted gays). But since very few people will be systematically lying into their search engines, the information gleaned on homosexuality from Big Data is considerable. The former Google data scientist Seth Stephens-Davidowitz revealed that about 2.5 per cent of male Facebook users register an interest in members of the same sex.

In searches for internet pornography Stephens-Davidowitz comes closer to reaching a figure that includes people who are not so open about their sexuality. One striking thing about these figures is that they are fairly consistent across states in the US. For instance, while there are twice as many gay Facebook users in Rhode Island than there are in Mississippi (a fact that can partly be explained by gay migration), internet pornography searches are remarkably consistent. So while around 4.8 per cent of searches for pornography in Mississippi are for gay porn, in Rhode Island the figure is 5.2 per cent. With all the necessary caveats (people looking out of curiosity, for instance) Stephens-Davidowitz comes to the conclusion that a fair estimate of the gay population in America is around 5 per cent.[15]

Yet like all other statistics these continue to be used as some sort of football. In 2017 the Office of National Statistics in the UK said that the number of gay, lesbian, bisexual or transgender people in Great Britain had hit 1 million people for the first time. The UK's *Pink News* described this as 'a landmark figure for the community', adding that the figure was 'high – but not high enough'.[16] Begging the question, how high would you like it to be?

Despite all this, in recent decades the public have been arriving at their own views on the matter. And their views have changed very significantly. In 1977 just over 10 per cent of Americans thought that people were born gay. By 2015 around half of the US population believed this to be the case. Over the same period the number of Americans who agreed that being gay was 'due to someone's upbringing and environment' halved from the 60 per cent who had agreed with that statement in 1977. Not coincidentally the moral attitudes of Americans towards homosexuality changed enormously in the same period. Gallup polls between 2001 and 2015 showed that gay and lesbian relationships were seen as 'morally acceptable' by 40 per cent of Americans in 2001 and 63 per cent in 2015. Those who thought they were 'morally wrong' in the same time period fell from 53 per cent to 34 per cent.[17] The single factor which opinion polls showed to have changed public opinion on the matter was people knowing somebody – a family member, friend or work colleague – who is gay. This factor has significant implications for other rights movements. A second obvious factor in that change in attitude has been the increasing visibility of gays in public life.

But the moral factor that has most clearly shifted attitudes towards homosexuality has been a shift from the idea that homosexuality is a learned behaviour to a belief that it is innate. A recognition of how important this was in the case of gays has significant implications for every other rights campaign. For here we can glimpse one of the most significant building blocks of contemporary morality: the fundamental recognition that it is wrong to punish, demean or look down on people for characteristics over which they have no control. This may seem like an obvious building block of morality, but it was not there for much of human history, when people's unalterable characteristics were very often used against them.

HARDWARE VERSUS SOFTWARE, AND THE NEED TO BE 'BORN THIS WAY'

Nevertheless, the contemporary world has begun to settle on a morality which roots itself in this dispute and which may be viewed as a hardware versus software question.

Hardware is something that people cannot change and so (the reasoning goes) it is something that they should not be judged on. Software, on the other hand, can be changed and may demand judgements – including moral judgements – to be made. Inevitably in such a system there will be a push to make potential software issues into hardware issues, not least in order to garner more sympathy for people who may in fact have software, rather than hardware, issues.

For instance, if a person is an alcoholic or a drug addict then people may regard them as having a failing over which they should be able to exercise some control. If they fail then it is a consequence of their own weakness, bad decision-making or some other moral laxness. If on the other hand they cannot help their behaviour then they are not to be blamed but rather to be regarded as victims of circumstance and to be understood as such. An unrelenting drunk may be a pain to everybody around them, but if he is said to have been born with a proclivity towards alcoholism – or better still to have an 'alcoholic gene' – he may be viewed in a very different light. Instead of some degree of criticism he may be regarded with varying degrees of sympathy. Were his alcoholism a learned behaviour then he may be regarded as weak or even bad. In general we modern people are more sympathetic to behaviour which cannot be changed, but we can still be critical or questioning of a lifestyle which we think is a matter of choice – especially if the behaviour is inconvenient for anyone else. Homosexuality could (from a reproductive angle, among others) be said to be inconvenient to society, and the question of what it actually is therefore presents a perfectly legitimate question for society to be engaged with.

The single factor that has most clearly helped to change public opinion about homosexuality in the West has been the decision that homosexuality is in fact a 'hardware' rather than a 'software' issue. Some people – mainly religious conservatives – continue to try to smuggle in their contrary view on this matter. For instance some of them still like to describe homosexuality as a 'lifestyle choice' – a phrase insinuating that homosexuals have chosen their own programming.

Countries and times in which this attitude predominates tend to coincide with periods of repressive laws against homosexual activity. And so there is an understandable push to reject the 'lifestyle choice' claim and encourage the recognition that homosexuality is a hardware matter or, as Lady Gaga would put it, a matter of being 'Born this way'.

In fact homosexuality has been morally accepted for too short a time in too few places to draw many long-term conclusions about it, let alone base any moral theory around it. What is certain is that the question of whether it is innate or a choice – hardware or software – has a profound effect on the sympathy which people are willing to expend on the issue. If people 'choose' to be gay – or it is 'learned behaviour' – then it must be possible to some extent either to unlearn it or even present it in such a light that nobody would wish to choose it.

The idea that, rather than being a 'lifestyle choice', people are 'born this way' has certainly received non-scientific boosts in recent years. The presence in everyone's lives of more and more visibly gay people has meant that the option of 'hiding' homosexuality becomes ever more unlikely to work. Meantime the stories of famous gay people – and especially the fear, bullying and discrimination that many have suffered – have clearly persuaded a lot of people that no one would willingly choose this. What child would want to be more of a target for bullies by being gay? What developing adult would want to add an extra layer of complexity to an already complex life?

So the zeitgeist appears to have settled on the 'Born this way' theory, while avoiding any glances at the destabilizing fact that the science is still not very much use in helping to back up Lady Gaga's theory.

Some fascinating work has been done in epigenetics in order to locate a gene variation that may cause homosexuality. The latest work focuses on methyl groups which get added to gene molecules. In 2015 scientists at UCLA announced that they had discovered a form of DNA modification in parts of the genome which differed between gay and straight brothers. But the study relied on small samples and as a result was strongly disputed despite the resulting hopes and headlines. There have been a number of similar studies, all of which have proved inconclusive.

For the time being the 'gay gene' remains elusive. Which is not to say that it won't be found at some point. Only that the war that goes on around it is telling. In general, fundamentalist Christians and others want a 'gay gene' not to be found, for the discovery of such a gene would seriously harm one of the foundations of their own view of the world ('God makes people gay?') and would have to affect their own stance on the matter. People who are gay, on the other hand, have a clear bias in favour of finding the gene, as it has the potential to permanently get them off any and all software accusations. So the work goes on – centring on identical male twins, whose sexuality interestingly appears to be identical when they are.

Perhaps more attention should be given to the question of what would happen if those most willing to discover a 'gay gene' get their way. Not all of the signs are good. Earlier this decade a neuroscience researcher named Chuck Roselli, at Oregon Health & Science University, produced a study of male sheep that appeared to prefer sex with other male sheep than with lady sheep. When his work became publicly known (thanks, as it happens, to an animal rights charity trying to whip up gay activists to their cause), it was claimed that Roselli's work was going to be used as a basis for eugenics efforts to stop humans being born gay.

Tens of thousands of emails and messages of complaint flooded in to Roselli's employer demanding he be sacked, and prominent gays and lesbians, including tennis star Martina Navratilova, attacked Roselli and his employer in the media. The sheep studies were never intended to facilitate any such thing.[18] But if this is how people react to someone researching homoeroticism among sheep how would they react to a gay gene being discovered in human beings? And if a 'gay gene' was discovered would parents in time be allowed to edit the patterns in their children's DNA to account for that? What would be the justifications for preventing them doing so?

The heat which surrounds every aspect of the genetics on this matter is one reason why so little study has been done on other aspects of homosexuality. For instance there has been very little work done on what role, if any, homosexuality might play in evolutionary terms. In 1995–6 an American and a British academic got into an exchange on this subject.[19] Gordon G. Gallup of State University of New York at Albany and John Archer of the University of Central Lancashire published their exchange in a scholarly journal. It focused on whether negative attitudes towards homosexuals are inherited as part of natural selection or part of a bias that is transmitted through culture. The fascinating debate centred around Gallup's suggestion that 'In its simplest form parents who showed a concern for their child's sexual orientation may have left more descendants than those who were indifferent.' Gallup also contends that what has become known as 'homophobia' may be a consequence of parental concern that the emerging sexuality of their children may be impressionable. Two demonstrations of this are higher concern about homosexuals doing jobs which bring them into regular contact with children and, secondly, that once their children are grown-up, they become much more relaxed about their being around gay people.

All, some or none of this may be true. The opinion data on which Gallup based his work was collected decades ago now, when attitudes towards homosexuality were – as we have seen – very different to what they are today. What is interesting is that studies of what evolutionary role homosexuality may or may not play, what evolutionary justification there might be for homosexuality and what evolutionary justification there might therefore be for some suspicion of homosexuality have evaporated in respectable biological debate. In private some biologists are willing to admit that this is a failure of their field. But the contemporary waters around this whole subject are now so deep and so perilous that these are not questions which academics seeking tenure would wish to engage in. If we have decided what the answers cannot be – or what answers we could not cope with – then there seems little point, beyond a fondness for truth, in asking the questions.

THE PHILOSOPHICAL CONFUSION

If scientists are unable or unwilling to answer questions over the origins of homosexuality then responsibility for discussion around the issue must go elsewhere. Ordinarily it might fall to philosophy. But there too almost no progress has been made on the question for many years. In fact for a couple of millennia at best.

Aristotle makes only a passing reference to homosexuality in his *Nicomachean Ethics*. He includes this condition in a list which wouldn't please many people today. In his discussion of 'morbid' and 'diseased' states in Book 7 of his *Ethics* he talks of the common situations of women who rip open other pregnant women and eat the child, of a man who kills and then eats his mother and also of a slave who ate the liver of another slave. These Aristotle sees as products of 'disease', including 'madness'. But other states occur from 'habit', or 'custom', including plucking out of hair, nail-chewing and homosexuality. Or sodomy. Or possibly pederasty. There is some difference of opinion on the precise issue that Aristotle is addressing (confused as it is by his differing views on the nature of same-sex relations). But if we are to take it that Aristotle is addressing the subject of homosexuality then it is striking that he essentially holds the same position in the third century BC as the American Psychological Association and the Royal College of Psychiatrists do in the twenty-first century. He sees it as a characteristic found in some men by nature and in others as a result of 'habitation'. The only point of difference is that a reputable twenty-first-century source would be unlikely to give the example that Aristotle does for what might cause such 'habitation'. Aristotle gives the example: 'such as in those who have been abused from childhood'.[20]

Nor have more recent philosophers than Aristotle been much more use in getting to the root of the question. Today Michel Foucault is one of the most cited scholars in the social sciences in the West.[21] For all the certainty and sanctity that is piled onto him, even in one of Foucault's most famous and most influential works – his *History of Sexuality* (1976) – his views on homosexuality are deeply confused. Foucault points out that to talk of homosexuals as though they are a defined group is historically illiterate, apart from anything else. Those people who were accused of gay acts in the past were not a distinct category of individuals, as the nineteenth-century man or woman started to consider them. As he describes the change that happened late in the nineteenth century, 'the sodomite had been a temporary aberration; the homosexual was now a species.'[22]

But other than using the opportunity to push his theories on power and sex further along their way, quite what Foucault thought about homosexuality is seriously debatable. At times he seemed to see it as absolutely central to identity. At other times (even in the same work) he considered it as unimportant. Those who have come after him, cited him and made themselves his disciples have used sexuality – like everything else – as a way to carry out group identification in opposition to the heterosexual norm. Foucault's follower at MIT, David Halperin, famously said that there was 'no orgasm without ideology'.[23] Which aside from suggesting tedium in bed also points to the fact that people who wish to understand homosexuality through this prism are piling unstable foundations on unstable foundations.

One of the few things in his work that does seem clear is that even Foucault himself seems to have recognized that sexual identity was probably not a wise basis on which to build any formal identity. Indeed towards the end of the first volume of his *History of Sexuality* he marvels at the way in which something which was for centuries thought to be a kind of 'madness' should have become the centrepiece of our 'intelligibility', and that our 'identity' should now be the source of 'what was perceived as an obscure and nameless urge'. Sex has become, he claims, 'more important than our soul, more important almost than our life'. The Faustian pact 'whose temptation has been instilled in us' is (he claims) 'to exchange life in its entirety for sex itself, for the truth and the sovereignty of sex. Sex is worth dying for.'[24] Although his disciples seem to have decided otherwise – and although Foucault didn't go into this in depth – it would seem that even Foucault noticed what an unstable thing sex or even sexuality is to base an identity on.

GAYS VERSUS QUEERS

In spite of all of this, today being gay has become one of the absolutely central building blocks of identity, politics and 'identity politics'. LGBT is now one of the groupings which mainstream politicians routinely speak about – and to – as if they actually exist like a racial or religious community. It is a form of absurdity. For even on its own terms this composition is wildly unsustainable and contradictory. Gay men and gay women have almost nothing in common. It may be too pedestrian to even mention, but gay men and lesbians do not always form the warmest of relationships. Gay men often characterize lesbians as dowdy and boring. Lesbians often characterize gay men as silly and displaying a failure to grow up. Neither have very much use for each other, and almost none meet in any 'communal' spaces. There are places where gay men can hook up and places where gay women can hook up, but there have hardly been any places in the decades since gay liberation where gay men and women organize or assemble to be near each other on anything like a regular basis.

Gay men and gay women, meanwhile, have a famous amount of suspicion towards people who claim to be 'bisexual'. The 'B' in LGBT is a source of occasional angst within the gay media. But bisexuals continue to be viewed not so much a part of the same 'community' as gays as some kind of betrayal from within its midst. Gay men tend to believe that men who claim to be 'Bi' are in fact gays in some form of denial ('Bi now, gay later'). And while a woman who sometimes sleeps with women will often get a hearing from male heterosexuals, few women react positively as partners to men who also sleep with other men. The question of what any of these people – gays, lesbians or bisexuals – have to do with people who decide to try to swap genders is a question for another chapter.

But it is worth bearing these internal frictions and contradictions in mind when people talk about the LGBT community, or try to co-opt it for any political purpose. It barely exists even within each letter of its constituent parts. And each has little in common with the others. Before decriminalization of homosexuality in the 1960s things were arguably slightly different. But the L's don't need the G's today, and the G's don't much care for the L's and almost everybody can be united in suspicion of the B's. And there is tremendous dispute over whether the T's are the same thing as everybody else or an insult to them. Still nobody is any the wiser about where any or all of this comes from. And yet it remains the means by which people are willing to identify vast swathes of the population, and build one of the defining justifications and bases for the liberal society.

Nor is it surprising that a conglomeration of people of such contradictory positions and origins might have serious tensions within every element of their own movement. From the origins of gay activism to the present every imaginable tension still exists over what is being asked for. It comes down to the unresolved question of whether gays are exactly like everybody else other than in one single characteristic. Or whether that single characteristic makes gays utterly unlike the rest of society. It is a divide which falls into two broad camps.

In the first are those who believe that gays are – and should be – just like everybody else. That they will win any and all remaining rights battles by demonstrating that nothing makes them different from their heterosexual friends and neighbours. Just like straight people, gays can live in houses with nice picket fences, can marry, have monogamous relationships and eventually produce and raise children like everybody else. In essence they can be respectable. This at least is one option, laid out in texts like Hunter Madsen and Marshall Kirk's 1989 work, *After the Ball: How America Will Conquer its Fear and Hatred of Gays in the '90s.*[25] But such works, preaching a path to acceptance to gays via normalization with the rest of society, always found themselves countered by another element within precisely the same alleged 'community'.

This side might be described (and self-described) not as 'gay' but as 'queer'. It was – and is – the group of people who believe that being attracted to the same sex means more than simply being attracted to the same sex. It is a group of people who believe that being attracted to the same sex should merely be the first stage in a wilder journey. The first step not just to getting on with life but to transgressing the normal modes of life. Whereas gays may just want to be accepted like everyone else, queers want to be recognized as fundamentally different to everyone else and to use that difference to tear down the kind of order that gays are working to get into. It is an almost never acknowledged but completely central divide that has existed as long as 'gay' has been recognized as an identity.

At the start of the gay revolution there were those pushing for a unified 'liberation front' which could align the 'gay liberation front' with other movements. Under the influence of activists like Jim Fouratt these alliances extended (though were not limited) to domestic movements like the Black Panthers and foreign ones such as the Viet Cong, Mao's regime in China, Castro's Cuba and more. The fact that these movements were explicit in their varied opposition to homosexuals (Mao's China, for instance, being willing to publicly castrate 'sexual degenerates') was merely one of those contradictions that needed to be got over.[26] The gay rights movement kept identifying itself with movements that were not just revolutionary but opposed to the society that the movement was seeking to be accepted into. In every decade that has followed since the 1960s that divide has been replicated in the gay world.

During the AIDS crisis in the 1980s there was a considerable (and understandable) radicalization among gays in Europe and America. Groups like 'Act Up' said that their elected representatives were not doing enough to recognize the unbelievable suffering which was going on with the unleashing of 'the plague'. Such groups took direct action, but other 'gays' felt this was at the expense of the cause as a whole. In an important book in the early 1990s, pushing back against some of the 'queer' takeover of the gay rights fight, the American author Bruce Bawer recalled the 'uncompromising' attitudes of groups like Act Up. In *A Place at the Table* he recalled a response to a letter criticizing the group's methods in the now-defunct gay weekly *QW*: 'You self-hating, hypocritical, misinformed piece of shit', one typical response read. 'You're a disgrace to the queer nation.'[27] What was the 'queer nation'? Was it to have only one voice and one set of aims? Was it to search for a life apart, or a life like any other? Then, as now, the question was unaddressed and unresolved. Were gays like everyone else, or were they a group of other people who wanted to knowingly and deliberately segregate themselves, as a city state if not a gay nation in their own right?

'Gays' and 'queers' remained in conflict throughout the 1990s. In Britain those who sought long-term acceptance and respectability were often horrified at the actions of groups like 'Outrage'. On Easter Sunday 1998 Peter Tatchell and other members of his group stormed the pulpit at Canterbury Cathedral, disrupting the Archbishop of Canterbury during his Easter sermon and waving placards about the Church of England's attitude towards gay rights. Was it a sensible way to bring gay rights to the fore, or did it risk alienating people who might be scared off by the apparent 'fundamentalism' of these gays? The same debate occurred (and to a lesser extent continues to happen) elsewhere. A bill legally opposing anti-gay discrimination went unpassed in New York State for 21 years. One of those involved described in 1992 how 'many legislators' contacts with gay groups came during angry clashes', such as one in which the radical group Queer Nation 'paraded around with an effigy of Senate majority leader Ralph J. Marino', which they burned. Other groups lobbied more effectively, taking what was described as a more 'polite' approach.[28]

But the radical attitude persisted. And the divide between the gays who wanted equality and those who wanted to use being gay merely as a first step to tearing down some other order or forming some new sort of society persisted. It was rarely more openly displayed than in the 'March on Washington' on 25 April 1993. This march had been intended to do for gay rights what Martin Luther King's march had done for the civil rights movement of three decades earlier. But the 1993 march was a mess, including 'obscene comics' and 'fire-breathing radicals who spoke for only a tiny segment of the gay population'. It was, as Bawer said, 'as if the march's organisers were out to confirm every last stereotype about homosexuals':

> I kept comparing the event with the 1963 March on Washington for black civil rights. On that occasion, Martin Luther King, Jr., had given the speech of his lifetime and had imbued not only his followers but every scrupulous American with a sense of the seriousness of his mission and the rightness of his cause. He hadn't called for revolution

or denounced American democracy or shared the podium with stand-up comics . . . On that day in 1963 he gave voice to a vision of racial equality that struck at the conscience of America, bringing out the best in his followers and speaking to the more virtuous instincts of his antagonists.[29]

And this is another aspect of the gay rights movement that has continued to fester. As another gay writer, Andrew Sullivan, noted in the 1990s, 'Go to any march for gay rights and you will see the impossibility of organising it into a coherent lobby: such attempts are always undermined by irony, or exhibitionism, or irresponsibility.'[30]

At almost any demonstration for gay rights today – most prominently the 'gay pride' marches which happen around the world – the call for legal equality (now achieved in most Western countries) is mixed in with things that would cause many homosexuals as well as heterosexuals to blush. There is nothing wrong with people enjoying whatever kinks they like in the privacy of their homes. But you don't have to be prudish to feel that the phalanxes of people at such protests dressed in fetish gear, in chaps and more, is off-putting to whatever cause they are hoping to advance. If the black civil rights movement had included a fetish section it would have been considerably easier to ignore its moral force.

But the gays will not be corralled. Not by themselves and certainly not by others. Those calling for equality will always include a contingent who mistake exhibitionism for activism, feeling that nobody is free or equal until they have the right to dress in puppy gear and be led on all fours by a 'master' down a public street. The liberal thinker Paul Berman recalls the 'high holy day' Stonewall commemorations as they went on into the 1990s. How the 'dour gay politicos' would march past calling for civil rights, followed by 'barechested young men' dancing erotically, women with their tops off, fetishists with their leathers, sadomasochists flogging each other in the street, and then the slogans: 'rectal pride', 'vaginal pride'. The justification for this (put forward by the intersectional sociologist Arlene Stein among others) was that if gay people looked like everybody else then they would disappear. Only by being flagrant and visible could they ensure they did not. Stein ended up describing herself as, among other things, a 'sexpert'. A title which as Berman noted, 'anybody would like to be, though maybe not twenty-four hours a day'.[31] Those who push the 'queer' view of gay do tend to present being gay as a full-time occupation. Those who are gay tend not to like them.

EQUAL OR BETTER?

Even in the more conservative demands of the gay rights movements are questions which lie unaddressed and filled with risk. For example, if gays have achieved the same rights as everyone else, should they be subjected to the same standards as everybody else? Or is there built into gay equality some kind of opt-out? Now that gay marriage exists should gay couples be expected to be monogamous just as heterosexual couples are expected to be? If they do not have children to bind them together does it make sense to expect two men or two women who meet in their early twenties to get married and then have sex solely with each other for the next six decades or more? Will they want to? If not, what are the social consequences? There must be consequences after all, mustn't there? Among the first couples to get married in the US was one who immediately admitted to an interviewer that they were in an open relationship. What are other people – including heterosexuals – to think of gay marriage in such a situation? The question rumbles on, entirely unremarked upon. In Britain one prominent gay couple who are married have gone to extraordinary lengths to conceal the fact that they are in an open relationship. Presumably because they realize the damage that it could do if the majority-straight population were to learn of 'infidelity' in a high-profile married gay couple.

Amid all the talk of 'equality' there isn't anything like certainty that most gays actually want to be completely equal. Many would appear to want to be precisely equal but with a little gay bonus. When the American TV celebrity Ellen DeGeneres came out as lesbian in 1997 she took a considerable risk. The fact that it was a risk which paid off and significantly increased lesbian visibility made her an object of respect. But is it the remaining social capital accrued from that act or some type of lesbian advantage which allows her a kind of latitude that no straight man would be allowed? Such as the game 'Who'd you rather', where Ellen invites guests on her show (male and female) to look at pictures of two famous people at a time and say 'Who'd you rather'.

At the start of the 'MeToo' scandal in 2017, any man who had not just ever inappropriately touched, but anyone who had ever objectified, a woman was in trouble. But it seemed that DeGeneres did not have to play by the same rules. Late in October, the month that Harvey Weinstein fell from grace, she posted to social media a picture of herself with Katy Perry. The pop star was wearing a noticeably figure-hugging dress which displayed her breasts to great effect. The photo showed DeGeneres with one arm around Perry, at eye-level with her breasts and ogling them with her mouth open. 'Happy birthday Katy Perry!' read the accompanying message on DeGeneres's official Twitter account. 'It's time to bring out the big balloons!'[32] Because although by then there was considerable agreement that men could not objectify women, it appeared that an exemption clause existed for celebrity lesbians.

GAY PARENTING

The success of the gay rights movement may be understandably touted in all Western liberal democracies. But there is a flip side to its celebration, which is the moral blackmail it holds over other issues. What might be equivalent issues today that will be looked back on in the future with the kind of shame with which the criminalization of homosexuals is now looked back on? A number of candidates are available to fill the space. But there is a knock-on effect for other gay rights. For having got criminalization so wrong, everything else in the area can start to sail by before our eyes without much or any contestation.

The advent of gay marriage in the US and UK has led to an upsurge in the ensuing rights demand, which is the right to gay parenting. Not just the right of gays to adopt children, but to have children of their own. Celebrity gay couples like Elton John and David Furnish and Tom Daley and Dustin Lance Black often portray this as though it were the simplest thing imaginable: 'We decided to start a family.' In February 2018 Daley and Black released a photo of the two of them holding a photo of an ultrasound. Newspaper headlines read 'Tom Daley Announces he and his Husband are Having a Baby'.[33] The old gay joke used to go that 'We haven't had a baby yet, but that doesn't mean we can't keep trying.' But here was a story suggesting a gay breakthrough. And it soon became clear that anyone who thought 'Can two men just make a baby?' received the reply 'Why not? Bigot.'

Naturally a columnist in the *Daily Mail* trod on the waiting landmine. But the question 'How, exactly?' was hardly without justifications. One was that writing women out of anything had in the preceding years been agreed upon to be a serious *faux pas*. Yet here were two gay men writing at least one woman – who must have been relevant along the route somewhere – out of the story entirely. Indeed, writing a woman out of perhaps the most important story any person could ever be involved in. The second reason for pause was that the carefully manicured narrative of the Daley–Black baby was lying to a whole generation of young gays. For the fact is that, while it is significantly easier for gay women, two gay men will find it exceptionally difficult to have a biological baby, and even if they do it will only carry the biological imprint of one of the parents – setting up questions and potential tensions of its own not very far down the road. The even plainer part of the lie is that even this situation – in which two gay men produce a child with the DNA of one of them – is not available to most gays. It is available only to very rich gays. Egg and surrogacy procedures do not come cheap. But until the very moderate backlash against the framing of their pregnancy, none of this was going to be on the table. A group called 'Stop funding Hate' produced a list of companies which advertised in the *Daily Mail* and tried by this route to get people to pressurize them to stop advertising in a paper that the campaign group said was 'increasingly out of touch with the views of mainstream British society'.[34] All this for saying 'wait a moment' on the claim that two men can just have a baby.

But the 'not only equal, but slightly better' attitude lives on in the gay debate as in so many others. In 2014 researchers at the University of Melbourne carried out a study which they said showed that the children of same-sex couples are healthier and happier than children brought up by heterosexual couples. The lead researcher on the project, Dr Simon Crouch, claimed that one cause of this superior happiness was that same-sex couples didn't fall into traditional 'gender stereotypes' and this led to 'a more harmonious family unit'.[35] It's not such an uncommon claim. In 2010 the BBC broadcast a short film by the Reverend Sharon Ferguson (who was also CEO of the Lesbian and Gay Christian Movement) in which she claimed that lesbians like her weren't just as good at being parents as heterosexual couples. According to her, lesbians actually make better parents than heterosexual couples do.[36] Similar claims, based on equally dubious statistics that always sound more like propaganda than analysis, crop up with considerable regularity.

For instance in March 2018 researchers from The Williams Institute at UCLA School of Law issued their findings after studying 515 couples in Vermont over a 12 year period. According to this research gay male couples were more likely to stay together than lesbian couples or heterosexual couples.[37] This was promptly written up in the gay press and elsewhere as 'Gay Marriages are Less Likely to Break Up than Straight Ones, Study Reveals'.[38]

It may be thought that gay parenting would fall solely onto the gay side of the gay versus queer divide, but behind some of the coverage is a recognizable echo of one of the ugliest noises that always existed on the fringe of the queer rights movement. This was the claim that equality was not enough, because gays were in some sense 'better' than straight people. The radical gay American activist Robert Rafsky was once filmed howling to fellow gay activists about heterosexuals during a protest, 'We're more important than they are!' An attitude which, as Bruce Bawer wrote, 'is no less ugly than that of heterosexuals who take it for granted that they are more important than homosexuals'.[39] But there is confusion about this, as about so many other things.

Among the last two confusions worth selecting is something that may be among the biggest issues of all. It is whether being gay means that you are attracted to members of your own sex, or whether it means that you are part of a grand political project.

IS GAY POLITICAL?

Ahead of the 2016 Brexit referendum in the UK, the actor Sir Ian McKellen was interviewed about which way he was planning to vote. The interview's headline quote was 'Brexit makes no sense if you're gay.' In the piece Sir Ian – who has done an enormous amount to advance fundamental gay rights over the decades – said that, looking at the vote from a gay perspective, 'there's only one point, which is to stay. If you're a gay person, you're an internationalist.'[40] Presumably people who thought they were gay and thought they'd vote 'leave' had been doing it wrong all these years. As so often, far worse wars have been fought on the same terrain in America.

The date of 21 July 2016 should have been a great moment for supporters of gay rights in the United States. That day Peter Thiel took to the stage of the Republican National Convention in Cleveland, Ohio, and addressed the main hall. A gay man had appeared on a Republican platform before, but not alone and not openly identifying as such. By contrast the co-founder of PayPal, an early investor in Facebook, made a clear and head-on reference to his sexuality as he endorsed Donald Trump as the candidate of the Republican Party for President. During his speech Thiel said, 'I am proud to be gay. I am proud to be a Republican. But most of all I am proud to be an American.' All of this was received with huge cheers in the hall. Such a situation would have been unimaginable even a few election cycles before. NBC was among the mainstream media to report all of this in a positive light. 'Peter Thiel makes history at RNC' ran the headline.

The gay press was not so positive. America's foremost gay magazine, *Advocate*, attacked Thiel in a long and curious piece consisting of an excommunication from the church of gay. The title read: 'Peter Thiel Shows Us There's a Difference between Gay Sex and Gay.' The sub-banner on the 1,300-word piece by Jim Downs (an associate professor of history at Connecticut College) asked 'When you abandon numerous aspects of queer identity, are you still LGBT?'

While Downs conceded that Thiel is 'a man who has sex with other men', he questioned whether he was in any other way actually 'gay'. 'That question might seem narrow,' the author admitted. 'But it is [*sic*] actually raises a broad and crucial distinction we must make in our notions of sexuality, identity, and community.' After pooh-poohing those who had hailed Thiel's speech as any kind of watershed moment – let alone 'progress' – Downs pronounced his anathema: 'Thiel is an example of a man who has sex with other men, but not a gay man. Because he does not embrace the struggle of people to embrace their distinctive identity.'

Exhibit A for this gay heresy-finder was that in his speech at the RNC Thiel had dismissed the endless high-profile rows about trans bathroom access, who should use which bathrooms and what facilities should be laid on where. Although Thiel had said that he didn't agree with 'every plank in our party's platform', he did state that 'fake culture wars only distract us from our economic decline'. As he went on, 'When I was a kid, the great debate was about how to defeat the Soviet Union. And we won. Now we are told that the great debate is about who gets to use which bathroom. This is a distraction from our real problems. Who cares?' This went down very well in Cleveland. And if opinion polls are anything to go by it is a statement that would go down very well across America. It is demonstrably the case that more people are worried about the economy than are worried about bathroom access. But for *Advocate* this was a deviation too far.

While reaffirming his own 'sexual choices' Thiel was guilty of 'separating himself from gay identity'. His opinions on the relative ephemerality to the wider culture of transgender bathrooms 'effectively rejects the conception of LGBT as a cultural identity that requires political struggle to defend'. Thiel was alleged to be part of a movement which since the 1970s had not 'invested in the creation of a cultural identity to the extent that their forebears did'. The success of gay liberation had apparently stopped them doing this 'cultural work'. But this was dangerous, as the recent massacre at a gay nightclub had shown in some unconnected way. The author left his readers with the powerful reminder that 'The gay liberation movement has left us a powerful legacy, and protecting that legacy requires understanding the meaning of the term "gay" and not using it simply as a synonym for same-sex desire and intimacy.'[41]

In fact the massacre at the Pulse nightclub in Orlando in June 2016 had been carried out by a young Muslim who swore allegiance to Islamic State (ISIS). Yet this detail didn't detain *Advocate* or the Gay Pride march in New York later the same month. On that occasion the parade led with a huge rainbow banner emblazoned with the words 'Republican Hate Kills!', clearly forgetting that Omar Mateen had not been a member of the Republican Party.

It isn't just that the self-appointed organizers of the 'gay community' have a particular view of politics. They also have a specific view of the alleged responsibilities that being gay brings with it. In 2013 the novelist

Bret Easton Ellis was reprimanded and banned from the annual media awards dinner by the gay organization GLAAD. He had been found guilty of tweeting views about the asinine nature of gay television characters that GLAAD said 'the gay community had responded negatively to'.[42] This censorious tone – the prim schoolmaster tone – is the same one *Pink News* unleashed with a straight face in 2018, with its list of ten 'dos and don'ts' for straight people on 'how they should behave in gay bars'.[43] In all of these cases the normal instinct is to say 'Just who the hell do you think you are?' But after his reprimand for wrong-think Ellis managed to sum up what had become a whole part of the new gay problem. This was, as he said, that we had come to live in 'The reign of The Gay Man as Magical Elf, who whenever he comes out appears before us as some kind of saintly E.T. whose sole purpose is to be put in the position of reminding us *only* about Tolerance and Our Own Prejudices and To Feel Good About Ourselves and to be *a symbol*.'

The reign of the magical gay elf has indeed been settled for the time being as one of the acceptable ways in which society has made its peace with homosexuality. Gays can now marry like everybody else can pretend that they have children in exactly the same way as everybody else, and in general prove – as Dustin Lance Black and Tom Daley do on their YouTube channel – that gays are unthreatening people who actually spend their lives being cute and making cupcakes. As Ellis wrote, 'The Sweet and Sexually Unthreatening and Super-Successful Gay is supposed to be destined to transform The Hets into noble gay-loving protectors – as long as the gay in question isn't messy or sexual or difficult.'[44] The former *enfant terrible* of American fiction had put his finger on something here.

WHAT ARE THE PLAUSIBLE CAUSES OF 'HOMOPHOBIA'?

None of this justifies hatred or violence towards individuals, let alone whole groups of people. But there are plenty of stages between absolute equanimity and ease around people and a desire to violently attack them. The fact is that some heterosexuals are genuinely unnerved by gay people. Perhaps many, most or even all heterosexuals feel something like this, very far away from dislike, but something unnerving. While much of the writing and study of what has come to be known as 'homophobia' has focused on the false justifications for it, the plausible reasons for something like it have been ignored. This is more the case with male homosexuality than lesbianism. For all sorts of historical and social reasons, lesbianism has rarely been viewed as a fundamental attack on the social order in the way that male homosexuality has. And that may be because there is something about the nature of male homosexuality that strikes right at the root of one of the most important aspects not of some people's sexuality – but of everyone's sexuality.

At the root of nearly all female and male opposite-sex attraction are a whole series of unanswered and probably unanswerable questions. There are mysteries and confusions that occur at the levels of the dating ritual. These have been the staple for nearly all comedy and tragedy from the earliest times right up to the present. But the greatest and most enduring questions reside underneath the courting and dating rituals and often find full expression at the stage of the mating ritual. Women want to know what it is that men are after, what they want and what – if anything – they might be feeling during the act of sex. These questions are a staple of conversation between friends and a source of unbelievable private concern and angst at some stage (sometimes all) of most people's lives from adolescence onwards.

If there is any one thing in society that gets even close to matching the confusion and angst of women about men, it is of course the list of questions which men have about women. The subject of nearly all dramatic comedy is the inability of men to understand women. What are they thinking? What do they want? Why is it so hard to read their actions? Why does each sex expect the other to be able to decode their words, actions and silences, when no member of the opposite sex has ever been given a decoding manual for the opposite sex?

At the root of the heterosexual male's set of concerns and questions is the same question that women have about men. What is the act of lovemaking like? What does the other person feel? What do they get out of it? And how do the sexes fit together? The Ancients contemplated these questions of course. They linger in Plato – and are suggested most famously in Aristophanes' contribution to the *Symposium*. But none of it is answered. The mystery continues, and most likely always will.

And that is where the presence of especially male homosexuals makes its unnerving entrance. For until the advent of plausible surgery for people who believed that they had been born in the wrong body (of which more later), the most disturbing travellers across the sexes were male homosexuals. Not because of a strongly feminine part of their nature but because they knew something about the secret that women hold in sex. It is a question – and a concern – which has existed for millennia.

Consider the legend of Tiresias as recounted in the *Metamorphoses*. There Ovid tells the story of Jove and Juno, who one day are idly joking about lovemaking. Jove tells Juno, 'You women get more pleasure out of love than we men do, I'm sure.' Juno disagrees and so they resolve to get the opinion of Tiresias: 'He who knows both sides of love.' The story of Tiresias is complex. Ovid tells us that Tiresias once came upon a pair of huge snakes mating in a green copse. He attacked them with his staff and was immediately transformed from a man into a woman. After spending seven years as a woman, in the eighth year he came upon the snakes again, and struck them again. 'If striking you has magic power / To change the striker to the other sex, / I'll strike you now again,' he tells them. He does so and returns to being a man.

Jove and Juno summon Tiresias because they want him to declare judgement on the question of whether men or women enjoy lovemaking more. The traveller across the sexes declares that Jove is right: women enjoy lovemaking more. Offended by the claim, Juno condemns Tiresias to be blind, and it is to compensate him for his blindness (for no god can undo the act of another god) that Zeus endows Tiresias with the gift of prophecy – the gift that will later allow Tiresias to predict the fate of Narcissus.[45] Gods, snakes and staffs aside, the legend of Tiresias raises – and suggests an answer to – a question of the greatest depth. It is one that gay men also play a part in.

Remarkably few people have taken this question up. One of the few who has done so in recent years is the writer and (not coincidentally) classicist Daniel Mendelsohn in his 1999 work *The Elusive Embrace:*

Desire and the Riddle of Identity. In that family history-cum-memoir he delves deep into this subject. Asking what it is like when two men have sex he writes:

> In a way, it is like the experience of Tiresias; this is the real reason why gay men are uncanny, why the idea of gay men is disruptive and uncomfortable. All straight men who have engaged in the physical act of love know what it is like to penetrate a partner during intercourse, to be *inside* the other; all women who have had intercourse know what it is like to be penetrated, to have the other be inside oneself. But the gay man, in the very moment that he is either penetrating his partner or being penetrated by him, knows exactly what his partner is feeling and experiencing even as he himself has his own experience of exactly the opposite, the complementary act. Sex between men dissolves otherness into sameness, *men* into *de*, in a perfect suspension: there is nothing that either party doesn't know about the other. If the emotional aim of intercourse is a total *knowing* of the other, gay sex may be, in its way, perfect, because in it, a total knowledge of the other's experience is, finally, possible. But since the object of that knowledge is already wholly known to each of the parties, the act is also, in a way, redundant. Perhaps it is for this reason that so many of us keep seeking repetition, as if depth were impossible.

Mendelsohn goes on to describe a poem written by a friend about a young gay man who watches football being played by men whom he silently and jealously desires. The poem finishes with a lustful, imaginative description of the players having sex with their girlfriends and of one man 'falling through her into his own passion'. Mendelsohn describes his own earlier heterosexual experiences, and whilst admitting that there was nothing unpleasant about them, they were, he says, 'like participating in a sport for which you're the wrong physical type'. But he adds:

> From those indifferent couplings I do remember this: when men have sex with women, they fall into the woman. She is the thing that they desire, or sometimes fear, but in any event she is the end point, the

place where they are *going*. She is the destination. It is gay men who, during sex, fall through their partners back into themselves, over and over again.

He goes on:

> I have had sex with many men. Most of them look a certain way. They are medium in height and tend to prettiness. They will probably have blue eyes. They seem, from the street, or across the room, a bit solemn. When I hold them, it is like falling through a reflection back into my desire, into the thing that defines me, my self.[46]

This is a remarkable insight, and also a disturbing one. Because it suggests that there will always be something strange and potentially threatening about gay people – most especially gay men. Not just because being gay is an unstable component on which to base an individual identity and a hideously unstable way to try to base any form of group identity, but because gays will always present a challenge to something innate in the group that make up the majority in society.

All women have something that heterosexual men want. They are holders, and wielders, of a kind of magic. But here is the thing: gays appear in some way to be in on the secret. That may be liberating for some people. Some women will always enjoy talking with gay men about the problems – including the sexual problems – of men. Just as some straight men will always enjoy having this vaguely bilingual friend who might help them learn the other language. But there are other people for whom it will always be unnerving. Because for them gays will always be the people – especially the men – who know too much.

The Marxist Foundations

'Credo quia absurdum'

('I believe because it is absurd')

Tertullian (attrib.)

In 1911 a famous poster appeared, entitled 'Industrial Workers of the World', depicting what it claimed to be the 'Pyramid of the Capitalist System'. At the bottom of the pyramid were the brave men, women and children of the working class. With their proud, sturdy yet struggling shoulders they were holding up the entire edifice. 'We work for all' and 'We feed all' were the captions accompanying this lowest but most fundamental part of the system. A floor above them, wining and dining in black tie and evening dresses, were the well-off capitalist classes, supported by the workers and only able to enjoy themselves because of the labour of working men. 'We eat for you' said this tier. Above them were the military ('We shoot at you'). Above them the clergy ('We fool you'). Above them the monarch ('We rule you'). And finally, perched at the very top of the pyramid, even above the monarch, was a great bag of money with dollar signs on the outside. 'Capitalism' was the label for this highest tier of the state.

Today a version of this old image has made its way to the centre of the social justice ideology. Just one of the things that suggest the Marxist foundations of this new structure is the fact that capitalism is still at the top of the pyramid of oppression and exploitation. But the other top tiers of this hierarchy pyramid are inhabited by different types of people. At the top of the hierarchy are people who are white, male and heterosexual. They do not need to be rich, but matters are made worse if they are. Beneath these tyrannical male overlords are all the minorities: most noticeably the gays, anyone who isn't white, people who are women and also people who are trans. These individuals are kept down, oppressed, sidelined and otherwise made insignificant by the white, patriarchal, heterosexual, 'cis' system. Just as Marxism was meant to free the labourer and share the wealth around, so in this new version of an old claim, the power of the patriarchal white males must be taken away and shared around more fairly with the relevant minority groups.

At its outset this new ideology was not taken especially seriously by its opponents. Some of its claims seemed so laughable, and its inherent contradictions so clear, that coherent criticism was almost absent. This was a mistake. It is an ideology with very clear ideological precursors, but still an ideology that – whatever else may be said for it – provides a lens for understanding the world and a purpose for an individual's actions and life within the world.

It is no surprise at all that the academics who spent years tinkering with the ideas that have evolved into this theory of intersecting special-interest groups all have the same historic interests in common. Not one academic involved in the pushing of identity politics and intersectionality has come from the conservative right. And there are several reasons why that isn't a surprise. One is the ideological bent that exists within academia. One 2006 study of universities in the US found that 18 per cent of professors in the social sciences happily identified as 'Marxist'. And though there are other departments that have relatively few Marxists in them, any field in which a fifth of all professors were shown to believe in a wildly controversial (to say the least) dogma might raise questions. The same survey found 21 per cent of social science professors willing to identify as 'activist' and 24 per cent as radical.[1] This is considerably higher than the number of professors willing to identify as 'Republican' in any field.

Even when it does not identify itself as such, the Marxist and post-Marxist trend on the political left can always be recognized by the set of thinkers whom it cites and reveres, and whose theories it tries to apply to any and all disciplines and walks of life. From Michel Foucault these thinkers absorbed their idea of society not as an infinitely complex systems of trust and traditions that have evolved over time, but always in the unforgiving light cast when everything is viewed solely through the prism of 'power'. Viewing all human interactions in this light distorts, rather than clarifies, presenting a dishonest interpretation of our lives. Of course power exists as a force in the world, but so do charity, forgiveness and love. If you were to ask most people what matters in their lives very few would say 'power'. Not because they haven't absorbed their Foucault, but because it is perverse to see everything in life through such a monomaniacal lens.

Nevertheless for a certain type of person who is intent on finding blame rather than forgiveness in the world, Foucault helps to explain everything. And what Foucault and his admirers seek to explain in personal relations they also attempt to explain on a grand political level. For them absolutely everything in life is a political choice and a political act.

The post-Marxists who seek to explain the world around us today have not only imbibed the distorting prism of Foucault and Marx. From Antonio Gramsci they have absorbed their notion of culture as a 'hegemonic force' the control of which is at least as important as the working class. From Foucault's contemporary, Gilles Deleuze, they have absorbed the idea that the role of the individual is to see through and undo the web that the culture you were born into has wound around you. And always and everywhere is the aim – taken from French literary theory – to 'deconstruct' everything. To 'deconstruct' something is as significant in academia as 'constructing' things is in the rest of society. Indeed, it is one curiosity of academia in recent decades that it has found almost nothing it does not wish to deconstruct, apart from itself.

The process of taking apart occurred in a number of fields, but nowhere did it happen faster or more comprehensively than in the ever-metastasizing offshoots of the social sciences. Courses like 'queer studies', 'women's studies', 'black studies' and others each in their own field worked always and everywhere to achieve the same goals.

Always with reference to the same, apparently indispensable, thinkers. The first priority of this segment of academia over recent decades – the first thing to 'unweave' – was to assail, undermine and finally pull down everything that had previously appeared to be fixed certainties, including biological certainties. So the recognition that there were two different sexes turned into the suggestion that there were two different genders. And from there the argument was carefully escorted to what turned out – in the universities at least – to be a wildly popular conclusion: which is that there was in fact no such thing as gender. Gender was not real but merely a 'social construct'. The work of Judith Butler from the University of Berkeley was particularly popular in this regard. In Butler's view (especially in *Gender Trouble: Feminism and the Subversion of Identity*, 1990), feminism has made a mistake in thinking that there are categories such as male and female. Both the masculine and the feminine are 'culturally presupposed'. Indeed, gender itself is nothing more than a 'reiterated social performance' and definitely not the result of a 'prior reality'. At the same time the same exercise took place in black studies, where the same work was being done – with reference to the same sets of thinkers – to assert that just like gender, race too was in fact a cultural construct, which was 'culturally presupposed' and to do only with 'reiterated social performance'.

It was only after this 'unweaving' had been performed that a new weaving began to take place. This is where the foundational texts of social justice and intersectionality stepped in. Having cleared the space, they then turned out to have cleared it for ideas of their own.

In 1988 Peggy McIntosh of Wellesley College (whose research area was 'women's studies') published *White Privilege: Unpacking the Invisible Knapsack*. The work itself is not so much an essay as a list of claims running to a few pages. In them McIntosh lists fifty things which she claims to see as the 'daily effects of white privilege'. They include claims such as 'I can if I wish arrange to be in the company of people of my race most of the time' and 'I can go shopping alone most of the time, pretty well assured that I will not be followed or harassed.'[2] Many of the claims which McIntosh makes in 1988 already seem absurd and dated today. Most are not applicable only to white people and none proves anything like the systemic point that McIntosh would appear to be making. But *White Privilege* is unusually clearly written and advances a clear claim – which is that people must acknowledge the privileges that can be identified in their own lives. She says that the people who benefit from the existing power structures have not 'earned' them. And most importantly she makes the claim that a variety of groups (including people of different sexual orientations and races) suffer from 'interlocking oppressions'. It is as though all the grievance studies departments have been brought together in one great seminar.

In the view of McIntosh, Kimberlé Crenshaw, and others who were making similar claims, the nature of these interlocking oppressions needed to be worked out. Always there is the sense that once they are unpicked then something wonderful might happen, though, as is common with utopians, the map of utopia is not included in the plan. Nevertheless, McIntosh urges people to 'raise our daily consciousness' on the nature of privilege and attempt to use 'our arbitrarily awarded power to try to reconstruct power systems on a broader basis'. This suggests that McIntosh is not against power, just in favour of some redistribution of it along different lines. It is all so ill-defined that in any ordinary times such a list of claims would not have broken out beyond the walls of Wellesley. And for many years it certainly did not breach the walls of academia in general. But *White Privilege* survived into very unordinary times – times when people were scurrying to explain things again. And it turned out that, simplistic as it was, such a simple call to self-consciousness and redistribution was very effective indeed in a time of intellectual disarray.

Others were simultaneously doing the same work from a slightly different angle. One leading post-Marxist, the Argentinian-born Ernesto Laclau (who died in 2014), spent the 1980s trying to work out some of the problems which, he recognized, could be said to have emerged. Along with his partner and co-author Chantal Mouffe, he provided one of the earliest foundations for what would become identity politics. In their 1985 work *Hegemony and Socialist Strategy* they start by nobly admitting that socialism has been challenged by 'the emergence of new contradictions'. The 'traditional discourse of Marxism' has, they say, 'been centred on the class struggle' and 'the contradictions of capitalism'. However, the notion of 'class struggle' now needs to be modified. They ask:

> To what extent has it become necessary to modify the notion of *class* struggle, in order to be able to deal with the new political subjects – women, national, racial and sexual minorities, anti-nuclear and anti-institutional movements etc – of a clearly anti-capitalist character, but whose identity is not constructed around specific 'class interests'?[3]

It should be said that this is not some obscure work but one that is regularly cited. Indeed, Google Scholar shows it to have been cited more than 16,000 times. In *Hegemony and Socialist Strategy* as well as other works, including *Socialist Strategy: Where Next?*, Laclau and Mouffe are perfectly frank about what they think could be achieved and how.

The fact that the capitalist system has not yet collapsed is not evidence that it never will. The failure of the project to date merely presents Laclau and Mouffe with yet more contradictions that must be got through. Among them is the fact that 'The conditions of political struggle in mature capitalism are increasingly distant from the nineteenth-century model.'[4] Political struggle in this era must involve other groups.

Naturally they recognize that these new movements may bring their own contradictions. For instance, they suggest that 'the class political subjectivity of white workers' may be 'overdetermined by racist or anti-racist attitudes' which are 'evidently important for the struggle of the immigrant workers'.[5] The authors are both exceptionally verbose and wholly unclear about how to find a way through such complexities. They write constantly of 'certain activities', 'organisational forms', and at times every word appears to be 'partly'.[6] Although Laclau and Mouffe are distinctly vague about a whole array of conclusions, one thing they are clear about is the utility for the socialist struggle of 'new social movements' such as the women's movement.

The utility of such groups is obvious: their 'highly diverse struggles: urban, ecological, anti-authoritarian, anti-institutional, feminist, anti-racist, ethnic, regional or that of sexual minorities' give purpose and drive to a socialist movement that needs new energy. What is more, unless they cohere together these groups might just pursue their own agendas and their own needs. What is needed is to bring all these movements under one umbrella: the umbrella of the socialist struggle. Laclau and Mouffe write of 'what interests us about these new social movements' and explain how it 'leads us to conceive these movements as an extension of the democratic revolution to a whole new series of social relations. As for their novelty, that is conferred upon them by the fact that they call into question new forms of subordination.'[7]

In the *Marxism Today* article that Laclau and Mouffe wrote in the run-up to their book they were even clearer about the utility of these movements. Because although they may be opposed to the same thing that socialists are opposed to, these 'new political subjects' ('women, students, young people, racial, sexual and regional minorities, as well as the various anti-institutional and ecological struggles') have an obvious immediate advantage. The primary one is that:

> Their enemy is defined not by its function of exploitation, but by wielding a certain power. And this power, too, does not derive from a place in the relations of production, but is the outcome of the form of social organisation characteristic of the present society. This society is indeed capitalist, but this is not its only characteristic; it is sexist and patriarchal as well, not to mention racist.[8]

Laclau and Mouffe were explicitly setting out to try to find, or create, a new class of 'exploited' person. The working classes may have been exploited but they had been unable to recognize the fact, had let down their theoreticians and had generally failed to follow the path of progress that had been laid out for them. For Laclau and Mouffe this progress was obvious, winding through the Second International, the Leninist breach, the Comintern, Antonio Gramsci, Palmiro Togliatti and the complexities of Eurocommunism. But not everyone had followed them on that. In any case the disappointing workers could now be, if not replaced, then at least added to.

By the time they were writing, Laclau and Mouffe were aware of the demoralization that had struck much of the left. The legacy of Budapest, Prague, Vietnam and Cambodia (just a few of their own examples) had left many socialists reeling. But in this 'whole series of positive new phenomena' a new energy could be harnessed. Although for Laclau and Mouffe it obviously first needed an urgent 'theoretical reconsideration':

> The rise of the new feminism, the protest movements of ethnic, national and sexual minorities, the anti-institutional ecology struggles waged by marginalized layers of the population, the anti-nuclear movement, the atypical forms of social struggle in countries on the capitalist periphery — all these imply an extension of social conflictuality to a wide range of areas, which creates the potential, but no more than the potential, for an advance towards more free, democratic and egalitarian societies.[9]

The point is that these new groups of people could be useful.

Of course those who took the advice and attempted to bring all these groups together found a number of problems in all of this. Aside from the assumed racism of the working class, the practitioners of 1980s and 1990s deconstruction provided new tensions of their own. For example, after critical race theory and gender studies had done their work, was it not hard to explain why some things that seemed fixed (especially sex and race) were in fact social constructs whereas other things that may have seemed more fluid (not least sexuality) had become viewed as completely fixed?

If these questions did detain anybody, they did not detain them for long. One of the traits of Marxist thinkers has always been that they do not stumble or self-question in the face of contradiction, as anybody aiming at truth might. Marxists have always rushed towards contradiction. The Hegelian dialectic only advances by means of contradiction and therefore all the complexities – one might say absurdities – met along the way are welcomed and almost embraced as though they were helpful, rather than troubling, to the cause. Anybody hoping that intersectionality would dissolve amid its own inherent contradictions cannot have seen the myriad of contradictions a Marxist can hold in their head at any one time.

Their ideological children in identity politics and intersectionality seem content to inhabit an ideological space littered with contradiction, absurdity and hypocrisy. For example, one of the foundational notions of women's studies and feminist studies was that victims of sexual abuse should be believed. Discussion of rape, abuse, domestic violence and inappropriately wielded power relations lay at the basis of all women's and feminist studies. Yet when a student of Avital Ronell of New York University filed a Title IX complaint against her in 2017, accusing her of sexual harassment, the alleged harasser found Ronell's academic colleagues coming out in support for her. Along with Slavoj Žižek and others, Judith Butler was among the signatories to a letter condemning the investigation of Ronell, testifying to her own character ('the grace, the keen wit') and attempting the equivalent of a drive-by shooting against the reputation of her male accuser. Specifically they demanded that Ronell 'be accorded the dignity rightly deserved by someone of her international standing and reputation'.[10] All of which suggested that allegations of abuse are indeed always to be taken seriously, unless the victim is a man or the accused is a professor of feminist literary theory. In all matters, such contradictions merely have to be got over.

By contrast, anybody who got in the way of this direction of travel found themselves mown down with astonishing vigour. The weapons to hand (accusations of racism, sexism, homophobia and finally transphobia) were all too easy to wield and there was no price to pay for wielding them unfairly, unjustifiably or indeed frivolously. Critics of the emerging orthodoxy, including scientists, were accused of being propelled by the most base motives. As Steven Pinker wrote in 2002, 'Many writers are so desperate to discredit any suggestion of an innate human constitution that they have thrown logic and civility out the window . . . The analysis of ideas is commonly replaced by political smears and personal attacks . . . The denial of human nature has spread beyond the academy and has led to a disconnect between intellectual life and common sense.'[11]

Of course it had. For the purpose of large sections of academia had ceased to be the exploration, discovery or dissemination of truth. The purpose had instead become the creation, nurture and propagandization of a particular, and peculiar, brand of politics. The purpose was not academia, but activism.

This fact is betrayed in a number of ways. The first is through the pretence that these academic political claims were in fact no less than science. Throughout the decades in which the social sciences were producing the bases of intersectionality they consistently presented their claims as though the 'social' wasn't in their title and the 'science' was real. Again in this they were following a strain which went right back to Marx through Nikolai Bukharin, Georgi Plekhanov and the Second International. In all of these cases claims were presented as though they were scientific when they were, in fact, not even politics, but more like magic. This was make-believe, masquerading as science.

Another curiosity about the intersectional movement is the camouflage that it employs. For aside from McIntosh's most popular document, the one thing that all the purveyors of the ideologies of social justice and intersectionality have in common is that their work is unreadable. Their writing has the deliberately obstructive style ordinarily employed when someone either has nothing to say or needs to conceal the fact that what they are saying is not true. Here is one sentence from Judith Butler in full flow:

> The move from a structuralist account in which capital is understood to structure social relations in relatively homologous ways to a view of hegemony in which power relations are subject to repetition, convergence, and rearticulation brought the question of temporality into the thinking of structure, and marked a shift from a form of Althusserian theory that takes structural tonalities as theoretical objects to one in which the insights into the contingent possibility of structure inaugurate a renewed conception of hegemony as bound up with the contingent sites and strategies of the rearticulation of power.[12]

Prose this bad can only occur when the author is trying to hide something.

A theoretical physicist like Sheldon Lee Glashow cannot afford to write in the unreadable prose of the social sciences. He needs to communicate exceptionally complex truths in as simple and clear a language as possible. When he weighs up the latest claim in string theory he concludes that it 'addresses none of our questions, makes no predictions, and cannot be falsified'. 'If one's theory can't predict anything,' Peter Woit observed with some asperity, 'it is just wrong and one should try something else.'[13] This clarity, and this honesty, may still exist in the sciences. But it is dead – if it ever existed – in the social sciences. Besides which, if practitioners of women's studies, queer studies and race studies tried something else when their theories couldn't predict anything, or were proved wrong, then their departmental buildings would empty.

Still, the purveyors of social justice theories have done a job, in providing a library of works which (however unreadable) present an intellectual framework on top of which political positions can be adopted and politicized claims can be made. Anyone who finds it useful to argue that gender or race are social constructs can cite a whole library of material to bolster their claim and cite endless numbers of tenured academics who can 'prove' it. A god is made of X, who is then the subject of study by Y, and before long Z comes along to write on the rearticulation of temporality demonstrated by any Althusserian comparison of their work. Any student wondering whether the world really works like this can be instantly presented with the library of intimidating evidence that the gobbledygook he is failing to comprehend is his fault and not the fault of the writer of the gobbledygook.

Of course sometimes when it is nearly impossible to tell what is being said, almost anything can be said and exceptionally dishonest arguments can be smuggled in under the guise of complexity. This is one of the reasons why Butler and others write so badly. If they wrote clearly they would attract more outrage and ridicule. It is also one reason why this field finds it so hard to detect what is sincere and what is satire. The claims made from the social sciences in recent years have become so unmoored from reality that when their walls have been assailed by genuine intruders it turns out that they have no defences to either detect or repel them.

One of the most beautiful things to happen in recent years was 'The Conceptual Penis as a Social Construct'. This was an academic paper published in 2017 which proposed that:

> The penis vis-à-vis maleness is an incoherent construct. We argue that the conceptual penis is better understood not as an anatomical organ but as a gender-performative, highly fluid social construct.[14]

The claim was peer-reviewed and published in an academic journal called *Cogent Social Sciences*. The only problem was that it was a hoax carried out by two academics – Peter Boghossian and James Lindsay – who had immersed themselves in the academic literature of our time. Once the authors admitted to their hoax the journal in question unpublished the piece. But the culprits have successfully repeated the exercise with other academic journals in the years since.

In 2018, with the addition of Helen Pluckrose, the same academics managed to get a paper published in a journal of 'feminist geography' titled 'Human Reactions to Rape Culture and Queer Performativity at Urban Dog Parks in Portland, Oregon'. This paper claimed that dog-humping in Portland parks was further evidence of the 'rape-culture' which many academics and students had by then begun to claim was the most perceptive lens through which to see our societies. Another paper published in a journal of 'feminist social work' was titled 'Our Struggle is My Struggle'. There the spoofers successfully managed to meld together passages from *Mein Kampf* and pastiches of feminist social-justice theory jargon and pass it off as an academic study. In a third paper published in 'Sex Roles' the authors claimed to have used 'thematic analysis of table dialogue' to conduct a two-year study on why heterosexual males would want to eat at a Hooters restaurant.[15] Aside from some swift unpublishings, the main response from the authors' peers once their successful infiltration had been exposed was to turn on them and attempt to expel Boghossian from his university position.

The spoofs carried out by Boghossian and his colleagues made a number of deadly serious points. Not just that these areas of academic study had become playgrounds for frauds, but that there was absolutely nothing that could not be said, studied or claimed so long as it fitted into the pre-existing theories and presumptions of the relevant fields and utilized its disastrous language. So long as people were willing to claim that we live in a patriarchal society, a 'rape-culture', a homophobic, transphobic and racist culture; so long as they indict their own society and scatter in a smattering of admiration for any other society (from an approved list), then almost anything can be said. So long as the pyramid of oppression is believed in and propagated to others, almost anything can find its way into the canon of unreadable and largely uncited academic work.

However, the biggest mistake was not in allowing this to go on at publicly funded institutions for decades. The true error was in not realizing that some day its fruits would spill out into the rest of the society. In its 2018 guidance on how its members should treat 'traditional masculinity' in boys and men, the American Psychological Association wrote:

> Awareness of privilege and the harmful impacts of beliefs and behaviours that maintain patriarchal power have been shown to reduce sexist attitudes in men and have been linked to participation in social justice activities.[16]

Indeed. If boys could just realize that their gender was 'performative' rather than natural, they could grow up to play a greater role in social justice activities, to the ends that Laclau, Mouffe and a generation of other radicals had always dreamed of.

2

Women

In his 2002 book *The Blank Slate*, Stephen Pinker noted that gender had already become one of the 'hot button' issues of the day. Nevertheless he seemed confident that the scientific view would win out. Over several pages he listed just some of the biological differences that exist between men and women, such as the fact that while men have 'larger brains with more neurons (even correcting for body size)', women 'have a higher percentage of gray matter' and that many of the psychological differences between the sexes are exactly what an evolutionary biologist would predict (males being larger than females on average because of an evolutionary history rife with violent competition for mates).[1] And treading close to what was soon to be a whole other issue, he also noted the divergence in development between the brains of boys and girls and the effects on the brain of testosterone and androgens. It is a stimulating scientific riposte to the people claiming that biological differences between the sexes do not exist. As Pinker said, 'Things are not looking good for the theory that boys and girls are born identical except for their genitalia, with all other differences coming from the way society treats them.'[2]

Except that less than two decades later they are. The facts are certainly on Pinker's side, but the noisier voices are not. As a result, since Pinker wrote *The Blank Slate* our societies have doubled-down on the delusion that biological difference – including aptitude differences – can be pushed away, denied or ignored. A similar process has occurred in social differences. Any parent may notice the differences between their sons and daughters, but the culture tells them that there are none or that those that are there are purely 'performative' issues.

The fall-out of this and much else is toxic. Most people are not gay. Men and women have to find some ways of getting along. And yet the societal self-delusion over biological reality is just one in a whole series of such self-delusions that our societies have decided to engage in. Worse is that we have begun trying to reorder our societies not in line with facts we know from science but based on political falsehoods pushed by activists in the social sciences. Of all the things that are deranging our societies, everything to do with the sexes – and particularly relations between the sexes – are perhaps the most deranging of all. Because the facts are there all the time, in front of our eyes. It is just that we are not meant to notice them, or if we notice them we are expected to stay silent.

It is 2011 and time for the Independent Spirit Awards in Santa Monica. A long way into an evening of lengthy self-congratulation Paul Rudd and Eva Mendes come onstage to present the prize for best screenplay. Mendes (who is 36 at the time) explains that she and Rudd (who is 41) had arranged to do some funny stuff up onstage but that the show was running behind schedule. As Mendes explained it to the audience: 'Paul was going to grab my tits. You guys were going to be shocked, horrified, and you guys were going to laugh hysterically. But apparently we can't do that any more because we're out of time. So . . .'

Rudd then ogles Mendes's chest meaningfully, pushes his hand onto her right breast and grips it hard before saying deadpan, 'The nominees for best screenplay are . . .' The audience laughs, gasps, whoops and cheers. Mendes looks faux-shocked. While Rudd is holding her right breast, Mendes uses her spare hand to flick back her hair. It is important, after all, to look good.

After this has been going on for a while another woman joins them onstage. The actress Rosario Dawson (31) has leapt up to the podium and is grabbing Rudd's crotch, hard. The audience whoops, cheers and laughs some more. 'Oh my god, what's happening,' says Mendes a couple of times in unconvincing bemusement at the tableau of which she is a part. She opens the award envelope. All the while Dawson keeps her hand vigorously attached to Rudd's crotch while waving her other hand in the air in a gesture of power or triumph. Although Rudd is no longer holding either of Mendes's breasts, Dawson continues to hold Rudd's crotch. The audience continues to laugh and scream with delight. Because this is 2011 and sexual molestation is still hilarious.

In a backstage interview afterwards Dawson explained the impetus for her equal-opportunity groping:

> I love Paul. I've been a huge fan of Paul since like way back in the *Clueless* moment and stuff. But he had this like vice grip on her breast and I was like 'OK that's funny, like ha ha ok' for like a second. But then it was like that kept going and going and then the lights went down and the clip started rolling and he was still vice gripping her . . . So I was like 'Alright I'm going to just grab his package.' Why not? It was kind of nice. It wasn't bad. It was actually a pretty good package. I've kind of been curious since I was a teenager watching *Clueless*. But yeah so then he stopped . . . I'm just a women's rights activist and I was getting a little tired that he was grabbing her boob onstage for half an hour. Nothing bad it was funny.

Her male interviewer reassures her: 'It was one of the . . . it got great reaction.' 'OK good,' she replies:

> I grabbed his package onstage. It was kind of great. Why do men always get to cop a feel? Women get to cop a feel too. You know what I'm saying. I'm just saying. Just keeping equal opportunity.[3]

This was the way back then. The grope-fest at the Independent Spirit Awards was not unusual or especially remarked upon. The idea of groping, grabbing or exposing yourself to people of the opposite sex may have been looked upon with a certain disdain in wider society for years. But in Hollywood it was still all part of the entertainment. In a profession in which nudity is normal and for which 'the casting couch' was coined, the boundaries were never easy to discern. This is one reason why Hollywood might be a bad place to base either a set of ethics to aspire to or a set of ethics which should be regarded as particularly emblematic of anything beyond the entertainment industry.

Different standards always operated in Hollywood. It was the only industry in the twenty-first century in which someone still on the run for child-rape could be applauded, revered and even viewed as something of a victim by their peers. Had an accountant, social worker or even a priest in their forties anally raped a 13-year-girl, then they might have got away with it as has Roman Polanski. They may have found friends to cover for them. But it would be inconceivable – even in the Catholic Church – for someone to be applauded on prime-time television as being at the top of their profession while still on the run from the law. Hollywood, and the audience of Polanski's peers at the Academy Awards in 2003 in particular, felt no such restraining impulse.

It was always a world slightly apart – as centres of the arts and entertainment always have been – and so as bad a place as it is possible to find from which to determine societal norms. Especially social norms as complex as relations between the sexes. Only in Hollywood would a famous director like Woody Allen separate from his wife because he has been caught having a relationship with her adopted daughter. But then this is a town, and a business, which threw up Gloria Grahame in the 1940s. Of her four husbands the fourth (Tony Ray) was the son of her second husband (Nicholas Ray) and his first wife. The relationship between Grahame and Tony Ray was first exposed when she was found in bed with him (Grahame being in her late twenties at the time, and Ray just 13).

So to make Hollywood, or movie people, into moral examples might have been a mistake in any era. But when the Harvey Weinstein scandal broke in 2017 that is exactly what was attempted. Yet, in its own way the oddity of the entertainment industry always does hold up a mirror. And if it is not any exemplar for how to behave then it is certainly a mirror which highlights the confusion of the age. Most especially the confusion over what roles women might play – and which roles everyone knows they can play – in an era that seems to swing between libertinism and prudery without finding any mean-like balance.

Consider the fondness with which people look back on the actress Drew Barrymore's appearance on the *David Letterman Show* in

April 1995: 12 April was Letterman's birthday and Barrymore was on the show, describing – among other things – her recent fondness for nude dancing. Although 20 years old at the time Barrymore spent the interview playing by turns the role of a confident sexual woman and a naughty little schoolgirl.

Eventually, presenting it as a birthday treat, in front of the live audience (who whooped, laughed and hollered throughout) Barrymore asked if Letterman would like a dance. Without waiting for an answer she called for the studio band to strike up, clambered onto the presenter's desk and performed a table-dance for Letterman, a married man twice her age. Slinking up and down, with her hands above her head and her midriff exposed, Barrymore's performance eventually culminated in her whipping up her short top and exposing her bare breasts to a visibly shocked Letterman. The audience could not see the breasts, though a camera caught what the *Mail Online*'s side-bar of shame would call a side-boob. But still the audience could not get enough of it. They loved the whole thing, laughing and cheering throughout and giving a great roar of appreciation when Barrymore exposed herself to the host.

Immediately after doing that Barrymore turned around and flung her arms out to soak up the audience's appreciation, then got back down on the desk on hands and knees, and crawling towards Letterman, planted a kiss on his cheek and cradled the back of his head. When she returned to her seat she ditched the virago act and regressed again, pulling her legs up onto her chair and tucking her knees under her head like a little girl who knew she'd just been really bad.

Of course it could plausibly be argued that 1995 was another era. But it wasn't really. This episode was looked upon as fondly in March 2018 when Barrymore was back – this time on *The Late Show* with Stephen Colbert. There Barrymore, older, if not wiser, reflected on what a 'real, like, card' she had been back in the day. In particular, she recalled that Letterman episode. 'In this very theatre I did something particular with Mr Letterman,' she said. The audience joined in a fond nostalgic laugh at this memory. Colbert, who had held a strict line during the 'MeToo' allegations which had emerged only months earlier and were still going around, prompted Barrymore's memories. 'On his birthday. On his birthday,' he prompted. 'Famously.'

Barrymore picked up the theme of memory, 'I literally was like "what"?' she set off:

> I sometimes think. Like it doesn't feel like me. It's like a distant memory that just doesn't seem like me. But it is me. And that's kinda cool. I'm still down with that. I'm like a mother of two. I'm completely like, you know I don't know. I'm such a different person now that it doesn't feel like me but I'm like still into it.

All this was greeted with laughter and applause from the audience and encouragement from Colbert, who then segued into the fact that Barrymore was one of the first famous women in Hollywood to create her own production company. He uses this moment to ask what we can learn from this about female empowerment in Hollywood and the 'moment we're in now'.[4] At no point is what happened in 1995 looked back at with anything other than fondness.

And why would it? The idea of women exposing themselves to men, making men feel uncomfortable or presenting themselves as especially 'feminist' for groping or harassing men was a trope that had itself run unmolested for years. As Stephen Colbert knew from his own experience.

He was a mere rookie television star in May 2007 when he interviewed Jane Fonda. This was a couple of years after Fonda had revived her acting career by playing Jennifer Lopez's mother-in-law in the hit movie *Monster-in-Law*. But Fonda was on Colbert's show to promote her new soon-to-be flop movie called *Georgia Rule*. At 69 Fonda was clearly keen to demonstrate to audiences that she still 'had it'. And so during the interview she made a show of sexually stalking her host. The fact that the movie she was promoting was about sexual abuse did not suggest to her that now might *not* be a good time to do what she did.

Right at the start of the interview she climbed onto Colbert's lap. She sat there throughout. And at one stage she proceeded to give him a full on-the-lips kiss and told him that she knew he fantasized about her. 'It's not exactly how I expected this interview to go,' said the host. Colbert tried to change the subject several times, including to war-protesting. Hanoi Jane could not be diverted. She kept caressing Colbert, kissing his cheek and fondling him. She started talking about premature ejaculation. This went on interminably.

The media then didn't seem to think that this scene was in any way unseemly or unsettling. In fact they could not get enough of it. 'Yeah, Jane Fonda's Still Got It' ran the headline in the *Huffington Post*: 'Wednesday's Colbert Report also featured this hilarious – and, we'll say it, sensual – segment wherein Jane Fonda seemed rather intent on engaging, well, Stephen Colbert's sensual segment ("Is that a sensual segment in your pocket or are you just glad to see me?").' The *Huffington Post* wittered on along these lines and linked it to a piece at *Salon* that they said also 'nails it', apparently 'giving a little context to Fonda's awesomeness'.[5] Because in 2007 unwanted sexual advances were not only hilarious and sensual. They were also awesome.

Years later, in 2014, Colbert would relate how 'definitely uncomfortable' he had been during all this. Yet he relayed this, including details of his wife's apparent unhappiness about this interview, to a hall full of yet more laughing, applauding people.[6] Because, in 2014, unwanted sexual advances were still adorable.

Of course all this changed in 2017 with the first 'MeToo' claims against Harvey Weinstein. At that stage there seemed to be a rapid consensus that any and all sexual advances against other people were intolerable, and that no excuse whatsoever could be made for them. The new lines appeared to have been dug very deep as well as very fast. But they left behind plenty of unpleasant things that had happened in the very recent past. After the Weinstein affair everything to do with interaction between the sexes in Hollywood and the wider world was presented by the press as really wildly easy and obvious. Yet it clearly wasn't, either in Hollywood or anywhere else.

One of the few people in the entertainment industry to slightly buck the precise contours of the digging was the actress Mayim Bialik. In October 2017 when 'MeToo' broke she received a certain amount of backlash for an opinion piece in *The New York Times* in which she talked frankly about the industry she had first entered as (in her words) 'a prominent-nosed, awkward, geeky, Jewish 11-year-old'. She described how she had 'always had an uncomfortable relationship with being employed in an industry that profits from the objectification of women'.

And she described how she had made 'conservative' choices as a young actress, and that guided by her first-generation American parents, she was always careful around people in the industry. This, along with her religious observance, meant that she was the sort of person who – as she explained – was unusual among women in Hollywood.

Bialik's trajectory had certainly been an unusual one. She had actually left the acting business for some years to pursue a doctorate in neuroscience. Then, after returning to the industry, she starred in *The Big Bang Theory* sitcom. Now in 2017 she said, 'I still make choices every day as a 41-year-old actress that I think of as self-protecting and wise. I have decided that my sexual self is best reserved for private situations with those I am most intimate with. I dress modestly. I don't act flirtatiously with men as a policy.'[7]

All of this got Bialik into a certain amount of trouble with other women in Hollywood who claimed that she was 'victim blaming' – specifically that she was blaming the way women dressed for the behaviour of men. Bialik was forced to apologize and express regret for some of the interpretations put on her article. But stranger than this was that so much of what Bialik said in the article ran in direct contradiction to what she had done only a year previously.

In February 2016 Bialik was on *The Late Late Show* with James Corden. One of the other guests on the programme was Piers Morgan. At one stage Corden asked his fellow Brit to explain the recent hashtag 'Cleavagegate'. Morgan said that he and Susan Sarandon had had a recent bust-up over a tweet of his. At the recent Screen Actors Guild Awards the 69-year-old Sarandon had presented the 'In Memoriam' section in a plunging top which had showed her cleavage. Morgan had gone on social media to complain that there was something inappropriate about a tribute to dead friends and colleagues being presented in such revealing attire. In the resulting backlash – one that Morgan could not have expected and the attention from which must have been enormously painful to him – Sarandon tweeted a photo to Morgan of herself in her bra pointing at the statue of the small-penised *David* of Michelangelo. Morgan went on to explain to the live audience on Corden's show that thousands of other self-declared 'feminists' had also responded by sending him photos of their cleavages by way of protest.

Throughout this explanation Bialik had been sitting between Corden and Morgan in a low-plunging green dress. And at this point she puts a hand on Morgan's arm and actually manages to interrupt him. 'You know what – I identify as a feminist. I'm going to do it this way.' And she stands up and, with her back to the crowd, pulls her dress apart and exposes her breasts to Morgan. The studio audience go wild with laughter and applause. Both Bialik's host and her fellow guest clap and laugh as volubly as possible. Something is made of the fact that Morgan actually looks like he is blushing and seems almost embarrassed for a moment. When he stresses again that he likes cleavages but that he doesn't think they should be on display during tributes to dead colleagues, but that again he loves cleavages, Bialik gets back up. 'Do you need to see it again?' and once again (more briefly this time) pulls the top of her dress apart for him.[8]

None of this could have possibly gone down better. All of it was lapped up by audiences in the studio and at home. In 2016 exposing your breasts was a 'feminist' act. Exposing them to a man who had not asked to see them was an especially 'feminist' act. And even a woman who claimed for religious and social reasons to be 'modest' could willingly and easily delight a studio audience by flashing her breasts – unasked for – at a man.

None of which is to say that women shouldn't be able to do what they like with their bodies. None of which is to say that celebrities can't flash their breasts at people to get laughs or attention, or that a woman flashing her breasts at a man is the precise equivalent of a man flashing his penis at a woman. But it is fair to say that women – perhaps especially the most famous and celebrated women – send out very confusing messages. The word 'mixed' doesn't even begin to address it. What is more, these more than mixed messages exist even within one person like Bialik, who in every other way would appear to be holding herself together through this maelstrom.

LOVE YOU

One reason why anybody might be confused by the messages being pumped all around the world by the entertainment industry is that it is itself highly confused about what is going on. Only a couple of decades ago there was still some awareness of the complexity of male–female relations. There is a famous scene in *Indiana Jones and the Last Crusade*, released in 1989. At an early stage in the film Indiana Jones, played by Harrison Ford, is in his classroom teaching basic archaeology to a class full of young women. Most of the class seem to be staring rather dreamily at him, and among them is one of their number who throws Professor Jones off his train of thought because she has written 'Love' on one eyelid and 'You' on the other. And she keeps blinking at him, slowly and meaningfully so that he can read the words and presumably absorb the intention behind them.

There are two memes in this scene that were perfectly familiar until we recently pretended that they weren't. The first is that the teacher-student relationship in learning can have an undercurrent of sex. The ancient Greeks knew this, though there was then, as there is now, a knowledge that any sexual current must always be resisted. Yet it can be there. And the second theme – more important to our purpose here – is that of the predatory, even vampish younger woman preying on the older, more vulnerable, possibly even helpless male. This was a recognized motif throughout most of history and at least as recently as 1989. It is an awareness that it is not only men who can harass women, but men who can also be the subject of harassment from women. Every man knows of this experience even if they have not experienced it, though most will have at some point. Its softer versions are of the kind Drew Barrymore acted out when she reverted to naughty little girl mode: the message 'I have been silly, and possibly naughty'. But there are harder versions of it, where a woman can positively stalk a man to extract from him what she wants.

If it weren't the case that women are practised at these forms of behaviour, just consider the market for women's clothing and accessories that are meant to present women to men in an even more sexual light than they might otherwise appear. Consider the vogue for fake stick-on nipples. Companies like 'Just Nips' often present these items on their website as though they are largely intended for women who have had mastectomies. But the wider marketing and the public awareness of the trend is that the 'bra-less' look is known to be an enormous turn-on to men. In the 1990s, in an episode of TV's

Sex and the City, Miranda wore stick-on nipples at a party and got exactly the attention she wanted as men at the party saw the nipples pushing through underneath her party dress and gravitated towards her. Because celebrities have made the 'bra-less' look extra desirable, manufacturers have moved in to make more affordable stick-on nipples. In 2017 'Just Nips for All' were advertising products which included nipples that included the 'cold' and 'slightly smaller' sizes which were 'the perfect perk' to nipples that are 'feeling down'. As the website said, 'When your look needs a little extra je ne sais quoi, top it off with a pair of these! Cold Nips are everything you'd ever want in a fake nipple . . . and more! What's more, you ask? They're subtle. They're sexy. They're so freaking cute!'

Of course this can be presented in female-focused ways. It's all about making women feel better about themselves: absolutely nothing to do with men; without men, women would still go around wearing ice-cold, fake, stick-on nipples. But the marketing for such products makes it perfectly clear what – and who – they are really for. About the 'freezing' option the makers boast:

> These babies are cheaper than implants, that's for sure! How do we put this . . . Freezing Nips are the WMDs [weapons of mass destruction] of nipple erectors. They are potent. They are lethal. They'll cut through glass, steel, Teflon, you name it – while giving everyone at the party something to talk about behind your back – in a good way, OBV (they're so jealous). Pair with your favorite graphic tee for that effortlessly sexy vibe models are always doing but let's get real you'll want them on under your tightest sweater for the hottest cold look in the game.[9]

Indeed. Why would women want the WMD of nipple erectors other than to make them feel better in general? Any other reason?

Although they don't get, or seek, much attention from men, the market is filled with products of this type. More commonly, things like bra uplifts. But there is no limit to the potential of the market because there is no limit to the extent that women will go to if they want to go there.

In recent years a market has developed for 'camel toe underwear'. As one female journalist wrote it up:

> One of the greatest fashion worries that every woman experiences is the fear that their vagina isn't plump enough. Isn't visible enough to the public gaze. You might have a nice bum and boobs…and brain, but if you don't have a bulging labia, what's the point? But good news my flat-lipped sisters. If you've ever worried that your vagina just isn't prominent enough through your shorts or yoga pants then worry no more.

Indeed, for in 2017 the 'push-up bra for your labia' had been discovered. A piece of underwear coming in a range of different skin tones, 'that looks like your pants are getting right up into your labia majora'.[10] Again, it might be possible to claim that this has nothing to do with men and is just the sort of thing women would like to wear around under their dressing gown at home or under the baggiest pair of trousers or skirt at work. That it is all about how a woman feels about herself. But there are other more obvious reasons why some women might want to make it look like their pants are riding right up into their labia majora.

In recent years even making a fraction of this point has brought people very close to total career destruction. In February 2018 the Canadian academic, author and psychiatrist Dr Jordan Peterson was interviewed by Jay Caspian Kang for VICE News. At one point in the interview Kang made a set of assertions which Peterson countered by saying that the difficult questions weren't being asked. For instance, he asked his interviewer, 'Can men and women work together in the workplace?' The interviewer looked amazed that the question should even be asked and countered it by saying he did know the answer to that and that yes they could because 'I work with a lot of women'. But Peterson pointed out that it's only been happening for around 40 years and so is a fairly new thing whose rules we're still trying to work out. 'Is there sexual harassment in the workplace? Yes. Should it stop? That'd be good. Will it? Well, not at the moment it won't because we don't know what the rules are.' And that was where Peterson walked onto very perilous terrain indeed.

'Here's a rule. How about no makeup in the workplace?' he suggested. Jay Kang started laughing and responded, 'Why would that be a rule?' Peterson then asked him, 'Why should you wear makeup in the workplace. Isn't that sexually provocative?' Kang couldn't agree. 'What's the purpose of makeup then?' Peterson asked him. 'It's, some people would just like to put on makeup. I don't know why.' At which point Peterson explained to him that the purpose of putting on lipstick and rouge is to stimulate sexual arousal. Then, even worse, he pointed out that high heels are a tool to exaggerate sexual attractiveness. Peterson explained that he definitely was not saying that women shouldn't wear high heels or makeup in the workplace. What he was saying was that we shouldn't be under any illusions about the reactions they are trying to get. This is the game that women who wear makeup and high heels are playing.[11] Throughout the interview Kang sometimes looked baffled, sometimes bored, as though the questions Peterson was asking were unbelievably easy to answer and obvious. What he did not at any point do was try to contend with the terrifying Pandora's box that his guest had opened up.

Perhaps that was a sensible duck and weave by the interviewer. After all, the response to this interview reached fever pitch even when compared to the standard response to a Peterson interview. Online chat forums were filled with people claiming that he had said that women who wear makeup and high heels at work are asking to be sexually assaulted. Parts of the media followed suit. And moments like this are interesting. Because if somebody says that opening this discussion up does not mean women shouldn't dress how they like, and yet still a lot of people hear (or claim to hear) that this is exactly what Peterson is saying, and what's more that he is excusing sexual assault, then something is clearly going badly wrong. This is not about mishearings or misunderstandings. It is more likely an example of people deliberately and lazily adopting simplified misrepresentations of what other people are saying in order to avoid the difficult discussion that would otherwise have to take place.

There are no end of difficult discussions to be had around this subject. If a culture lands on the idea that women must always be believed in cases not just of sexual assault but of unwanted sexual advances, then this must generate some confusion in society. What are people to think about, and how should they react to, those occasions when they have experienced women doing that female thing? How are they to reconcile the information that women must always be believed with the fact that there are entire industries set up to help women fool men? Or – to put the most positive spin on it – to entice them. After all, what are all those summer advertising campaigns about that invite women to 'turn heads this summer'? Whose heads are they being invited to turn? Any and all passing women, hoping to purchase, say, the same dress or bikini? Or men?

MAKE HIM DROOL

The manner in which marketing addresses women tells us a great deal about what women are actually motivated by when they think men aren't watching. Consider the endless numbers of advertising campaigns and pieces in women's magazines dedicated to motifs like 'Make him drool'. If car advertisements or shaving products aimed at men were pushed with the suggestion that the object, if acquired, would make women drool, it would not just be condemned but might well fail to appeal to men. Google is a hive of assistance in this regard. Typing the words 'Make him drool' turns up reams of articles, adverts and online discussions. The words 'Make her drool' by contrast throw up a host of articles ranging from how to stop drooling during sleep to explanations as to why some cats dribble from their mouths.

All this suggests our societies have arrived at a stage of seemingly industrial-strength denial. We have decided to forget or completely edit out things that were recognized to be valid the day before yesterday. And we seem to have decided that the individual complexities which actually exist not just between women and men but within men and within women can simply be pushed to one side with the assumption that they have all been overcome.

Or perhaps this whole pretence is in fact built upon an impossibly large landmine. After all, a man trying to work out what a woman wants today might be forgiven for being racked with confusion. A young man starting out on his attempts to understand the opposite sex currently has to face a world which tells him that he must have consent classes in school, and in university, that dictate exceptionally precise rules about what does and does not constitute inappropriate behaviour. And yet he can go online or down to his local bookstore – if he can find one – and discover that the books which have recently sold in the greatest numbers to women (including those of his mother's age group) are ones centred around women's rape fantasies. Fantasies that could not possibly be discussed or attempt to be understood but which are so public that the books in question are also made into movies showing in cinemas and grossing profits to date of around half a billion dollars. Is it groups of men who go to the cinema to see Christian Grey tying his girlfriend up for sex and then being redeemed by her? Or is the demographic more female?

There is a song by Nicki Minaj which perhaps inadvertently sums up the deep confusions of the current settlement. The song is called 'Anaconda' and it was released in 2014. Anybody who hasn't seen the video should join the hundreds of millions of people who have watched it online. To say that Minaj's video is sexual is like saying that her lyrics are banal. These ones start with 'My anaconda don't, my anaconda don't / My anaconda don't want none unless you got buns, hun.' Anybody in doubt about what 'buns' she is talking about will work it out from the fact that the first three minutes of the music video consist almost entirely of Nicki Minaj in a bikini, in a jungle setting, wiggling her bum for the camera. Sometimes she has a group of other women with her similarly dressed who wiggle their bums for the viewer too. The wiggling goes on and on. If anyone hasn't got the point they can get it from the chorus:

> Oh my gosh, look at her butt
> Oh my gosh, look at her butt
> Oh my gosh, look at her butt
> (Look at her butt)
> Look at, look at, look at
> Look, at her butt

Other than wiggling her butt alongside her girlfriends wiggling their butts, and sometimes playing with each other's butts, the only other things that happen in the opening three minutes of the video are Nicki Minaj suggestively eating a banana, then spraying a can of squirty cream onto her cleavage, then wiping her fingers across her breasts and feeding the cream to herself in a sequence that is obviously impossible to interpret.

But this is not the most significant part of the 'Anaconda' video. All of this is completely normal and banal imagery in the world of pop music videos, where female stars tend to dress and dance like strippers. The important part is the last minute and a half of the video which opens with Minaj crawling on all fours in a sexily, darkly lit room. She is crawling towards a fit young man who is sitting in a chair. The lyrics for this scene commence with 'This one is for my bitches with a fat ass in the fucking club / I said, where my fat ass big bitches in the club?' Wearing just a bra on top and a pair of lacy and holed leggings she moves around the man, gyrating as she goes. She puts a leg over one of his shoulders. She leans in front of him pushing her famous butt in his face and wiggling it up and down. She adopts pole dancer positions, sliding up and down in front of him. Through all of this he sits still like a well-behaved customer enjoying a show in a lap-dancing club. Eventually as her butt is being waved right in front of his face for the umpteenth time he is clearly getting sexually frustrated. Eventually, having wiped his mouth with his hand he hesitates again before placing one hand gently over her buttocks. At which point it's over. The vocals go 'Hey', Minaj hits his hand away and walks out, flicking her hair back as she goes. As she makes this exit the man leans forward in the chair and puts his face in his hands, apparently mortified at his inexcusable behaviour.

The confusion that Nicki Minaj acts out here is representative of a whole host of other things in our culture. It contains an unresolvable challenge and an impossible demand. The demand is that a woman must be able to lap-dance before, drape herself around and wiggle her ass in the face of any man she likes. She can make him drool. But if that man puts even one hand on the woman then she can change the game completely. She can go from stripper to mother superior in a heartbeat. She can go from 'Look at my butt, waving in front of your face' to 'How dare you think you can touch the butt I've been waving in front of your face all this time.' And it is he who must learn that he is in the wrong. What is the demand that is being made here? The impossible demand that cannot be met but which has been written into contemporary mores? It is that a woman must be allowed to be as sexy and sexual as she pleases, but that does not mean she can be sexualized. Sexy, but not sexualized.

It is an impossible demand. And not just an unreasonable but a deranging demand to make on men. But nobody wants to explore it. Because to explore it would be to uncover a whole world of unremediable, unsolvable, complexity.

THE SAME OR BETTER?

The belief that it is possible to be sexy without being sexualized is just one of the contradictory settlements that we have landed on. But there are plenty of others in the air. For instance, there is the one that simultaneously insists that women are in every meaningful way exactly the same as men, possessing the same traits and competencies and able to challenge them on the same turf at any time. Yet simultaneously, magically, they are better than men. Or better in specific ways. All this seems perfectly capable of being held in the same head – contradictory though it all is. So that the current accepted way of regarding women is: the same as men, but different where it's useful or flattering.

An example of this paradox is often displayed by Christine Lagarde, who has been head of the International Monetary Fund for most of this decade. In 2018, on the tenth anniversary of the financial crash, Lagarde took to the IMF's website to write about lessons learned from the 2008 crash and reflect on what had been fixed – and what had not – in the decade since. Lagarde used the opportunity to talk about the need for a greater number of women to be on the boards of banks and agencies overseeing financial institutions. And she used the opportunity to repeat what had been one of her favourite and most repeated mantras of the previous decade. 'As I have said many times,' she wrote, 'if it had been Lehman Sisters rather than Lehman Brothers, the world might well look a lot different today.'[12] This was not simply a reiteration of the problem of groupthink that had so contributed to the events of 2008. Lagarde was making a bigger point. Not only that women were needed in financial institutions. Almost nobody could doubt that. But that if women were more prominent in that workforce – or better still leading it – then the results and outcomes would be different. And Lagarde was not alone in making this claim. Indeed, versions of it ran throughout the decade following the financial crisis. And they centred on finance as in every other area of public life.

Shortly after the crash the daytime television host Fern Britton was on the BBC's main political discussion show, *Question Time*, and commenting on the crisis she got a round of applause from the audience for saying, 'It appears that an awful lot of men have been in on this money business and they've made a very bad fist of it. If there were some women doing some old-fashioned house-keeping where women traditionally anyway are pretty good at making sure that the money goes in the pot for the electricity and the gas and the phone and the food. We didn't pillage and rob it and stick it all on a horse to see if the money would come in next week.'[13] The Equalities minister in the 2010–15 coalition government in Britain, Liberal Democrat Lynne Featherstone, was an exponent of the same theory. At her party's conference in 2011 she blamed men for the 'terrible decisions' made in the world's economy and said that men as a whole were the principal reason for 'the mess the world is in'.

So here is the first conundrum of the current presumption on the position of women as opposed to men in our societies. Women are exactly the same as men – as capable, as able, as suited to the same array of tasks. And also better. Exactly how this is the case is ill defined because it is ill thought through. Nevertheless we have decided to embed precisely such ill-thinking as deep into our societies as we can possibly manage.

WOMEN MEAN BUSINESS

It is a fine day in the City of London, and at an upmarket hotel just south of the river more than four hundred very smart women are gathered together. Smart, it should be clarified, in every sense of the term. Not only are the attendees all business leaders, from the top of every profession they are in, but whenever the door swings open with another arrival it is as though we are at a fashion shoot. High heels, swishing scarfs, the power clothes of the international business elite: nobody – absolutely nobody – lets the side down. And it is clear from the outset that there most certainly is a side.

The 'Women Mean Business' conference has been put together by *The Daily Telegraph*. Its major sponsors include NatWest and BT. The day is opened by the Minister for Women and Equalities, and is followed by a panel entitled 'How Work Needs to Start Working for Women'. Many of the most successful and well-known women in business are here, along with several of the country's most famous female broadcasters. There is a 'fireside chat' between the 'head of enterprise' at NatWest and the first female Serjeant at Arms at the House of Commons. Then more panels: 'What are the Real Roadblocks to Women's Success?'; 'Closing the Gender Gap'; 'Are Women at a Disadvantage in a Male-Dominated Investor World?' The panels that do address the male half of the species have titles like '#MenToo: Men's Crucial Role as Allies for Women'.

It must be said that since all this has been aimed at women and since all but a couple of the people in the room are women, the female focus is inevitable. It is also inevitable that much of the discussion centres around issues to do with women in the workplace, including childcare issues. But there is also a distinct air of alliance in the room. An alliance of people who are put upon. Whenever somebody wants to get a warm ripple of nods or applause from the audience they stress how much we need 'confident women'. The surest way to get the room to tut volubly is to tell a story involving the bad behaviour of any 'alpha male'. Examples of 'alpha male' behaviour include stories of men dominating things by talking too much. There seems to be a clear agreement in the room that whereas there is a great need for 'confident women' there is also a need for 'less confident men'. As though by these means the sexes might in time meet somewhere in the middle.

There is one other surefire way to get the crowd on your side. And that is for a woman on the stage to express concern, nervousness or a sense of 'imposter syndrome'. One impressive, smart and striking young woman involved in a start-up business begins her contribution by saying all of these things. She is nervous and feels almost as if she shouldn't be there, with all these amazing women in the room who have achieved so much. They applaud heartily and congratulate her on her bravery in saying this. Women need to be confident. But it seems that one good strategy for getting other women onside is to present yourself as not being at all confident. Almost as though you fear being shot down, particularly by other women. When it comes to Q and A one attendee sends in a question asking whether any other people in the room haven't in fact found other women to be their biggest challenge in the workplace. This female remains anonymous.

As one of the few men asked to speak on the day, I find myself on a panel entitled 'Is the Focus on Promoting Women Holding Men Back?' Our chair is a journalist from *The Daily Telegraph*. The other panellists are a British MP called Craig Tracey who heads a Parliamentary group supporting women, the female 'Chief People Officer' from *The Daily Telegraph* and the 'UK Head of Female Client Strategy' at J. P. Morgan. The consensus in the room is the same as the consensus that has emerged in nearly all public discussion, and is clearly in need of disrupting.

The most striking thing is that there appear to be a set of confusions centring around the issue of 'power'. Every discussion so far has centred on a presumption that almost all relationships in the workplace and elsewhere are centred around the exercise of power. Knowingly or otherwise these women have all imbibed the Foucauldian world view in which power is the most significant prism for understanding human relationships. What is striking is not just that everyone seems to have paid lip-service to this, but that these women are focused only on one sort of power. This is a sort of power which – it is presumed – has historically been held solely by mainly old, mainly rich, always white men. It is why the joking and berating about the behaviour of 'alpha males' goes down so well. There is a presumption that if the alpha and maleness could be squashed out of these people, in some great majestic social-justice blending device, then the power squeezed out of them might be drunk up by women like those in the room today. That it will be used to nourish, and grow, those who deserve the power more.

Here are deep waters. But I suggest in my contribution that our conversations are being limited by this misunderstanding. Even if we concede – which we should not – that power (rather than, say, love) is the most important force guiding human affairs, why are we focusing only on one type of power? There certainly are types of power – such as rape – which men can sometimes hold over women. And there is a type of power which some old, typically white, males might be able to hold over less successful people, including less successful women. But there are other types of power in this world. Historical old white man power is not the only such source. Are there not, after all, some powers which only women can wield. 'Like what?' someone asks. At which point, having waded in this far it only makes sense to wade further.

Among other types of power that women wield almost exclusively, the most obvious is this. That women – not all women, but many women – have an ability that men do not. This is the ability to drive members of the opposite sex mad. To derange them. Not just to destroy them but to make them destroy themselves. It is a type of power which allows a young woman in her late teens or twenties to take a man with everything in the world, at the height of his achievements, torment him, make him behave like a fool and wreck his life utterly for just a few moments of almost nothing.

Earlier we heard from the young, attractive woman, who was heading a start up, that she had a couple of times in her search for capital received inappropriate advances from men who were potential funders. The room had understandably tut-tutted. For that would indeed have been an abuse of power. But there is unspoken knowledge – and there are unspoken hypocrisies – beneath all such tut-tutting. Was everybody in the hall – including the tut-tutters – absolutely sure that the woman in question did not also wield some power? Are they certain that she would have been able to raise an equally large amount of capital if instead of looking rather strikingly like an international model she had (while equally smart and savvy) more closely resembled Jabba the Hutt? Or a mangy-looking old white man? It is no disservice to the abilities of the woman in question (and no let-off for any man behaving badly) to say that even the prospect of being in future proximity to such a person may not have worked entirely against her. Studies repeatedly show that – all else being equal – people who are attractive manage to climb higher in their chosen professions than their less attractive peers. Is physical attractiveness plus youth and womanhood such a negligible set of cards? Might not one or more of the men among her investors have thought at some point that even if nothing could, would or should ever happen between them, at least investor meetings with her would be looked forward to slightly more than another investor meeting with an elderly white male? And is this not – unpleasant as it is to admit – a type of power? One which is either denied or harnessed only outside of the realms of current mentionability, but a power that exists in the world nonetheless?

This was not a point which was received warmly in the room. This was very definitely not what attendees wanted to hear. Before being able to proceed to my next unpopular point the Chief People Officer of *The Daily Telegraph* decided to take us there herself. Inappropriate behaviour in the workplace was a problem to be emphasized. A lot of women had terrible stories of this. Many women in the room doubtless had stories of their own. But it was suggested that the whole matter of relations between the sexes was really a very straightforward matter to arrange. Especially in the wake of the MeToo movement, everything had become clear. Men needed to realize that there was behaviour that was appropriate and behaviour that was inappropriate. And while conceding that the categories for both had changed again only very recently, it was also suggested that the mores were in some sense timeless as well as always obvious.

My suspicion is that anyone who has ever worked in an office knows that it isn't at all as straightforward as that. 'Is it permissible to ask a colleague out for a coffee?', I wondered aloud. This appeared to be a borderline case. If the coffee was requested more than once then this was an obvious problem. 'Men have to learn that no means no', it was suggested. 'Don't do anything you wouldn't do in front of your mother' was suggested as one basis for a moral norm – ignoring the fact that there are plenty of perfectly legal, acceptable and very enjoyable acts that adults perform in their lives which they would not do in front of their mother. This was nit-picking, it seemed. 'It's really not that difficult,' the Chief People Officer reiterated.

Except that it is, isn't it? And every woman in that room – like the vast majority of women outside it – knows that to be the case. For instance, they know that a considerable percentage of men and women meet their future life partner in the workplace. Even though the internet has changed much about dating life, most studies even from recent years show around 10–20 per cent of people still find their partners at their place of work. Given that successful people like those in the room are the sort of people who have a work-life balance that disproportionately favours work, they are going to be spending more time with their colleagues than at social engagements. So is it entirely wise to cordon off this significant tributary of potential life partners? Or to limit it to the tiny slivers of potential permitted by their organization's Chief People Officer? To do so would be to demand the following: that every man had the opportunity to pursue only one woman in their work life. That that woman could be asked out for coffee or a drink on only one occasion. And that this sole shot must have an absolute, 100 per cent accuracy rating on the one occasion on which it was deployed. Is this a sensible, orderly or indeed humane way to arrange relations between the sexes? Of course most of the room laughs at the very suggestion. Because it is laughable. And it is risible. And it is also the law of the modern workplace.

An investigation by *Bloomberg* published in December 2018 looked at attitudes among senior figures in the world of finance, which is an undeniably male-dominated sector, with male majorities in each main area other than support staff.[14] The attitudes of men at a senior level were striking. In interviews with more than 30 senior executives from the world of finance men admitted to no longer being willing to have dinner with female colleagues. They also refused to sit next to them on flights. They insisted on hotel rooms being booked on different floors from female colleagues and avoided any one-on-one meetings with women.[15]

If this is truly the attitude of men in the workplace then it does not suggest that the whole area of etiquette around the office is generally either honest or obvious. Rules that claim to be established have only just come in. Norms that are meant to be universal weren't followed until the day before yesterday. And then underneath all of this is the sense gathered from the *Bloomberg* report, which is not that people do not trust themselves (though they may not) but that they don't trust the honesty of other people making claims – including claims made by women once they are alone with a male colleague. If the etiquette of the workplace is so easy to work out it is surprising that it is so complex.

Back at the conference in London, one of the most striking things about the day is that the discussion ends up being of the sort which until very recently was confined to liberal arts college campuses. At the 'Women Mean Business' conference we conclude, inevitably, with a discussion about 'privilege'. Who has it, who should have it, and how can it be more fairly apportioned?

Not least among the oddities of this discussion whenever it arises – and this is very common today – is the fact that privilege is an unbelievably hard thing to define. It is also very nearly impossible to quantify. One person may have 'privilege' from inheriting money. For another person this same privilege may be a curse, giving them too much too early and disincentivizing them from making their way in the world. Is a person with inherited wealth but who has a natural disability more privileged or less privileged than a person without any inherited wealth who is able-bodied? Who can work this out? Who would we trust to work it out? And how can the various stratas of this arrangement be flexible enough not just to include everybody in view but also take into account the comparative changes for the better and worse which will occur across every human life?

Another problem connected to privilege is that though we may be able to see it in others we may be unable or unwilling to recognize it in ourselves. By any stretch of the imagination the women in this room form the top percentile of people not just among those who ever lived but among those in their own countries, cities and neighbourhoods right now. They have significant salaries, considerable contacts and will have more opportunities in an average month than most white males will have in a lifetime. And yet privilege as an issue is repeatedly raised because it is assumed to be something that other people have.

UNCONSCIOUS BIAS TRAINING + INTERSECTIONALITY
This brings us ineluctably – and right on cue – to the ultimate destination point of this impossible process of perpetual stratifi-cations and deduction: the importance of 'intersectionality'. The Chief People Officer of *The Daily Telegraph* gets us there before I can. But it is important, she stresses, to consider the intersectional overlay in all of this. For we should recall that it is not only women who need to be empowered and given a leg-up in the hierarchy. There are other marginalized groups who should also receive help. A member of the audience reminds the panel that some people are refugees and it is important that their voices do not get lost in all this. A point which

can be made widely and endlessly. Some people have disabilities. Some people are depressed. Not everyone is beautiful. Some people are gay. And so on.

The woman from J. P. Morgan tells us that this is precisely one of the reasons why her firm has instituted compulsory 'unconscious bias training'. There is general agreement that this should be instituted more widely. Our brains are so wired that we are sometimes not aware of biases and prejudices that may lie dormant in the back recesses of our brains. These engrained prejudices may lead us to prefer men over women (or, presumably, vice-versa) or people of one skin colour over another. Some people may be put off hiring somebody because of their religion or sexuality. And so 'unconscious bias training' is available at J. P. Morgan and at an increasing number of other banks, financial institutions and other private and public companies in order to rewire our attitudes and allow those who submit to it to have their natural prejudices altered, cleaned up and corrected.

Just one of the staggering oddities of the discussion going on is the certainty that the readers of *The Daily Telegraph* would absolutely hate all this. In Britain the *Telegraph* is regarded as the newspaper of the conservative right. Its readers might fairly be said to be less in favour of change than in things broadly staying the same, whereas unconscious bias training must be very high up the list of things that will stop anything being the same. That is the point of it. It is intended to change everything. And it has come to occupy a central position not just at conservative newspapers and leading Wall Street and City of London firms, but at the heart of government. In 2016 the US Government's Office of Personnel Management announced that it was planning to put all of its employees through unconscious bias training. That is a workforce of 2.8 million people.[16] The British government has committed itself to similar processes of bias and 'diversity training' for all.

The schemes themselves slightly differ, but all centre around versions of what at Harvard University has been developed as the Implicit Association Test (IAT). Since it went on the internet in 1998 more than 30 million people have taken the test on the Harvard website to discover whether or not they harbour unconscious bias.[17] What the IAT attempts to work out is who individuals think of as being in an 'in group' and who they might see as being in an 'out group'. Cited thousands of times in academic papers, it has undoubtedly become the most influential measure of 'unconscious bias'.

It has also spawned a whole industry. In 2015 the Royal Society of Arts in London announced that it was training people on selection and appointment panels to address their unconscious bias. The organization released a video explaining how this was done. It advocated four principal moves: deliberately slow down decision-making; reconsider the reasons for your decision-making; question cultural stereotypes; monitor each other for unconscious bias. All of which presupposes certain sets of outcomes. For instance, once someone has questioned a cultural stereotype are they allowed to hold onto it? Probably not. If people monitor each other for unconscious bias and find none, is that a failure or a success? A sign of unimaginable virtue, a sign that people aren't spotting the signs or a sign that everyone is cheating? When people talk about 'questioning' things through the application of unconscious bias training they do not seem to mean 'questioning' people. They mean 'changing' them.

Anyone who has ever had to interview large numbers of people for any role will know that a significant part of the process is 'first impressions'. The reason there are so many heave-some mottoes like 'You never get a second chance to make a first impression' is that it is widely recognized to be true. It isn't just how people look, how they are dressed or what firmness their handshake does or does not have. It is about a whole set of other signals and impressions that a person gives off. And the response to them does indeed involve prejudice, and swift decision-making. Not all of which will be bad.

For example, most people have a natural prejudice against those with swiftly moving, shifting or darting eyes. Is that presumption a 'bias' or might it be justified, built in by an evolutionary instinct that it may be unwise to overcome? More pertinently, what should a small-business owner feel in an interview with a woman in her late thirties who the boss suspects is likely to become pregnant in the next few years? Obviously employment law prevents the interviewer from delving into this. But it could be said that the employer has an instinctive bias against such a candidate. And the law might wish to change that. But the small-business owner's bias against hiring a woman who may work for a short period of time before going on maternity leave, thereby costing the company in maternity pay for a job she may not return to, is not an entirely irrational bias.

Testing yourself for existing prejudices may root out some deep-seated distrust of people of a certain background or powerful women, or much else. It may also just make you distrust all of your instincts. And just as instinct can lead individuals in the wrong direction, it is also very often the only thing that has seen them right.

What is more, you may feel differently from one day to the next, and people who have taken the IAT have found exactly that. Indeed, criticism of the whole idea of implicit bias is such that even some of the people who worked on the Harvard test, which has become such a benchmark, have expressed their concern about what their work has been used for. Since its deployment in the corporate world, government, academia and an increasing number of other places, two out of the three people who created the IAT at Harvard have publicly admitted that the test cannot do what it purports to do with sufficient accuracy. One of the three, Brian Nosek of the University of Virginia, has said publicly that the extent to which the test can measure anything meaningful has been misconceived. There had been an 'incorrect interpretation' of his work, he noted. Of attempts to prove bias in individuals he has said, 'There is some consistency but not high consistency. Our mind isn't that stable.'[18] What is more there is mounting evidence that none of this works in practice. For instance, that increasing the number of women on selection panels doesn't increase the chances of a woman getting a job.[19]

So here is a whole area which has been insufficiently studied but has already been rolled out across government and business. Will its effects be benign, its only costs being the huge expense in recruiting experts to guide people in this inexpert discipline? Or will attempts to presume to rewire the brains of every single government employee and everybody in business have repercussions which nobody has yet dared to imagine? Who knows.

But if implicit-bias training looks like a half worked-out theory turned into a fully worked-out business plan, the dogma under which it sits is a grade even beyond that. At the 'Women Mean Business' conference it is the Chief People Officer of *The Daily Telegraph* who is busily pushing the importance of an intersectional approach in business as well as in society more widely. This comes in response to women in the audience wondering where they should place ethnic minorities, refugees and asylum seekers in the list of groups who deserve a bit of whatever can be squeezed out of those with power.

It should probably be said from the outset that despite presenting itself – like 'bias training' – as a fully worked-out science, intersectionality is far from it. Its originators, like the feminist authors and academics 'bell hooks' (i.e. Gloria Jean Watkins) and Peggy McIntosh, simply assert that Western democracies include a range of groups (women, ethnic minorities, sexual minorities and others) who are structurally oppressed in a 'matrix of oppression'. From there what the intersectionalists urge is a political project rather than an academic discipline. The interests of one of these groups is portrayed as the interest and concern of all of these groups. If they unite against the common enemy of the people at the top of the pyramid who allegedly hold the power, then something good will happen. To say that intersectionality has not been thought through is an understatement. Together with its other faults it has not been put to the test in any meaningful way anywhere for any meaningful length of time. It has the most tenuous basis in philosophy and has no major work of thought dedicated to it. To which someone might respond that there are plenty of things that haven't been tried yet and that don't have a fully worked-out structure of thought behind them. But in such cases it would ordinarily be deemed presumptuous, not to say unwise, to try to roll out that concept across an entire society, including every educational institution and every profitable place of business.

Although many people in important, well-remunerated positions now argue for this theory, where can this 'intersectionality' be said to work? And how could it? Just look at the set of unsolvable questions which it sets off even just in this room at the 'Women Mean Business' conference. All of the women here have benefited from career advancement. Many could hardly enjoy more. Which of them is willing to offer up that place to somebody of a different skin colour, sexual orientation or class position, and when and how should they do so? When, and how, is anyone meant to be able to discern that the person who is prioritized over them, if they were to take a step back and urge this other person forward, has not in fact had a far easier time in their life than they have themselves?

In recent years, as intersectionality has begun to catch on, the workplaces which are attempting to implement it have produced stranger and stranger conundrums. The order of their discoveries sometimes varies but the discoveries themselves do not. At firms in all the major cities a concerted drive will take place to promote women or people of colour into higher positions. But as an increasing number of companies and government departments have to account for pay differentials between the sexes and people of different racial backgrounds, fascinating new problems arise. In the UK all organizations with more than 250 employees must publish the average pay differences in their company between men and women. In 2018 MPs suggested that all companies with more than 50 employees should have to provide the same information.[20] This means, among other things, that an entire bureaucracy has to be created to sort through a new set of problems.

I will keep the following person's identity secret, but it is a telling case. A person I know in Britain recently got a job in a large corporation. They went in on a very fine salary. A short time into the job this person's superiors approached with an embarrassing request. Would the individual be willing to accept a larger salary than had previously been offered? The institution was getting close to the end of its financial year and was seeking to satisfy the infinite number of graphs and breakdowns on racial and gender quotas in the organization. To its dismay the institution had discovered that the 'gap' between pay of people of the majority ethnicity and that of racial minorities was insufficiently close. Would the individual then mind their own salary being significantly upped in order to better satisfy the year's-end differentials? Being a perfectly wise and sane person the relevant employee graciously agreed to take the higher salary to help their employer out of this otherwise tricky situation.

This may be an especially ludicrous example of where the obsession with quotas can get people. But in company after company there are more prosaic examples of something similar. For instance, every firm that makes a concerted effort to promote people of colour, women or sexual minorities will always arrive at a moment where they make some version of the following discovery: the people they have promoted are themselves likely to be comparatively privileged. In many, though not all, cases they are people who have already been well served by the system. They may be women who are from a well-off background, who have been privately educated and gone to the best universities. Did they require a leg-up? Possibly. But at whose expense?

Likewise the discovery has been made that in the first waves of sexual and ethnic minority employees benefiting from 'positive discrimination' in order to 'diversify' an office environment, the men and women in question were not from the most put-upon groups in society. A phenomenon occurs similar to what happens in political parties. When the Conservative Party in Britain sought to increase its number of ethnic minority MPs it managed to recruit some very talented individuals. These included at least one black MP who had been to Eton, and another whose uncle is the vice-president of Nigeria. As for the Labour Party, it chose among its candidates for Parliament a woman whose aunt is the Prime Minister of Bangladesh.

As it is in politics, so it is in private and public companies. Fast-tracked diversity may promote the people who were nearest to their destination already. And very often these are the most privileged people of any group – including their own. At companies across Europe and America which have adopted this approach to hiring, a common story is emerging, albeit one only talked about in whispers. For people in such companies are gradually realizing that there are costs to all this. That is, while their companies have managed to increase female mobility and ethnic minority mobility, their level of class mobility has never been lower. All they have managed to do is build a new hierarchy.

Hierarchies are not static. They have not always been in the past and they are unlikely to remain the same in the future. For their part, the proponents of intersectionality, bias training and more have made extraordinarily swift inroads. And the flow of these ideas straight through into the corporate world is a demonstration that a new type of hierarchy has been set up. This one has – like all hierarchies – its oppressor class and oppressed class. It has those who seek to be virtuous and those ('Chief People Officers') who are in a position to enlighten

See Thomas Sowell

those who are not. For the time being this new priestly class is getting a pretty good run at explaining how they think the world works.

But the overwhelming problem is not just that these theories are being embedded in institutions without sufficient thought or track record of success. The overwhelming problem is that these new systems continue to be built on group identities which we still haven't come close to understanding. They are systems built on foundations which are nowhere near being agreed upon. Such as the whole issue of the relations between the sexes and issues which we would once have called 'feminist'.

THIS FEMINIST WAVE

In part this confusion emerges from the tremendous success of the first and second waves of feminism, and the fact that succeeding waves have suffered severe symptoms of 'St George in retirement syndrome'.

Pinpointing exactly which waves of feminism occurred when is complicated by the fact that they are recognized to have occurred at different times in different places. But it is widely accepted that the first wave of feminism was the one which began in the eighteenth century and continued, in some estimations, up to the franchise and by others right up to the 1960s. It was precise in its ambitions and deep in its claims. From Mary Wollstonecraft to the Campaign for Women's Suffrage, the claims of first-wave feminism were defined by the demand for equal legal rights. Not different rights, but equal rights. The right to vote, obviously. But also the right to petition for divorce, to have equal guardianship over children and the equal inheritance of property. The fight for these rights was long, but it was achieved.

The wave of feminism which began in the 1960s addressed the priorities that remained unresolved underneath those basic rights. Issues such as the rights of women to pursue their desired careers and to be supported in those aims. In America Betty Friedan and her allies championed the rights not only of women's education but of maternity leave and childcare support for women in employment. These feminists argued for reproductive rights around contraception and abortion, for the safety of women inside marriages as well as out of them. The aim of these feminists was to help get women to the place where they would have an equal shot in their lives and careers, comparable to men.

Having managed between two and three waves (depending where and how you are counting) in as many centuries, by the 1980s the feminist movement splintered and fell out over niche issues such as what attitudes feminists should take towards pornography. Those people often described as third-wave feminists emerged, like the fourth-wavers that swiftly followed them in the 2010s, with a striking style of rhetoric. With the major battles for equality behind them, it might have been expected that feminists would mop up the remaining issues that existed and that the fact that things had never been better would mean that the pitch of their rhetoric matched this reality.

Yet no such thing happened. If anything ever picked up steam and careered off down the tracks just after having pulled in at the station, it was feminism over recent decades. From the 1970s onwards a new pitch embedded itself within the feminist camps, with several distinctive motifs. The first was that of defeat being imminent just before the point of victory.

In 1991 Susan Faludi published *Backlash: The Undeclared War Against American Women*. A year later Marilyn French (bestselling author of *The Women's Room* in 1977) repeated the trick with *The War Against Women*. These hugely successful books thrived on the notion that although rights had been achieved there was now a concerted campaign under way to roll that progress back. Equality had not been achieved, Faludi and French argued, but the possibility that it might be had set the males off on an inevitable response in which even those rights that had been achieved would be taken away. It is remarkable to revisit those works at the distance of a quarter of a century, for they have simultaneously become absolutely normal in their pitch and are clearly deranged in the claims that they make.

In her international bestseller, Faludi identified the 'undeclared war against women' in almost every element of life in Western societies. She saw it in the media and the movies. She saw it in television and in clothes. She saw it in academia and in politics. She saw it in economics and in popular psychology. What it all added up to, Faludi insisted, was 'the rising pressure to halt, and even reverse' the quest for 'equality'. This backlash had many apparent contradictions. It was both organized and 'not an organized movement'. In fact the 'lack of orchestration' made it 'harder to see – and perhaps more effective'. Over the previous decade, which had seen cuts in public spending in countries like the UK (instigated, of course, by a female Prime Minister), 'the backlash has moved through the culture's secret chambers, travelling through passageways of flattery and fear'.[21] Through these and similar means, the war against women was at once both staring everybody in the face all the time and so subtle as to require Faludi to make it noticeable.

For her part French declared at the outset of her book, 'there is evidence' that for around three and half million years the human species lived in a situation in which men and women were equal. In fact more than equal, for in those days women apparently enjoyed a higher status than men. Then for the last 10,000 or so years our species allegedly lived in 'egalitarian harmony and material well-being', with the sexes getting on pretty well. But since the fourth millennium BCE, French informs her readers, men began to construct 'the patriarchy', a system she defines as 'male supremacy backed by force'. For women 'it has been downhill ever since'. We are informed that women were 'probably' the first slaves and have since then been 'increasingly disempowered, degraded and subjugated'. For the last four centuries, French says, this has got completely out of control, with men ('mainly in the West') attempting to 'tighten their control of nature and those associated with nature – people of color and women'.[22]

Having established her definition of feminism as 'any attempt to improve the lot of any group of women through female solidarity and a female perspective', French claims that men 'as a caste . . . continue to seek ways to defeat feminism'. They seek to take away its victories (the example French gives being 'legal abortion'). They also seek to put a 'glass ceiling' over professional women and create movements aimed at returning women to 'fully subordinate status'. This and more amounts to 'a global war against women'.[23]

Ignoring a fair amount of evidence to the contrary, and showing no compunction about essentializing or making generalizations about the male half of the species, French declares that 'the only ground of male solidarity is opposition to women'.[24] She sees the demands of feminists as equally straightforward. The challenge to 'patriarchy' by feminists is simply a demand 'to be treated as human beings with rights', including the demand 'that men not feel free to beat, rape, mutilate, and kill them'.[25] What kind of monster would oppose that? And who are the members of this patriarchy who feel free to beat, rape, mutilate and kill women?

In French's argument, from every direction, the problem is men. Every time women make an advance, men can be found 'mustering all their forces to defeat this challenge'. Male violence towards women is not an accident or a by-product of some other factor (let alone many potential factors). Rather it is the case that 'all male violence toward women is part of a concerted campaign' that includes 'beatings, imprisonment, mutilation, torture, starvation, rape and murder'.[26]

It is bad enough that men are driven to such acts as part of an ongoing wider campaign to defeat women, but what is worse, according to French, is that men also organize in other ways to ensure that 'women are disadvantaged in every area of life'. Men apparently arrange this by systematic wars against women in every imaginable field, including in education, work, healthcare, law, sex, science and even in a 'war against women as mothers'.[27]

The final insult, as described by French, is that there are not only wars against women which women have to worry about, but also war – period. Literal, actual, non-metaphorical war is also a problem and is also in and of itself anti-women.[28] From its language to its actions, war is a male act and as such is designed to oppose women. For women – it becomes clear by the very close of French's book – are the embodiments of peace. Whereas men wage war, women have a set of movements like the Women's Pentagon Action in 1980 in which women encircled the Pentagon, declaring that 'militarism was sexism,' and at Greenham Common in Britain. This is the good news, French reveals at the rousing end of her book: 'Women are fighting back on every front.'[29]

Many of the claims made in French's book are tendentious and ahistorical. Once she has set up her paradigm she is able to make almost anything fit into it. But it is the dichotomy she insists on throughout which is most striking. Everything that is good is female. Everything that is bad is male.

French, Faludi and others were enormously successful in embedding this idea. They also established a pattern, which was that the success of feminist arguments began to depend on claims being distorted and hyped. Gradually the most extreme claims took over as the norm. Not just the most extreme claims about men, but the most extreme claims about women as well. These came to be insinuated in every aspect of the claims made by the new waves of feminists. For instance, in her hugely successful book *The Beauty Myth* (1990) Naomi Wolf claimed that although it was true that the benefits of feminist achievements and analysis meant that women were better off than they had ever been before, in other ways they were quite literally dying. In *The Beauty Myth* she famously tried to claim that in America alone around 150,000 women a year were dying from anorexia-related eating disorders. As a number of scholars including Christina Hoff Sommers subsequently showed, Wolf had exaggerated the actual figures by several hundred times.[30] Exaggeration and catastrophism became the regular currency in which feminists were encouraged to deal.

The other thing to get embedded in this stage of feminism was a form of misandry – man-hating. This had been present among various individuals in earlier waves of feminism, but it had never been so dominant, let alone triumphant. At some point in the 2010s it was reckoned that third-wave feminism had progressed into a fourth wave of feminism because of the advent of social media. Fourth-wave feminism is mainly third-wave feminism with apps. What all these waves have inadvertently demonstrated is the deranging effects that social media can have not just on a debate but on a movement.

Consider the scene in February 2018 when self-declared 'feminists' are once again on Twitter pushing around their new favourite slogans. 'Men are trash' is the latest arrangement of words they had come up with in order to persuade more people to come onto their side. Fourth-wave feminists are trying to get 'All men are trash' or just 'Men are trash' trending on social media. One of those who whipped this along is the British fourth-wave feminist writer Laurie Penny, author of various blog compilation books, including the charmingly titled *Bitch Doctrine* (2017). In February 2018 Penny could be found on Twitter saying, '"Men are trash" is a phrase I adore because it implies waste.'[31] She went on to explain that the beauty of the phrase had to do with the fact that 'toxic masculinity wastes so much human potential

. . . I hope we're on the cusp of a giant recycling program.' This was followed by the hashtag 'MeToo' and an emoji of hands being raised in the air.

As is so often the case, a member of the public was at hand to ask if Penny might perhaps have had father issues that caused her to use phrases such as these. At which point, as so often, Penny pivoted on a dime. 'Actually, my father was wonderful, and a great inspiration. He passed away a few years ago. We all miss him.' The reader pushed his point. 'Was he toxic?' he enquired. At which point the reader was reprimanded by Penny for being 'harsh'. She went on to reprimand him: 'It's not appropriate to make cracks about someone's dead dad.' Meaning the line had already developed to: 'All men are trash apart from my late father, who you're not allowed to mention.' Within an hour the victimhood narrative developed even further. Penny returned to Twitter to say: 'Right now I'm facing a barrage of abuse, threats, antisemitism, fantasies about my death, disgusting things said about my family. It has rapidly become frightening. This is all because I said "I like the phrase 'men are trash'", it implies the potential for change.' Which actually wasn't what she had said. She had said how delighted she was to use a phrase that described half of the human species as 'trash'. And then having behaved like a bully she found shelter behind the claim of being bullied. As though, having written off half the human race, it would be wrong to get any kind of pushback.

In fact, had Penny waited a while, a fellow feminist would have been at hand to explain that whether or not Penny wanted to justify the words she had used she no longer needed to, because these words were among the growing list of magical words which did not mean what they appeared to mean.

THE WAR ON MEN

The *Huffington Post* writer Salma El-Wardany whose byline describes herself as a 'half Egyptian, half Irish Muslim writer traveling [*sic*] the world eating cake and dismantling the patriarchy'. As part of this dismantling, El-Wardany also turns out to be fond of the phrase 'all men are trash'. But she explained in the words of her headline 'What women mean when we say "men are trash"'. According to this *Huffington Post* feminist, 'It can actually be directly translated into; "masculinity is in transition and it's not moving f**king fast enough."'

El-Wardany claimed that the phrase 'men are trash' is heard everywhere in her world, 'like a gentle hum vibrating across the globe. An anthem . . . a call to arms and a battle cry.' She claimed that if you enter 'any room, social event, dinner party, creative gathering and you'll hear the phrase from at least one corner of the room, and you'll naturally gravitate towards that group of women because you immediately know you've found your tribe. It's basically the password to the "*pissed off at men*" club.' It turns out that the words are the consequence of a condensed form of 'anger, frustration, hurt and pain'. And in El-Wardany's view this hurt and pain come from the fact that while women are constantly asked what sort of girl or woman they want to be, men are apparently never asked – and never have to ask – what sort of man they are going to be. While women are constantly having demands made on them, 'masculinity was handed down from father to son, with little or no deviation from the typical provider/protector role'.

In conclusion, when women say 'men are trash' what they in fact are saying is 'Your ideas of manhood are no longer fit for purpose and your lack of evolution is hurting us all.' It is saying that men are the slow kids in the class and that they have got, in El-Wardany's words, to 'get there a lot faster'.[32]

As it happens, 'All men are trash' and 'Men are trash' were at the lighter end of feminist rhetoric in its fourth wave. One of the previous popular hashtags used on Twitter by feminists was 'Kill All Men'. Fortunately the journalist and commentator Ezra Klein was available at *Vox* to decode this one. Whilst conceding that he had not enjoyed seeing the hashtag 'Kill All Men' or the moment when this phrase leaked out from the virtual world into the real one, the words did not mean what they appeared to mean. As Klein explained, when people he knew and 'even love[d]' began to use the term in casual conversation, he at first recoiled and felt defensive. But he explained that he came to realize '*that wasn't what they were saying*' (italics in original). He realized that not only did they not want to kill him or kill any men. In fact it was better than that. 'They didn't hate me, and they didn't hate men.' Klein's discovery was that 'Kill All Men' was merely 'another way of saying "it would be nice if the world sucked less for women'". A hell of a way to say it, but Klein went on, 'It was an expression of frustration with pervasive sexism.'[33]

Saying 'Kill All Men' might have been an over-zealous way to call for female suffrage at a time when women did not have the vote. First-wave feminists campaigning for equality by saying 'Kill All Men' would have been a deranged way to try to get people on their side. But a century later it appeared to have become normal and indeed acceptable for women born with all the rights their forebears had fought for to react with more violent language than had been employed when the stakes were infinitely higher.

Nor is this campaign limited to Twitter hashtaggery. Over the last decade we have seen the entry into everyday public discussion of a range of slogans such as 'male privilege'. Like most slogans it is easy to spout but hard to put a finger on. For instance, it might be said that the preponderance of males in the position of Chief Executive Officer is an example of 'male privilege'. But nobody knows what the preponderance of male suicides (according to the Samaritans, British men are three times more likely to commit suicide than women), deaths in dangerous occupations, homelessness and much more might mean. Is this a sign of the opposite of male privilege? Do they even each other out? If not, what are the systems, metrics or timespan for doing so? Nobody seems to know.

Other forms of the new misandry present themselves as more lighthearted. For instance, there is the term 'mansplaining' to decry any occasion when a man can be said to have spoken to a woman in a patronizing or supercilious manner. Certainly everybody can think of examples when they have heard men speak in precisely such a tone of voice. But most people can also think of times when a woman has spoken to a man in the same way. Or indeed when a man has spoken patronizingly to another man. So why does only one of these circumstances need its own term? Why is there no term for – or wide usage of – a word like 'womansplaining'? Or any idea whether a man can 'mansplain' to another man? What are the circumstances under which a man can be said to be talking down to a woman because she is a woman as opposed to a man talking down to a woman because she is talking down to him? At present there is no mechanism to work any of these things out, merely a projectile that can be launched at any stage by a woman.

Then there is the concept of 'the patriarchy' – the idea that people (largely in Western capitalist countries) live in a society which is rigged in favour of men and with the aim of suppressing women and their skills. This concept has become so ingrained that when it is mentioned it now floats by as though the idea that modern Western societies are centred around – and run solely for the comfort of – men is not even something most people would bother to dispute. In a 2018 article, commemorating the centenary of women in Britain over the age of 30 gaining the right to vote, a piece in the popular women's magazine *Grazia* said, 'We live in a patriarchal society, that much we know.' The reasons it gave as evidence were 'the objectification of women' and 'unrealistic beauty standards', as though men are never objectified or held to any standards in their appearance (a claim that men who have been surreptitiously photographed on trains by strangers and had their photos uploaded to 'Hot dudes reading' on Instagram might dispute). 'For us, the patriarchy is hidden' according to *Grazia*, though other visible symptoms were 'a lack of respect that amounts to a gender pay gap and snatched career opportunities'.[34] Men's magazines seem perfectly happy to adopt the same presumptions. Reflecting on the events of 2018, the men's magazine *GQ* was happy to editorialize approvingly that during that year 'For the first time in history, we've all been called to account for the sins of the patriarchy.'[35]

Worst among the new lexicon of anti-male slogans is that of 'toxic masculinity'. Like each of these other memes, 'toxic masculinity' started out on the furthest fringes of academia and social media. But by 2019 it had made it into the heart of serious organizations and public bodies. In January the American Psychological Association released its first ever guidelines for how its members should specifically deal with men and boys. The APA claimed that 40 years of research showed that 'traditional masculinity – marked by stoicism, competitiveness, dominance and aggression, is undermining men's well-being'. To tackle these 'traditional' aspects of masculinity the APA had produced its new guidelines in order to help people in practice 'recognize this problem for boys and men'. The APA went on to define traditional masculinity as 'a particular constellation of standards that have held sway over large segments of the population, including: anti-femininity, achievement, eschewal of the appearance of weakness, and adventure, risk, and violence.'[36] It was just one of the inroads that the concept of 'toxic masculinity' has made into the mainstream.

It did so, again, with no suggestion that any such problem is mirrored on the female side. For instance, does a form of 'toxic femininity' exist? If so, what is it and how can it be permanently excised from women? Nor is there any sense before the concept of 'toxic masculinity' is embedded of whether or how it might work even on its own terms. For instance, if competitiveness is indeed an especially male trait – as the APA would appear to be suggesting – when is that competitiveness toxic or harmful, and when is it useful? Might a male athlete be allowed to use his competitive instincts on the racetrack? If so how can he be helped to ensure that off the track he is as docile as possible? Might a man facing inoperable cancer with stoicism be criticized for doing so, and helped out of this harmful position into a situation in which he demonstrates less stoicism? If 'adventure' and 'risk' are indeed male traits then when and where should men be encouraged to drop them? Should a male explorer be encouraged to be less adventurous, a male firefighter be trained to take fewer risks? Ought male soldiers be encouraged to be less connected to 'violence' and be keener to show an appearance of weakness? If so when? What would the mechanism be by which male soldiers were reprogrammed to use their very useful traits and skills in certain dangerous occasions when society badly needs them, but that this should be trained out of them the rest of the time?

Of course if there are toxic traits within masculinity the likelihood is that they are so deep (that is, they exist across all cultures irrespective of situational differences) that they are ineradicable. Or it could be that there are specific aspects of some male behaviour which in certain times and places are undesirable. If the latter is the case then there are almost certainly specific ways in which to tackle the problem. But in either case inventing concepts like 'male privilege', 'the patriarchy', 'mansplaining' or 'toxic masculinity' would not get near to addressing the problem, proving either too little or too much for the diagnosis at hand. The more obvious explanation from any outside analysis is that there seems to be a move less intended to improve men than to neuter them, to turn any and all of their virtues around on them and turn them instead into self-doubting, self-loathing objects of pity. It looks, in a word, like some type of revenge.

Why would that be? Why would the war and the rhetoric become so heated when the standards of equality have so much improved? Is it because the stakes are low? Because people are bored and want to assume the heroic posture amid a life of relative safety and comfort? Or is it simply that social media – the challenge of speaking to yourself or possibly to the entire planet – is making honest discussion impossible?

Whatever the cause, the impact this is having on the reputation of feminism is clear. The misandry is damaging. In 2016 the Fawcett Society surveyed 8,000 people to find out what proportion of people identified themselves as a 'feminist'. The survey found that only 9 per cent of British women used the word 'feminist' to describe themselves. Only 4 per cent of men did. The vast majority of people surveyed supported gender equality. In fact a larger number of men than women supported equality between the sexes (86 per cent versus 74 per cent). But the vast majority also resisted the 'feminist' label. For their part the Fawcett Society managed to put a positive spin on what for a feminist organization must have appeared to be a disappointing finding. Britain was a nation of 'hidden feminists', the group's spokeswoman said. Explaining why the vast majority of the public didn't identify with the feminist label, she said, 'The simple truth is that if you want a more equal society for women and men then you are in fact a feminist.'[37] Yet when asked what words popped into respondents' heads first when they heard the word 'feminist', the single most popular word that came to them – indeed to more than a quarter of respondents – was 'bitchy'.[38]

It is a similar story in the US. Asked in 2013 whether men and women should be 'social, political and economic equals', the vast majority of Americans (82 per cent) said 'yes'. But when asked whether they identified themselves as 'feminists' there was a recognizable fall-off. Only 23 per cent of women and 16 per cent of men in the US identified themselves as 'feminists'. A clear majority (63 per cent) said that they were neither feminist nor anti-feminist.[39]

Whatever the cause may be, it isn't wholly clear how men are supposed to react to this. The likelihood of reprogramming the natural instincts of all men and all women is a remote one. For three years between 2014 and 2017 academics in the UK carried out a study about the images of men that women found attractive. The results, published in Feminist Media Studies, discovered a disturbing trend. *Newsweek* summed up the shocking findings in a headline, 'Men with muscles and money are more attractive to straight women and gay men – showing gender roles aren't progressing.'[40] Indeed. 'Progress' will only be achieved when women find men attractive who they don't think are attractive. What could be unachievable in that?

HARDWARE TRYING TO BE SOFTWARE

When it comes to differences between men and women – and how to bring some order to relations between them – there remains a huge amount that we do not know. But there is a lot that we do know. Or did know. And as the snapshots of popular culture above demonstrate, this was not niche knowledge but knowledge just about as widely held as any knowledge can be. Yet something happened. At some point some scrambling device was imposed on the whole issue of relations between the sexes. Something caused this massive upsurge of rage and denial just at the point the issue should have reached a consensus and settlement.

Without doubt the scrambling device laid over the issue of the sexes is among the most deranging aspects of all. It involves a set of unbelievable mental leaps to try to play along with it, and even then it cannot be even attempted without causing unbelievable personal and societal pain.

It comes down to this. Gay campaigners spent the 1990s onwards hoping to persuade the world that homosexuality was a hardware issue, and as we saw above it may be or it may not be. But the drive to make it so was obvious. Hardware was good because hardware protected your status. But something happened at the same time as that fight was going on in gay rights which is truly staggering. Thanks to the work of a number of people – including people who were mistakenly thought to be arguing for feminism – the direction of travel for women simultaneously went in exactly the opposite direction.

Until the last decade or so, sex (or gender) and chromosomes were recognized to be among the most fundamental hardware issues in our species. Whether we were born as a man or a woman was one of the main, unchangeable hardware issues of our lives. Having accepted this hardware we then all found ways – both men and women – to learn how to operate the relevant aspects of our lives. So absolutely everything not just within the sexes but between them became scrambled when the argument became entrenched that this most fundamental hardware issue of all was in fact a matter of software. The claim was made, and a couple of decades later it was embedded and suddenly everybody was meant to believe that sex was not biologically fixed but merely a matter of 'reiterated social performances'.

The claim put a bomb under the feminist cause with completely predictable consequences for another problem we'll come to with 'trans'. It left feminism with almost no defences against men arguing that they could become women. But the whole attempt to turn hardware into software has caused – and is continuing to cause – more pain than almost any other issue for men and women alike. It is at the foundation of the current madness. For it asks us all to believe that women are different from the beings they have always been. It suggests that everything women and men saw – and knew – until yesterday was a mirage and that our inherited knowledge about our differences (and how to get along) is all invalid knowledge. All the rage – including the wild, destructive misandry, the double-think and the self-delusion – stem from this fact: that we are being not just asked, but expected, to radically alter our lives and societies on the basis of claims that our instincts all tell us cannot possibly be true.

The Impact of Tech

If the foundations of the new metaphysics are precarious and the presumptions that we are being asked to follow seem subtly wrong, then it is the addition into the mix of the communications revolution that is causing the conditions for a crowd madness. If we are already running in the wrong direction then tech helps us to run there exponentially faster. It is this ingredient that is causing the sensation of the treadmill running faster than our feet can carry us.

In 1933 James Thurber published 'The Day the Dam Broke', recalling his memories of 12 March 1913 when the whole of his town in Ohio went for a run. Thurber recalled how the rumour began that the dam had broken. Around noon 'Suddenly somebody began to run. It may be that he had simply remembered, all of a moment, an engagement to meet his wife, for which he was now frightfully late.' Soon somebody else began to run, 'perhaps a newsboy in high spirits. Another man, a portly gentleman of affairs, broke into a trot':

Inside of ten minutes, everybody on High Street, from the Union Depot to the Courthouse, was running. A loud mumble gradually crystallized into the dread word 'dam'. 'The dam has broke!' The fear was put into words by a little old lady in an electric, or by a traffic cop, or by a small boy: nobody knows who, nor does it now really matter. Two thousand people were abruptly in full flight. 'Go east!' was the cry that arose – east away from the river, east to safety. 'Go east! Go east! Go east!'

As the whole town stampedes to the east nobody stops to consider that the dam is so far away from their town that it could not cause a trickle of water to flow across the High Street. Nor does anybody notice the absence of water. The faster residents, who have put miles of distance between themselves and the town, eventually return home, as does everybody else. As Thurber says:

> The next day the city went about its business as if nothing had happened, but there was no joking. It was two years or more before you dared treat the breaking of the dam lightly. And even now, twenty years after, there are a few persons . . . who will shut up like a clam if you mention the Afternoon of the Great Run.[1]

Today our societies seem always on that run, and always risking extraordinary shame over not just our own behaviour but the way in which we have treated others. Every day there is a new subject for hate and moral judgement. It might be a group of schoolboys wearing the wrong hats in the wrong place at the wrong time.[2] Or it could be anybody else. As the work of Jon Ronson and others on 'public shaming' has shown,[3] the internet has allowed new forms of activism and bullying in the guise of social activism to become the tenor of the time. The urge to find people who can be accused of 'wrong-think' works because it rewards the bully.[4] The social media companies encourage it because it is part of their business model. But rarely if ever do the people in the stampede try to work out why they are running in the direction they are.

THE DISAPPEARANCE OF PRIVATE LANGUAGE

There is a phrase variously attributed to the Danish computer scientist Morten Kyng or the American futurist Roy Amara, that the one thing we can say with certainty about the advent of new technologies it is that people overestimate their impact in the short term and underestimate their impact over the long term. There is little doubt now, after the initial excitement, that we all massively underestimated what the internet and social media would do to our societies.

Among the many things that was not foreseen but can now be recognized is that the internet, and social media in particular, have eradicated the space that used to exist between public and private language. Social media turns out to be a superlative way to embed new dogmas and crush contrary opinion just when you needed to listen to them most.

We have spent the first years of this century trying to understand a communications revolution so huge that it may yet make the invention of the printing press look like a footnote in history. We have had to try to learn how to live in a world where at any moment we may be speaking to one other person or to millions around the world. The notion of private and public space has eroded. What we say in one place may be posted in another, not just for the whole world but for all time. And so we are having to find a way to speak and act online as though we may be speaking and acting in front of everyone – with the knowledge that if we slip up our error will be accessible everywhere and always.

Just one casualty of this is that it has become very nearly impossible to sustain principles in public. For unless a principle works identically well for everybody all the time, there are going to be some people who benefit from it and some who are comparatively disadvantaged by it. Where those at a disadvantage may once have been somewhere in the ignorable distance, today they can always be there right in front of you. To speak in public is now to have to find a way to address or at least keep in mind every possible variety of person, with every imaginable kind of claim – including every imaginable rights claim. At any moment we might be asked why we have forgotten, undermined, offended or denied the existence of a particular person and others like them. It is understandable that the generations now growing up in these hyper-connected societies worry about what they say and expect other people to be equally worried. It is also understandable that before the critical potential of an entire world, an almost limitless amount of self-reflection – including weighing up your own 'privileges' and rights – might appear one of the very few tasks that could be successfully attempted or achieved.

Difficult and contentious issues demand a great amount of thought. And a great amount of thought often necessitates trying things out (including making inevitable errors). Yet to think aloud on the issues which are most controversial has become such a high risk that on a simple risk/reward ratio there is almost no point in anyone taking it.

If someone who is a man says that they are a woman and would like you to refer to them as a woman, then you can weigh up your options. On the one hand you could just pass the test and get on with your life. On the other hand you could get labelled a 'phobe' and have your reputation and career destroyed. How to decide?

Although a variety of thinkers have set a certain amount of the weather, the ferocious winds of the present do not come from academic philosophy or social science departments. They emanate from social media. It is there that assumptions are embedded. It is there that attempts to weigh up facts can be repackaged as moral transgressions or even acts of violence. Demands for social justice and intersectionality fit fairly well into this environment, for no matter how recherché the demand or cause, people can claim to be seeking to address them. Social media is a system of ideas that claims to be able to address everything, including every grievance. And it does so while encouraging people to focus almost limitlessly upon themselves – something which users of social media do not always need to be encouraged to do. Better still, if you feel at any point anything less than 100 per cent satisfied with your life and circumstances, here is a totalistic system to explain everything, with a whole repository full of elucidations as to what in the world has kept you back.

SILICON VALLEY IS NOT MORALLY NEUTRAL

As anybody who has spent any time there will know, the political atmosphere in Silicon Valley is several degrees to the left of a liberal arts college. Social justice activism is assumed – correctly – to be the default setting for all employees in the major companies and most of them, including Google, put applicants through tests to weed out anyone with the wrong ideological inclinations. Those who have gone through these tests recount that there are multiple questions on issues to do with diversity – sexual, racial and cultural – and that answering these questions 'correctly' is a prerequisite for getting a job.

It is possible that there is some guilty conscience at work here, for the tech companies are rarely capable of practising what they are so willing to preach. For instance, Google's workforce is only 4 per cent Hispanic and 2 per cent African-American. At 56 per cent, whites are not over-represented compared to the wider population. But Asians make up 35 per cent of Google staff and have been steadily reducing the number of white employees despite accounting for just 5 per cent of the US population.[5]

Perhaps it is the cognitive dissonance this creates which makes the Valley wish to course-correct the world since it can't course-correct itself. The major tech companies now each employ thousands of people on six-figure salaries whose job is to try to formulate and police content in a way which is familiar to any student of history. At one recent conference on Content Moderation leading figures in both companies suggested that Google currently has around 10,000 and Facebook as many as 30,000 people employed to moderate content.[6] And these figures are more likely to grow than to remain static. Of course this is not the task that Twitter, Google, Facebook and others particularly expected to perform when they were started. But once they found themselves having to perform such tasks it is unsurprising that the presumptions of Silicon Valley began to be imposed on the rest of the world online (other than in countries like China where Silicon Valley realizes that its writ does not run). But otherwise on each of the hot-button issues of the day it is not local custom or even the most fundamental values of existing societies that are being driven, but the specific views that exist in the most social-justice-obsessed square miles in the world.

On each of the maddening issues of our time – sex, sexuality, race and trans – the Valley knows what is right and is only encouraging everyone else to catch up. It is why Twitter is capable of banning women from its platform for tweeting 'Men aren't women' or 'What is the difference between a man and a transwoman'.[7] If people are 'wrong' on the trans issue in this way, then Silicon Valley can ensure that they do not have a voice on their platforms. Twitter claimed that the above tweets, for instance, constituted 'hateful conduct'. Meanwhile accounts which attack so-called 'TERFS' (trans-exclusionary radical feminists) are allowed to stay up. At the same time as the feminist campaigner Meghan Murphy was ordered by Twitter to delete the two tweets above, Tyler Coates (an editor at *Esquire* magazine) had no problem getting thousands of re-tweets for a tweet simply saying 'Fuck Terfs!'[8] In late 2018 Twitter's 'hateful conduct policy' changed so that Twitter could permanently ban people from the platform if they were found to have 'deadnamed' or 'misgendered' trans people.[9] So the moment that a person says that they are trans and announces a change of name anybody who calls them by their previous name or refers to them by their previous gender has their account suspended. Twitter has decided what does and does not constitute hateful conduct, and has decided that trans people need protecting from feminists, more than feminists need protecting from trans activists.

The tech companies have repeatedly had to come up with jargon to defend decision-making which is political always in one particular direction. The funding website Patreon has a 'Trust and Safety team' which is supposed to monitor and police the suitability or otherwise of 'creators' using Patreon as a crowd-funding resource. According to the company's CEO, Jack Conte:

> Content policy and the decision to remove a creator page has absolutely nothing to do with politics and ideology and has everything to do with a concept called 'Manifest, Observable, Behaviour'. The purpose of using 'Manifest, Observable, Behaviour' is to remove personal values and beliefs when the team is reviewing content. It's a review method that's entirely based on observable facts. What has a camera seen. What has an audio device recorded. It doesn't matter what your intentions are, your motivations, who you are, your identity, your ideology. The Trust and Safety team only looks at 'Manifest, Observable, Behaviour'.[10]

It is a 'sobering responsibility' according to Conte, because Patreon are aware that they are talking about taking away an individual's income when they ban them from using Patreon. But it is one that his company has exercised repeatedly, and in each known case against people who are believed to have the 'wrong' manifest, observable behaviour by being on the wrong side of the Valley on one of the new dogmas of the day. The tech companies can constantly be caught displaying such dogmas – often in the most bizarre ways imaginable.

MACHINE LEARNING FAIRNESS

In recent years the Valley has not just adopted the ideological presumptions of intersectionalists and social justice warriors. They have embedded them at a level so deep that this provides a whole new layer of madness in any society which imbibes them.

In order to correct bias and prejudice it is not enough simply to go through the procedures outlined in the 'Women' chapter. Unconscious bias training may be able to make us distrust our own instincts and may even show us how to rewire our pre-existing behaviour, attitudes and outlook. It may make us pay attention to our own privileges, check them against the privileges or disadvantages of others and then choose where we can legitimately place ourselves in any and all existing hierarchies. Paying attention to the intersections may make people more aware of when they need to be silent and when they may be allowed to speak. But all of these are only corrective measures. They cannot start us off from a place of greater fairness. They can only correct us once we are on our error-strewn way.

And that is why the tech companies are putting so much of their faith in 'Machine Learning Fairness' (MLF). For Machine Learning Fairness doesn't just take the whole process of judgement-making out of the hands of prejudiced, flawed, bigoted human beings. It does so by handing judgement over to the computers which it ensures cannot possibly learn from our own biases. It does this by building into the computers a set of attitudes and judgements that have probably never been held by any human being. It is a form of fairness of which no human being would be capable. Yet it is only since users started to notice that something strange was going on with some search engine results that the tech companies have felt the need to explain what MLF is. Understandably they have tried to do so in as unthreatening a manner as possible, as though there is nothing much to see here. Whereas there is. An awful lot.

Google has intermittently posted, removed and then refined a video attempting to explain MLF in as simple a way as possible. In Google's best shot to date at laying out what they are doing a friendly young female voice says 'Let's play a game', then invites viewers to close their eyes and picture a shoe. A sneaker, a smart gentleman's brogue and a high-heeled shoe all come up on the screen. Although we may not know why, the voice says that all of us are biased towards one shoe over the others. If you are trying to teach a computer how to think of a shoe, this is a problem. And the specific problem is that you may introduce the computer to your own shoe biases. So if your perfect shoe is a high heel then you will teach that computer to think of high heels when it thinks of shoes. A complex web of lines alerts the viewer to how complicated this could all get.

Machine learning is something that helps us 'get from place to place' online. It is what allows an internet search to recommend things to us, advise us on how to get somewhere and even translate things. In order to do this, human beings used to have to hand-code the solutions to problems which people were asking to have solved. But machine learning allows computers to solve problems by 'finding patterns in data':

> So it's easy to think there's no human bias in that. But just because something is based on data doesn't automatically make it neutral. Even with good intentions it's impossible to separate ourselves from our own human biases. So our human biases become part of the technology we create.

Consider shoes again. A recent experiment asked people to draw a shoe for the benefit of the computer. Since most people drew some variation of a sneaker, the computer – learning as it went along – did not even recognize a high-heeled shoe as a shoe. This problem is known as 'interaction bias'.

But 'interaction bias' is not the only type of bias about which Google are worried. There is also 'latent bias'. To illustrate this, consider what would happen if you were training a computer to know what a physicist looks like and in order to do so you showed the computer pictures of physicists from the past. The screen runs through eight white male physicists, starting with Isaac Newton. At the end they show Marie Curie. It demonstrates that in this instance the computer's algorithm will have a latent bias when searching for physicists, which in this case 'skews towards men'.

A third and final bias (for the time being) is 'selection bias'. The example here comes if you are training a computer model to recognize faces. We are asked, 'Whether you grab images from the internet or your own photo library, are you making sure to select photos that represent everyone?' The photos which Google presents are of people in headscarves and people who are not, people of all skin colours and people of very different ages. Since many of the most advanced tech products use machine learning, the voiceover reassures us, 'We've been working to prevent that technology from perpetuating negative human bias.' Among the things they have been working on is tackling 'offensive or clearly misleading information' from appearing at the top of search results and providing a feedback tool for people to flag 'hateful or inappropriate' autocomplete suggestions.

'It's a complex issue' we are reassured, and there is no 'magic bullet'. 'But it starts with all of us being aware of it so we can all be part of the conversation. Because technology should work for everyone.'[11] Indeed, it should. But it is also giving them a very predictable set of Silicon Valley's own biases.

For instance, if you search for Google's own example ('Physicists') on their image search, there is not much that can be done about the lack of female physicists. The machine appears to have got around this problem by emphasizing other types of diversity. So although the first image to come up on Google when searching for 'physicists' is of a white male physicist using chalk on a blackboard at Saarland University, the second image is a black PhD candidate in Johannesburg. By photo four we have got onto Einstein and photo five is Stephen Hawking.

Of course there is something to be said for this. Very few people would want any young woman to think that she couldn't become a physicist just because historically there has been a predominance of men in the field. In the same way that very few people would want a young man or woman of one race or another to think that a particular field was closed to them because people of their skin colour had not been dominant in a field before. However, on any number of searches what is revealed is not a 'fair' view of things, but a view which severely skews history and presents it with a bias from the present.

Consider the results of a simple search such as one for 'European Art'. There are a huge range of images that could come up on any Google Images search for those words. And it might be expected that the first images to come up would be the *Mona Lisa*, Van Gogh's *Sunflowers* or something similar. In fact the first image that comes up is by Diego Velázquez. This may not be so surprising, though the specific painting chosen might be. For the first image to come up on 'European Art' is not *Las Meninas* or the portrait of Pope Innocent X.

115

The Velázquez portrait that comes up as the first painting offered to someone searching for 'European Art' is his portrait of his assistant, Juan de Pareja, who was black.

It's a tremendous portrait, but perhaps a surprising one to put first. Skipping further along the first row of images the other five are all of the type you might be hoping to get if you have typed in this term, including the *Mona Lisa*. Then we have a *Madonna and Child* (the first so far), and it is a black Madonna. Then next there is a portrait of a black woman from something called 'people of colour in European art history'. The line she is on finishes with a group portrait of three black men. Then another line with another two portraits of black people. And then a painting by Vincent van Gogh (his first appearance so far). And so it goes, on and on. Each line presents the history of European art as consisting largely of portraits of black people. Of course this is interesting, and it is certainly 'representative' of what some people today might like to see. But it is not remotely representative of the past. The history of European art is not a fifth, two-fifths or a half about black representation. Portraits by or of black people were very unusual until recent decades when the populations of Europe began to change. And there is something not just strange but sinister in this representation of the past. You can see how in the mind of a machine taught to be 'fair' it could seem that this would constitute adequate representation of different groups. But it is simply not a truthful representation of history, Europe or art.

Nor is this a one-off with Google. A request to find images relating to 'Western people art' offers a painting of a black man (from 'Black people in Western art in Europe') as the first picture. And from there the dominant selection is paintings of Native American people.

If you tell Google that you would like to see images of 'Black men' the images that come up are all portrait photos of black men. Indeed, it takes more than a dozen rows of images before anybody who isn't black comes up in the images. By contrast a search for 'White men' first throws up an image of David Beckham – who is white – but then the second is of a black model. From there every line of five images has either one or two black men in the line-up. Many of the images of white men are of people convicted of crimes with taglines such as 'Beware of the average white man' and 'White men are bad'.

As you begin to go down this rabbit hole the search results become increasingly absurd. Or at least they are absurd if you are expecting to get what you wanted from your search, though you can very soon work out which directions the misleading goes in.

If you search on Google Images for 'Gay couple', you will get row after row of photos of happy gay couples. They are handsome, gay people. Search for 'Straight couple' by contrast and at least one to two images on each line of five images will be of a lesbian couple or a couple of gay men. Within just a couple of rows of images for 'Straight couple' there are actually more photographs of gay couples than there are of straight ones, even though 'Straight couple' is what the searcher has asked for.

The plural throws up an even odder set of results. The first photo for 'Straight couples' is a heterosexual black couple, the second is a lesbian couple with a child, the fourth a black gay couple and the fifth a lesbian couple. And that is just the first line. By the third line of 'Straight couples' the results are solely gay. 'Couples learn from gay relationships' is the tag to a photo of a mixed-race (black and white) gay male couple. Then we have 'Straight couples can learn from gay couples'. Then a gay male couple with an adopted baby. And then just a photograph of a cute gay male couple from the gay luxury lifestyle magazine *Winq*. Why, just three lines down of images requested for 'Straight couples', is everyone gay?

It gets predictably stranger. For 'Straight white couple' the second photo is a close-up of a knuckle with 'HATE' written on it. The third is of a black couple. Asking for this in the plural ('Straight white couples') throws up a range of images so bizarre that it is clear that something is up. As the second image we get a mixed-race couple. Fourth is a gay male couple (one black, one white) holding two black children. By lines two and three the photos are mainly of gay couples with tags including 'Interracial couples', 'Cute gay couples' and 'Why gay couples tend to be happier than straight couples'.

But try these searches in other languages and apply them to Google search engines in the countries where these languages predominate and you get a different set of results. So for instance, Googling for 'White men' in Turkish on Google Turkey just turns up lots of images of little white people or men whose surname happens to be 'White'. Google Image searching in French seems to turn up the same phenomenon as that in

English. But in general the further away you go from European languages, the more you get what it is that you asked to see. It is in the European languages that these strange results come up. And it is in English that the results are most pointedly, clearly, in-your-face just not what you asked for. In fact the oddity of the results for some of these searches in English is so extreme that it is clear that this isn't just a machine trying to throw in a certain amount of diversity. This is not simply MLF.

Whereas a search for 'White couple' will throw up a mixed-race and mixed-race gay couple in the first five images and then a white couple who have given birth to black babies by using black embryos, a search for 'Asian couple' returns what the searcher actually asked for. 'Asian couple' simply gives a range of photographs of Asian couples. It is not until the fourth row of images that an Asian woman is photographed with a black man. There is one other similar image, but otherwise almost entirely just Asian couples. At no point is there an effort to make it gay. There are no gay couples at all.

This is very mysterious. If MLF alone was being applied to the searches then a search for straight white couples might turn up some gay couples. But it would not end up prioritizing images of couples who are neither straight nor white. There seems to be a deliberate effort – on specific occasions – to push images of couples who are none of the things that have been asked for.

What appears to be happening is that something is being layered over a certain amount of MLF: it is MLF plus some human agency. And this human agency seems to have decided to 'stick it' to people towards whom the programmers or their company feel angry. This would explain why the searches for black couples or gay couples give you what you want whereas searches for white couples or straight couples are dominated by their opposites. It explains why people interested in searching for photos of Asian couples do not need to be aggravated or re-educated whereas the sort of people searching for 'White couples' do. Likewise, straight people of Asian descent do not need to be shown a diversity of mixed-race couples or be told that such couples are not merely normal, but more normal than anything else, or to have photos of gays thrown at them. If a person just wants to search for an Asian couple they will be shown lots of happy straight Asian couples – young and old. At no point will Google try to rewire their view of what a couple is or what the average relationship might look like.

Whereas somewhere in the coding there has been a very deliberate attempt to upset, throw, disorientate or enrage people who are searching for certain terms. It appears that Google wants to offer the service it prides itself as providing for some people, but not for anyone who might be searching for heteronormative or Causasian couples; these people would obviously already be a problem and must be refused and frustrated in their attempts to access the type of material they are after. They must be given a giant, tech-sized 'F- you'. All in the interests of fairness, obviously. It is the same thing that *The New York Times* is doing with its endless stories about gay businessmen and gay ballet dancers. But it is being done in the Valley at such a sustained pitch and speed as to make it far less deniable.

Search for 'Black family' and you will see smiling black families all the way down, without even a mixed-race family in sight. Type in 'White family' on the other hand and three out of the five images in the first line alone are either of a black or mixed-race family. Soon it is black family after black family.

It seems that in order to strip computers of the sort of bias that human beings suffer from, they have been set off to create a new type of non-bias. Yet this turns up a skewed version of history plus a new layer of bias that has been deliberately injected into the system by people intent on attacking other people who they regard as having particular biases. In the interests of weeding out human biases, humans have laced an entire system with biases.

The problem with this is not just that people will not get what they want to get from the search engines. People are used to the media landscape which we have had. If you read *The New York Times* or *The Guardian* you know the particular biases that the paper may or may not have, and you can choose to be a reader or not. Likewise if you are reading *The Daily Telegraph*, *The Economist* or the *New York Post* you know the direction that the paper, its editors, contributors and perhaps owners may hold. Even if these attitudes and outlooks are not ones that you share, the familiar reader can select out what is useful to him or her as they are reading because they know the direction from which the publication is coming.

But up until now the search engines have been assumed to be a 'neutral' space. They might be expected to throw up oddities, but not whole new editorial lines – let alone editorial lines which are outstandingly biased in particular directions. It is as though a paper of record turned out to be fairly reliable in its foreign reporting, extraordinarily biased in its domestic coverage and made it clear in the sports pages that anyone who like sports should be punished and corrected for their error.

Of course it is possible that as people become wiser about social media they will end up using search engines that are tailored to their specific needs in the same way that people tend to absorb news outlets that broadly fit their needs and existing world view. Or it is possible that the tech companies will be successful to some degree, and that the version of things that they push will become widely or fully accepted. Would it hurt very much if a generation or two from now most schoolchildren thought that their country had always looked as it does now? And that black people and white people were pretty evenly distributed in seventeenth-century Europe? Would there be much harm in straight people being more comfortable with gay people – including images of gay people showing affection? Would it hurt if young straight people thought that about 50 per cent or more of people are gay? You can see the ease with which these bias corrections can be slipped into. If there was a genuine chance of diminishing racism, sexism or anti-gay sentiment, who would not wish to seize it with every tool and engine at their disposal?

The one overwhelming problem with this attitude is that it sacrifices truth in the pursuit of a political goal. Indeed, it decides that truth is part of the problem – a hurdle that must be got over. So where diversity and representation are found to have been inadequate in the past, this can be solved most easily by changing the past. Some users of the world's most popular search engine will have noticed some of this. Some may have noticed all of it. But for most people on a day-to-day level, whether using Google, Twitter or any of the other big tech products, there may simply be a sense that something strange is happening: that they are being given things they didn't ask for, in line with a project they didn't sign up for, in pursuit of a goal they may not want.

3

Race

When Martin Luther King Jr addressed the crowds from the steps of the Lincoln Memorial in Washington, DC, on 28 August 1963, he appealed not only to foundations of justice in the founding traditions and principles of America; he also made the most eloquent defence anyone has ever made about the right way in which to treat other human beings. He spoke not only after centuries in which black Americans had been first slaves and then second-class citizens, but in an era during which racist laws were still on the statute books in American states. Racial segregation laws including anti-miscegenation laws were still in place, able to punish couples from different racial backgrounds who had fallen in love.

It was Dr King's great central moral insight that in the future about which he dreamed his children should 'one day live in a nation where they will not be judged by the color of their skin but by the content of their character'. Although many people have attempted to live up to that hope and many have succeeded, in recent years an insidious current has developed that has chosen to reject Dr King's dream, and insist that content of character is nothing compared to the colour of someone's skin. It has decided that skin colour is everything.

In recent years the world has become aware of one of the remaining sewers in which this dangerous game is played. Since the American presidential election of 2016 there has been intense media attention focused on the remnants of white supremacism and white nationalism which have lingered in the US as they have in parts of Europe. But the general attitude towards these people is agreed upon. There is little widespread support for the games they are playing with history's darkest materials. Almost all media and political response to them is unequivocally condemning of racism exhibited by people pursuing white ethno-nationalism.

Yet the greatest backsliding on Dr King's dream has not come from there. It has come from people who almost certainly believe themselves to be pursuing the same path as that which Dr King outlined on the steps of the Lincoln Memorial in 1963. In pursuit of anti-racism these people turn race from one of many important issues into something which is more important than anything else. At the very moment when the issue of race might at long last have been put to rest, they have decided once again to make it the most important issue of all.

ACADEMIA

Like other special-interest studies, the decades since the 1960s saw the growth of 'Black studies' in American universities. As with other identity group studies, the aim of such courses started out in part as a way of de-stigmatizing the group in question and educating people about a crucial aspect of their history. Like 'queer studies' and 'women's studies', 'Black studies' was intended to emphasize a specific version of history, politics, culture and literature. So black literature courses would cover black writers who might not be covered in other literature courses. Black political figures might be highlighted in a black history course and missed in a wider overview of an era or place. That such study areas grew after black authors and politicians had entered all the other syllabuses was one oddity. This meant that just as racial differences were diminishing they suddenly became siloed in special-interest sections of their own: 'black literature', like 'gay literature' and 'women's literature', now got a section of its own in bookshops and libraries.

As with feminism, after black studies had reached something like the point of victory, so a newly fervent rhetoric and set of ideas entered the discipline just as racial equality was looking better than ever. Just as a popular strand of feminism turned from celebrating women to vilifying men, so a portion of black studies started attacking people who were not black. A discipline intended to de-stigmatize began to re-stigmatize. The racial equivalent of fourth-wave feminism came in the development of the growth of 'whiteness studies' – a discipline that is now taught at all of the Ivy League universities in the US, and at universities from England to Australia. This offshoot of critical race theory now sees the University of Wisconsin in Madison providing a course called 'The Problem of Whiteness', while at Melbourne University in Australia academics have pushed for 'whiteness studies' to be made a compulsory part of training in completely unconnected fields. Anyone who has been force-fed their intersectionality will recognize the argument in an instant.

Oxford University's *Research Encyclopedia* describes whiteness studies as:

> A growing field of scholarship whose aim is to reveal the invisible structures that produce white supremacy and privilege. Critical Whiteness Studies presumes a certain condition of racism that is connected to white supremacy.

It certainly does 'presume' this, but the author of this entry – Syracuse University professor Barbara Applebaum – like others in her field also now makes a living from that presumption. In her 2011 book *Being White, Being Good: White Complicity, White Moral Responsibility and Social Justice Pedagogy* (2011) Applebaum explains how even white people who are avowedly anti-racist may still be racist. It is just that they are often racist in ways that they have not yet realized. Among much else Applebaum calls for white students to learn how to listen to other people, admit their 'complicity' in racism and from there learn how to 'build alliances'. For this does not appear to be a mere area of academic study. In Applebaum's view – as she puts it in the *Oxford Encyclopedia* – it is an unabashed campaign, one with all the familiar hallmarks not of education but of re-education. It is like an 'implicit bias test' being run by someone who has already found you guilty.

Applebaum talks of 'advancing the importance of vigilance among white people', of teaching them 'the meaning of white privilege', of teaching them 'how white privilege is connected to complicity in racism'. And of course all of this does not exist in a vacuum. It exists in a situation in which racism is 'rampant' and has 'violent effects . . . as numerous acts of racial violence in the media have shown', she adds slightly anti-climactically. Still the *Oxford Encyclopedia* is clear what the aim of this course of study should be. Whereas black studies celebrates black writers and black history, and gay studies brings out gay figures from history and pushes them to the fore, 'whiteness studies' is far from a celebratory study – if it is a study at all. The aim of 'whiteness studies', as Applebaum proudly states, is that it is 'committed to disrupting racism by problematizing whiteness'. This is to be done 'as a corrective'. So whereas every other field of race studies is performed in a spirit of celebration the aim of this one must be to 'problematize' hundreds and hundreds of millions of people.

Citing W. E. B. Du Bois's 1903 observation that the 'colour line' is the defining characteristic of American society, she writes that 'Unless white people learn to acknowledge, rather than deny, how whites are complicit in racism, and until white people develop an awareness that critically questions the frames of truth and conceptions of the "good" through which they understand their social world, Du Bois's insight will continue to ring true.'

Of course it might be said that what will continue to ring even more true is that defining an entire group of people, their attitudes, pitfalls and moral associations, based solely on their racial characteristics is itself a fairly good demonstration of racism. For 'whiteness' to be 'problematized' white people must be shown to be a problem. And not only on some academic, abstract, level but in the practical day-to-day business of judging other people. As so often this progression of an idea from academia into the rest of society has found its most prominent demonstrations in the world of celebrity, which like every area of life has gone past race-unbothered straight into race-obsessed.

'PROBLEMATIZE' ARMIE HAMMER

Consider the case of the actor Armie Hammer. His prominence grew in 2017 with the gay romance movie *Call Me By Your Name*. Unfortunately for his reputation, Hammer himself is not gay. But he is male and white, so when the movie he had starred in started winning critical acclaim and getting nominated for awards he had no defences. *Buzzfeed* chose to run a 6,000-word piece entitled 'Ten long years of trying to make Armie Hammer happen'. Race and racial politics could now be weaponized to poison absolutely everything. As *Buzzfeed*'s 'senior culture writer' put it in her sub-heading, 'How many second chances does a handsome white male star get?' According to Anne Helen Petersen, the movie star had 'the height, the side-part, and the old-fashioned good looks that would lead directors to compare him to the likes of Gary Cooper. He also comported himself the way people who have grown up with money often do: with confidence and charisma, or if you're being less generous, like a little bit of an asshole.' The writer went on to mock the various movie projects that Hammer had been cast in but which had either collapsed or not been well received. After he had been cast as a young Bruce Wayne in an adaptation of DC Comics' *Justice League: Mortal*, the project fell through: 'suddenly [his] path to instant stardom was over'. In a tone of undisguisable relish Petersen listed the 'failed Westerns', 'blockbuster flop', 'prestige pictures' which fell 'flat', one of the 'greatest summer bombs of all time' and an Oscar favourite that became a mere 'blip on the awards season radar'. Despite this she complained that Hammer's publicity team had 'never given up trying to Make Armie Hammer Happen'.

The point of this interminable essay – written by a white woman – seemed to be to attack Hammer not just for being a loser but for being white – specifically for the 'privilege' that Petersen seemed to see at every stage of Hammer's career. Her explanation for Hammer still being on the acting scene despite having dissatisfied *Buzzfeed*'s writer was that 'Hollywood would never give up on a guy that handsome, that tall, that white, with a jaw that square.' And again, 'No one gets second chances in Hollywood the way straight white men do.' And again, 'Ultimately, the problem isn't that Armie Hammer was given this many chances to happen. It's the system that ensured those chances – along with those given to so many other white men – also withholds chances, leeway, and faith from those who need and would benefit from them most.'[1]

In response Hammer himself took to Twitter: 'Your chronology is spot on but your perspective is bitter AF. Maybe I'm just a guy who loves his job and refuses to do anything but what he loves to do . . .?' And then he quit Twitter. Others came to his defence. One Twitter user stressed that Hammer had spent the past two years pushing 'black and gay filmmakers and stories. He's one of the good guys.' But a film and

TV critic from *Forbes* magazine attacked those defending Hammer: 'Ask yourself if you champion PoC actors/actresses as much. If you don't then kindly STFU [Shut The Fuck Up].' Others reminded everyone that Luca Guadagnino, the director of *Call Me By Your Name* (who is at least gay), had come under fire earlier for not casting gay actors in the gay roles in his film.[2] In an interview Guadagnino tried to explain that he had wanted to cast people who he thought had the right chemistry rather than the right sexuality. In his own defence he stressed that he was 'fascinated with gender theory' and had studied the American gender theorist Judith Butler 'for so long'.[3] This appeared to get him off the hook. But the 'problematizing' of one white actor proved to be a very typical imbroglio of the age.

Although there may be some people who think that an actor like Hammer can take it – that even if not at the top of his profession, he has done better in his field than most actors and been compensated well – there is still the problem that 'problematizing whiteness' means 'problematizing white people'. Rather than taking the heat out of anything it seems clear that when race games like this become commonplace they add to a situation in which everything becomes considered not merely in race terms but in the most aggressively racist terms possible.

Even anti-racism becomes racist. One of the primary principles of anti-racism in recent decades was the idea of 'colour-blindness' – the idea of which Martin Luther King was dreaming in 1963. The idea that skin colour should become such an unimportant aspect of a person's identity that it is possible to ignore it completely – to get beyond race – is perhaps the only solution available, as well as a beautiful idea, for how to prevent race colouring every single aspect of human interaction for all of the future. Yet even this concept has found itself under attack in recent years. For example, Eduardo Bonilla-Silva, President of the American Sociological Association, who is also a professor at Duke University, has said that the very idea of society being 'colour-blind' is in fact part of the problem. In his own war on the concept of 'colour-blindness' Bonilla-Silva has declared the concept of 'colour-blindness' itself as an act of racism. In his 2003 book *Racism without Racists* (reprinted four times to date) Bonilla-Silva even coined the term 'colour-blind racism'. Other academics have extended this argument.

By 2018 hundreds of university lecturers in Britain had to attend workshops where they were told to acknowledge their 'white privilege' and recognize how 'whiteness' can make them racist even without knowing it. At universities across the country they were invited to agree that white people enjoy unearned advantages because of the colour of their skin and that black staff, students and colleagues are routinely discriminated against. A speaker at one session in the University of Bristol, hosted by the Black, Asian and Minority Ethnic Staff Advisory Group, promised that his institution would invite university lecturers to 'examine and acknowledge the destructive role of whiteness'.[4] Such ideas started in America, with its very different history of race relations. Yet one of the fascinating things about the racism of the anti-racists is that it presumes that the situation of race relations is the same everywhere and always and that institutions which must be among the least racist in history are in fact on the verge of racist genocide.

As Greg Lukianoff and Jonathan Haidt have shown in their 2018 book *The Coddling of the American Mind*, catastrophizing has become one of the distinctive attitudes of the era. Just as women can be told that we live in a culture so rife with rape that it can fairly be described as a 'rape culture', so too people behave as though they live in a society teetering on the edge of Hitlerism. One oddity in both cases is that the most extreme claims are made in the places least likely to experience any such catastrophe. So whereas there are countries in the world which might be described as having something resembling a 'rape culture' (where rape goes unprosecuted and indeed is sanctioned by law), Western democracies could ordinarily not reasonably be accused of being among them. In the same way, whereas there are places in the world where racism is rife and there are societies which could at some point teeter back into some kind of racial nightmare, one of the places least likely to switch into ethnic cleansing in the style of 1930s Germany must surely be a liberal arts college in a liberal state within North America. Strangely, it is at precisely such places that the most extreme claims are made, and the most extreme behaviour is found.

'DECOLONIZE' EVERGREEN

Evergreen State College in Olympia, Washington, has for decades had a tradition known as 'The day of absence'. Taken from a 1965 play of the same name by Douglas Turner Ward, the idea was that once a year all students and faculty who were black (later all people of colour) would leave campus for a day, partly to meet and discuss relevant issues, and partly to highlight their contribution to the community as a whole. This tradition continued until 2017 when an announcement was made that this year's 'day of absence' would be flipped the other way around. This time around the organizers announced that they would like all white people to stay away from campus for the day.

One member of the college's faculty – the biology professor Bret Weinstein – objected to this. Having taught at the college, along with his wife, for 14 years, he had no problem with the earlier arrangements for the day. But as he pointed out in a message sent on a campus email list:

> There is a huge difference between a group or coalition deciding to voluntarily absent themselves from a shared space in order to highlight their vital and underappreciated roles (the theme of the Douglas Turner Ward play *Day of Absence*, as well as the recent Women's Day walkout), and a group encouraging another group to go away. The first is a forceful call to consciousness, which is, of course, crippling to the logic of oppression. The second is a show of force, and an act of oppression in and of itself.

Weinstein said that he at any rate would not be forced to stay away from campus for the day. 'One's right to speak – or to be – must never be based on skin color.' That's what he thought.

As a self-identifying progressive, left-winger and Bernie Sanders supporter, Bret Weinstein was not an obvious person on whom to affix accusations of racism. But they came anyway. When news of the email emerged, a group of students organised outside Weinstein's classroom. There he tried to engage them in a civilized discussion, discuss the misunderstanding and reason with them. The results were caught on a range of students' camera-phones. Weinstein tried to point out that there is a difference 'between debate and dialectic'. As he said, 'Debate means you are trying to win. Dialectic means you are using disagreement to discover what is true. I am not interested in debate. I am interested only in dialectic, which does mean I listen to you and you listen to me.' This suggestion did not go down well with the assembled students. 'We don't care what you want to speak on,' one young woman screamed at Weinstein as he held his hands on his head. 'We are not speaking on terms of white privilege.' Others barracked and shouted as the general mood got uglier. 'This is not a discussion,' one student yelled. 'You have lost that one.'

Weinstein persevered: 'I am talking about terms that serve the truth.' His comment was immediately greeted with snorts of derision and shouts of laughter. 'You said some racist shit,' one student shouted: 'Fuck what you've got to say.' As the shouting increased nobody could hear anybody speak in any case. 'Would you like to hear the answer or not,' another person said to the students. Only to get a resounding 'No'. On it went: 'Stop telling people of color they're fucking useless,' shouted one student. 'You're useless,' she shouted at him. 'Get the fuck out. Fuck you, you piece of shit.'[5]

Across campus the situation continued to get ever more out of hand. Police were called and were then insulted by the students who started chasing in crowds around the campus. One group gathered outside the office of George Bridges, the College president, with chants of 'Black power' and 'Hey hey, Ho ho, these racist teachers have got to go.' On one video a black male student with pink hair instructs the other students on how to make sure Bridges and other staff cannot leave the president's office. This same student later explained that 'free speech is not more important than the lives of, like, black, trans, femmes and students on this campus'. Eventually the students occupied the president's office, and for anyone in the outside world what ensued was surreal. For example, once there the students refused to allow Bridges to leave. At one point he says that he needs to go to the bathroom but is told he is not allowed to go. 'I have to pee,' he begs. A student directs him simply: 'Hold it.' Eventually it is agreed that he can go to the bathroom but only if two students escort him there and back.[6] For people apparently worried about fascism these students proved startlingly good at organizing and behaving like stormtroopers.

More footage taken later on mobile phones showed the president (who as a product of the social sciences had spent his career advocating social justice) pleading with students in a larger venue on campus. As Bridges tries to engage with them they shout things like 'Fuck you, George, we don't want to hear a goddam thing you have to say. You shut the fuck up.' One woman tries to explain to the president that 'These people are angry and so what matters is what they're saying not how they're saying it.' There are shouts about 'white privilege' and as the college president nods thoughtfully he gets abused by student after student. One black student accuses him of sounding like he is trying to simplify things for them. 'We're not simpletons,' she says. 'We're adults. And so I'm telling you, you're speaking to your ancestor. Alright. We been here before you. We built these cities. We've had civilization way before you ever have. Coming out your caves. OK?'

'You have the fucking nerve to fucking dehumanize like our . . .' says another. Somebody else interrupts them to raise the oppression of 'the trannies too' because there is 'targeting of trannies'. 'Fuck yeah' some people say, but there is less applause for the trannies' point than for anything to do with race. Eventually the meeting breaks down as several students stand close to Bridges and shout in his face, with one large male waving his arms threateningly. Shortly afterwards the president meekly uses his hands to try to emphasize a point. 'Put your hand down, George,' one student instructs him. 'Don't point, George.' 'That's not appropriate,' warns another. A student goes over to him to show him how he should stand, with hands straight down by his sides when he speaks to them. 'You got to put your hands down. You know you got to put your hands down,' people shout. When he does exactly as they tell him to do there is audible laughter.[7] It is not the sound of relief that the danger of a pointy finger has passed, but the audible glee of people who have managed to make a much older and more experienced man abase himself for them.

At another meeting with students there is a further demand that the president shouldn't make hand gestures. 'Put your hand down,' demands one young woman. 'That's my problem, George,' says another young female black student, getting up. 'You keep doing these little hand movements or whatever, like. And I'm going to decolonize this space. I'll just be roaming around.' Everyone applauds and cheers. 'My hands are down,' Bridges promises, as he tries to continue the dialogue with his hands behind his back while the young woman walks around, 'decolonizing' the space.[8]

As the mood of rebellion across campus grew, Evergreen students persuaded themselves and each other that they were facing an openly racist professor and an overtly racist institution. Soon a gang of students wielding baseball bats and other weapons were found prowling the campus, chasing, assaulting and intimidating people and apparently planning to do harm to Professor Weinstein and his family who were then living opposite the college. The threat of violence became so great that the campus went into lockdown for days. The police were forbidden to enforce the law and locked themselves inside the police station, though they called Weinstein and told him to stay away from the campus and move his wife and children into hiding for their own safety. The day after the scene outside his classroom, the police told Weinstein that protestors were searching from car to car in the area and asking for ID documents of the occupants because they were looking for him. His own students – and others suspected of holding divergent opinions – were themselves stalked and harassed by mobs. One student kept his phone running as he was assaulted by a mob. After the incident one young woman involved in the assault claimed that the reason they had confronted the student was because they had found him 'writing hate speech'.[9]

To say that Evergreen became race-obsessed during this period is grossly to understate things. At a subsequent meeting of the college's Board of Trustees one white student recounted, 'I've been told several times that I'm not allowed to speak because I'm white. This school seems to focus so much on race that it is actually becoming more racist in a different sort of way.'[10] But other students took a different view. One white girl (again with pink hair) who was interviewed said, 'I don't care what happens to Bret any more. He can go and be racist and be a piece of shit wherever he wants to do that. Hopefully long term we can just weed out people like Bret.'[11]

As it happened, Weinstein never taught at Evergreen again. Only one of his or his wife's academic colleagues at Evergreen ever came out publicly in support of his right to take the stand he took. After a period of some months he and his wife negotiated a settlement with the college and left their positions.

There is a whole dissertation to be written about what went on at Evergreen in those days, and about what students and others really thought was going on. All the characteristics of a modern campus outburst were there. The catastrophizing, the claims made which bore no resemblance to provable facts, the unleashing of entitlement in the guise of creating a level playing field, the turning of words into violence and violence into words.

But events at Evergreen were not very unusual on an American campus. They were only an extension of a movement that had first come to wide public notice two years earlier at Yale University. Catastrophizing about racist incidents has become so common that it is unsurprising that students at Evergreen might have thought they could take it to the next level. Again and again when they did they found that the adults had either left the room or (if they had not) were willing to take instruction.

In 2015 – two years before events at Evergreen – a lecturer at Yale called Erika Christakis had questioned in an email whether university administrators should be giving advice to adult students over what to wear to a Halloween party. This followed another round of Halloween wars on campus in which fears of insensitive, possibly culturally appropriative, costumes being worn had become the central aspect of that annual celebration. As a result of Erika's email, dozens of students surrounded her husband Nicholas (also a professor) in the courtyard of the residential Silliman College of which he was Master. For several hours they barracked him, insulted him and accused him and his wife Erika of racism. Again students had camera-phones at the ready.

Early in the exchange one black female student told Nicholas Christakis, 'This is no longer a safe space for me' because his words and his wife's email were 'an act of violence'. Throughout this Christakis was mild, placatory and trying to be helpful. He is visibly trying to engage the students and encourage them to see that there was another point of view from their own. It did not go down well. One black female student started wailing and crying just during the dialogue with him. Everything Christakis tried to tell them was in vain. As he tried to explain that he had a vision of common humanity parts of the crowd tittered and giggled as their contemporaries would later at Evergreen. Others waited to pounce. Christakis tried to explain his view that even if two people do not share exactly the same life experiences, exactly the same skin colour or gender, they can still understand each other. It didn't work. At one point he smiled and was berated by students for smiling.

'I am sick looking at you,' shouted one young Yale woman. A tall black male student strode forward to instruct Christakis: 'Look at me. Look. At. Me. Do you understand: you and I are not the same person. We're humans, great – glad we understand that. But your experiences will never connect to mine.' Here the surrounding students began to click (the non-'aggressive' alternative to clapping). 'Empathy is not necessary for you to understand that you are wrong. OK', the student explained. 'Even if you don't feel what I feel ever. Even if nobody's ever been racist to you, because they can't be racist to you that doesn't mean like you can just act like you're not being racist.' Christakis was then again instructed by the same student that the situation 'does not require you to smile'. When he politely said he agreed with a student, another person screamed at the professor that agreement wasn't needed or wanted. 'It's not a debate. It's not a debate,' that student shouted. Another young black female student laid into him: 'I want your job to be taken from you. OK. Understand that. Look me in my face first of all.' She went on to tell him to his face how 'disgusting' a man she thought he was and that she was leaving him now – leaving him with 'his sick beliefs, or whatever the hell this is'.[12]

Eventually Christakis explained to the students that other people have rights too, not just them. And at this point as other students were heard saying 'He doesn't deserve to be listened to', another young black woman – whose rant ended up going viral – started accusing the professor of making 'an unsafe space here'. He started to respond. She raised a hand and screamed 'Be quiet!' She went on. 'In your position of master your job is to create a place of comfort and home for the students that live in Silliman. You have not done that. By sending out that email that goes against your position as master. Do you understand that?' Christakis tries to say, 'No I don't agree with that.' Then at the top of her voice, in fury the student screams: 'Then why the fuck did you accept the position? Who the fuck hired you?' He tried again, 'Because I have a different vision than you.' It didn't placate her. The student kept screaming, 'You should step down. If that is what you think about being a master you should step down. It is not about creating an intellectual space. It is not. Do you understand that? It is about creating a home here. You are not doing that.' Before storming off she screams, 'You should not sleep at night. You are disgusting.'[13]

It is worth remembering that all of this was about Halloween costumes, and whether or not university authorities should infantilize students by telling them what to wear or not. After watching the display at Yale most people who had not gone to the college might wonder how these students were going to get through life if they found it this hard just to get through Halloween.

Unlike with the Weinsteins, in the case of Erika and Nicholas Christakis there was some support from some colleagues. But nevertheless at the end of the year of the imbroglio Christakis stepped down from his position as the Master of the residential college at Yale and his wife resigned her position.

The fact that students at Yale were able publicly to berate and curse at their professors, even getting them to act in exactly the way they wanted them to act – and eventually to hound them from their jobs – was significant. Perhaps this led to emboldening students at Evergreen and elsewhere. But what is striking about the footage of these events is that they are such outrageously clear power-plays. However sincere some of the students might be, there is also a visible disbelief that the adults are so easy to get on the run. That and a certain relief that university (instead of being a period of rigorous study) might be got through by a process of making extreme allegations and unreasonable demands.

In a piece after the case had died down Christakis tried to explain what a university should be and that it was the duty of a university to 'cut at the root of a set of ideas that are wholly illiberal'. These included that 'Disagreement is not oppression. Argument is not assault. Words – even provocative or repugnant ones – are not violence. The answer to speech we do not like is more speech.'[14]

That sentiment did not catch on. A year after Christakis's written intervention there was a panel discussion at Rutgers University on Identity Politics which included Professor Mark Lilla and the black entrepreneur and libertarian commentator Kmele Foster. In his remarks Foster made a passionate defence of free-speech protections, explaining to the assembled students that in the 1960s minority groups had used free-speech protections to fight for civil rights and that 'it was essential for them to be able to secure those rights in order to advocate'. Foster pointed out that Martin Luther King Jr had written his letter from a Birmingham jail because he had been imprisoned for effectively violating speech codes. At this point a portion of the Rutgers audience turned on the black speaker and started chanting 'Black Lives Matter'. One black member of the audience who started shouting at Foster got a simple question in response from Foster: 'Do facts matter?' His interlocutor shouted back, 'Don't tell me about facts. I don't need no facts.' He went on: 'colonialism is the problem . . . the fact that you have one group of people controlling over another group of people'. During this another audience member waved a sign which read 'White supremacy is the problem.'[15] Eventually the black speaker was allowed to finish.

What these and many other such reactions revealed was part of a much deeper well of thought. This is the idea – which has been swilling around in black politics and black radical thought for years – that since everything is set up by a structure of white hegemony every single thing in that structure is laced through with implicit or explicit racism, and that therefore every single aspect of it must be done away with. If any of the existing system is allowed to remain then racial justice cannot be arrived at. It is why the black community magazine *The Root* ran a piece by Michael Harriot in 2018 which criticized white people who complain about lack of 'diversity of thought'. 'You have to give it to white people,' the author said, with 'their penchant for playing the victim'. He went on to explain that 'The caucasity lies in their immediate dismissal of any object that might pose a threat to the continued primacy of whiteness.' He then built up to his central insight which was that, '"Diversity of thought" is just a euphemism for "white supremacy".'[16]

On it goes. In the same year as Kmele Foster was told 'I don't need no facts' the writer Heather Mac Donald was due to speak at Claremont

McKenna College. The speech itself was diverted to another room and given by video link because of threatening behaviour from students. But ahead of the event a letter was sent to the university authorities from 'We, few of the Black students here at Pomona College and the Claremont Colleges'. The signatories claimed that the female conservative guest would, if engaged to speak, 'not be debating on mere difference of opinion, but the right of Black people to exist'. They described Mac Donald as 'a fascist, a white supremacist, a warhawk, a transphobe, a queerphobe, a classist, and ignorant of interlocking systems of domination that produce the lethal conditions under which oppressed peoples are forced to live'. Needless to say, none of this is true. The students had clearly heard some version of what Mac Donald had written about in her book *The War on Cops: How the New Attack on Law and Order Makes Everyone Less Safe*, but they clearly had not read it. Still they went on in the same vein that giving Mac Donald a place to speak would be 'condoning violence against Black people' and would be 'anti-Black'. But it was the culmination of the students' peroration which was most revealing. There they wrote:

> Historically, white supremacy has venerated the idea of objectivity, and wielded a dichotomy of 'subjectivity vs. objectivity' as a means of silencing oppressed peoples. The idea that there is a single truth – 'the Truth' – is a construct of the Euro-West that is deeply rooted in the Enlightenment, which was a movement that also described Black and Brown people as both subhuman and impervious to pain. This construction is a myth and white supremacy, imperialism, colonization, capitalism, and the United States of America are all of its progeny. The idea that the truth is an entity for which we must search, in matters that endanger our abilities to exist in open spaces, is an attempt to silence oppressed peoples.[17]

'The Truth' is a construct of the Euro-West. It is hard to think of a phrase which can at one and the same time be so wildly misguided and so dangerous in its implications. If 'the Truth' (in scare quotes) is a white thing, then what is everyone else meant to live in and strive towards?

Truthfully the worrying thing about such cases is not that young people would regurgitate such positions. The disturbing thing is that they have been taught them.

Of course one of the oddities of campus politics – including campus activism – is that it is easy and tempting to dismiss. Anybody of a certain age can look back and say that the students were always revolting, ignoring the fact that until the 1960s university was not seen as a place to start a career in activism or indeed foment a local, let alone worldwide, revolution. But the rapidity with which the most bizarre campus claims have swept out into the real world is now clear. As people at safe liberal arts colleges in America have started to believe or pretend to believe that racism is ever-present where it is demonstrably absent, so in the wider world an obsession with race – and the ability to say racist things in pursuit of an alleged anti-racism – has become utterly normalized. And so, as Andrew Sullivan has noted, when surveying the craziness of campus and looking at the rest of society, it is impossible to avoid the conclusion that 'We all live on campus now.'[18]

CRAZY SHIT

Like so many things, some of this starts from a perfectly reasonable place, such as a desire to atone for undeniable past mistakes. But even these acts of atonement often feel less like an act of healing and more like an act of re-infecting. For instance, most people probably do not view *National Geographic* as a particularly racist magazine. But for anyone who missed its past racism, in 2018 the publication felt compelled to issue the magazine with an editorial consisting of a formal apology. In a whole issue devoted to the issue of race the magazine editorial was headlined 'For decades, our coverage was racist. To rise above our past, we must acknowledge it.' The apology from the magazine – which started publishing in 1888 – covered a wide range of things. In her editorial the editor-in-chief, Susan Goldberg, said that she had commissioned someone to review the back issues of the magazine and that 'some of what you find in our archives leaves you speechless'. The magazine found its past editions guilty of many things. They discovered that until the 1970s the magazine had 'all but ignored people of color who lived in the United States'. Elsewhere in the world it had pictured 'natives' as 'exotics, famously and frequently unclothed, happy hunters, noble savages – every type of cliché'. In short the magazine 'did little to push its readers beyond the stereotypes ingrained in white American culture'. A piece from 1916 about aboriginals in Australia was found to be especially racist.[19] As a demonstration of how far the magazine had come the editor pointed out to readers that she was not only Jewish but also a woman.

Aside from drawing attention to things nobody could have remembered, there was something else strange in all of this. Almost any student of history is familiar with the truth summed up in the opening line of L. P. Hartley's novel *The Go-Between*: 'The past is a foreign country; they do things differently there.' It requires a level of naivety to imagine that a piece from a magazine published in 1916 would meet the precise social criteria of 2018. In 1916 women in Britain and America did not have the right to vote, you could still be sentenced to hard labour in prison for being gay, and an entire generation of young men were being gassed, blown-up, shot at and shelled in the fields of Flanders and France. Things were different then.

A lesson that might have been learned was that in any event the apology from *National Geographic* did not satisfy. In *The Guardian* the historian David Olusoga declared the apology 'well meant but slow in coming'.[20] Perhaps it is not surprising that this level of scouring of the past should lead not to a helpful critical attitude but to a neurotic fear about what people should or should not be allowed to do or say in the present. If people got things so wrong in the past, how can you be sure you are acting appropriately today?

Just before *National Geographic*'s apology the film *Black Panther* was released. In the run-up there had been a lot of comment about the predominantly black cast and the opportunity for the film to be a moment of hope for black Americans and others. A lot appeared to be riding on the critical and commercial success of the film. A senior editor called Emily Lakdawalla at something called The Planetary Society asked Twitter to help her with what was clearly a sincere question. When would be the appropriate moment for a white woman such as herself to go to see *Black Panther*? Obviously the opening weekend was inappropriate, but when could she go? The 42-year-old woman wrote on Twitter: 'So I carefully did not buy Black Panther tickets for opening weekend because I did not want to be the white person sucking Black joy out of the theater. What's the appropriate date for me to buy tickets? Is next weekend ok?'[21] 'Sucking Black joy' has quite a ring to it, suggesting that white people are not just monsters and racists, but vaguely vampiric to boot.

Again it sounds deranged to think that the mere presence of somebody of one skin colour could suck the joy out of an experience for another group of people. But much lampooned for her tweet though Lakdawalla was, the ideas she had imbibed were absolutely everywhere. She had breathed them in, and now was merely breathing them out.

In most years Thanksgiving is simply the time for people in America to come together with their families and loved ones. But by 2018 even this could be racialized. Here is how *The Root* magazine chose to line up its readers for Thanksgiving 2018. 'Dear Caucasians', the publication lectured its online followers, 'If you're attending Thanksgiving with black families, remember that our Thanksgiving has nothing to do with the colonization and genocide of Native Americans. Ours is a semi-religious ritual based on food, family and sweet potato pie.'[22] A few weeks later into the holiday season and *Vice* released a video about an exciting new type of vacation. It was about a group of women who needed a break, 'from white people'. Or as *Vice* headlined the video when they sent it out, 'What it's like to take a vacation away from white people.'[23] About the vacation itself and the ideas behind it, the publication and participants had only good things to say. The participants made it plain that it was important for women of colour to find time to get away from white people, that there was nothing wrong with this and that you would have to be sinisterly racist to take any exception to the vacation in question.

Over the northern border it turned out that Canadians were not even able to die without demonstrating systemic racism. In April 2018 a terrible bus crash occurred in Saskatchewan in which 16 young people were killed and another 13 injured. The tragedy was only made greater when it was discovered that the bus involved in the collision had been filled with the Humboldt Broncos. In a hockey nation the death of so many people in their late teens was a source of unprecedented national mourning. Canadians left their hockey sticks outside their front doors as a mark of respect and a campaign to raise funds in memory of the young men yielded a record-breaking amount of money. But even this tragedy was not immune from the new racialization of absolutely everything.

In the immediate aftermath of the tragedy the Quebec City writer and self-described 'activist' Nora Loreto took to social media to complain about the attention paid to the dead hockey team by proclaiming, 'The maleness, the youthfulness and the whiteness of the victims are . . . playing a significant role.'[24]

By 2018 it seemed as though whether you looked forward or backward, in tragedy or in comedy, always the same lens was looked through: the lens of race. It was the year in which Disney released a remake of their classic film *Dumbo* – the story of a young elephant. Reviewing not even the film but the trailer of the live-action remake, *Vice* chose to refer to the original 1940 Disney cartoon of *Dumbo* as 'easily one of the scariest things Disney has ever made' because of various characters who were alcoholic, 'creepy' and 'also generally pretty racist'. Yet 'In spite of all of that, the movie has still managed to become a beloved cartoon, cherished and periodically feared by children for generations'. Fortunately all of this had now been fixed in the updated version. Having watched a trailer of this children's cartoon, *Vice* felt licensed to report to its adult readership that Disney's remake of *Dumbo* appeared to be 'cute and heartwarming and seemingly neither racist nor terrifying'.[25] What made them think that it would be? In what sort of world does a remake of a children's cartoon about a flying elephant have to be given such a health warning? The answer is – a world in which everything had become completely obsessed not by racial blindness but by racial obsession. And if campus race theorists are the obscure genesis of some of these ideas, nowhere are they more visibly played out than in the most public mediums of all, where hundreds of millions of people imbibe the idea that this newly revived obsession with race is absolutely normal.

CASTING ASPERSIONS

In February 2018 Netflix released its adaptation of Richard K. Morgan's novel *Altered Carbon*. To anyone but the most dedicated science fiction aficionado it was almost wholly indecipherable, albeit stunningly and expensively shot. Without getting too enmeshed in the weeds, the central plot occurs in the year 2384 and revolves around a character called Takeshi who has been killed and is then reborn in another body (or 'sleeve') – which is the sort of thing you can always do in the future.

The moment that Netflix announced the casting – even before the series was released – the central decision was condemned. For the role of the reborn Takeshi has been given to the Swedish-born actor Joel Kinnaman who had become famous playing a political opponent of Kevin Spacey's Frank Underwood in the Netflix adaptation of *House of Cards*. On the day of *Altered Carbon*'s release *Time* magazine was among those publications that decided to run straight at the target. As its headline put it, 'Altered Carbon takes place in the future. But it's far from progressive.'

In fact, as the piece went on to argue, the series felt 'downright retrograde' because of its treatment of 'race, gender and class'. The central problem was the casting of the Swedish Kinnaman. According to *Time* (which seemed to have forgotten that the whole thing was science fiction), it was wrong to cast a 'white guy' as the person in the reborn body of a character who in a previous life had been 'an Asian man'. While conceding that the adaptation does accurately follow the scenario as written in the original book, *Time*'s critic found (deploying the favoured lexicon of social justice) that nevertheless 'onscreen it's especially problematic'. By her lights:

> The creators would have done well to instead cast an Asian actor as the reborn Takeshi, avoiding the same controversy that plagued last year's *Ghost in the Shell*. In that adaptation, Scarlett Johansson played an Asian woman's consciousness inside a white android.

Anything to avoid the great Scarlett Johansson android consciousness wars of 2017. Clearly if you are going to set a sci-fi drama in 2384 you should expect people in that year to hold the same values as *Time* magazine's movie critic holds in 2018.[26]

Entertainment of the Netflix variety is one of the most popular and accessible mediums that anyone has yet been presented with. It provides an opportunity for expression and the free exchange of ideas that previous generations could only have dreamed of. And yet even this tool has become a playground of the now omnipresent calls for this newly revived obsession with race. Despite the fact that these attitudes towards race seemed race-obsessed in a way that had not occurred for decades.

YESTERDAY IT WASN'T LIKE THIS

Part of the madness of all this is that the desirable destination had been so nearly reached. In recent decades it had already become completely normal and acceptable for people of any race to play leading roles in Western theatre or film. This row was meant to be over. It is almost two decades since the actor Adrian Lester (who happens to be black) was cast as Henry V by the Royal Shakespeare Company. Theatre audiences flocked to the production as they would to any good production and great performance. Since then, black actors have become so visible on stage, including in period pieces, that their inclusion is rarely even noted. It has been the same for decades in the world of music. Back in the 1970s the great American soprano Kathleen Battle was appearing in works by Strauss, Verdi and Haydn. None of the roles had been written for a black singer, but there was no serious question of her suitability for the role and no negative comment about the casting.

Likewise with Jessye Norman, one of the great sopranos of recent decades. Richard Wagner did not specify that Isolde should be black. But when Jessye Norman sang the music from *Tristan and Isolde* under the baton of Herbert von Karajan with the Vienna Philharmonic, nobody thought of ignoring the music and denouncing the casting for being racially inappropriate. We had all got used to this.

But that was yesterday. Today, it has become wholly acceptable to suggest that the racial characteristics of an actor or performer are the most important characteristic when they are cast. More important, indeed, than their ability at performing the role. Race wars now break out on a regular basis in entertainment as everywhere else.

In 2018, only weeks after *Altered Carbon* had been put through the racial purity test, the BBC announced its schedules for that summer's Promenade Concerts. It was announced that one highlight would be the Broadway star Sierra Boggess appearing in a concert performance of *West Side Story*. But as soon as the cast was announced there was denunciation on social media. Boggess had been cast to play the role of Maria (a fictional character who is Puerto Rican) while herself being reported to be Caucasian. The fact that the whole thing was fiction – and a fiction whose lyrics and music were written by two Jews – was not a matter for consideration. One Twitter user wrote: 'You are a Caucasian woman and this character is Puerto Rican. It's not like you're hurting for job opportunities. Stop taking roles from actors of colour.' Another posted: 'I love Sierra Boggess but Maria is seriously one of the only leading roles for Latina women in musical theatre so can we please cast one of the many talented Latina women out there who would KILL to play this role.'

By casting Boggess in the role of Maria the BBC Proms were alleged to be engaging in 'whitewashing'. Unfortunately Boggess took these criticisms to heart and so announced on Facebook:

After much reflection, I've realised that if I were to do this concert, it would once again deny Latinas the opportunity to sing this score, as well as deny the IMPORTANCE of seeing themselves represented onstage.

She said this would be a 'huge mistake':

Since the announcement of this concert, I have had many conversations about why this is a crucial time, now more than ever, to not perpetuate the miscasting of this show.

I apologise for not coming to this realisation sooner and as an artist, I must ask myself how I can best serve the world, and in this case my choice is clearer than ever: to step aside and allow an opportunity to correct a wrong that has been done for years with this show in particular.

I have therefore withdrawn myself from this concert and I look forward to continuing to be a voice for change in our community and our world![27]

The role was subsequently recast and the role eventually performed by Mikaela Bennett, who is from Ottawa, Canada, but was deemed to have a more appropriate ethnic profile.

So with only a handful of tweets a casting decision that had been made could be unmade. A talented star had been bullied into submission. And in the name of 'progress' and 'diversity' the most regressive and undiverse thing imaginable clocked up another victory.

In an era that is witnessing the politicization and polarization of absolutely everything, the realm of fiction and art – one of the great barrier breakers we have – is also becoming a battleground for racial exclusivity and racial exclusion.

Perhaps those who are attempting to push such agendas will at some point wake up to the fact that they are heading towards an almighty logical crash. For the same logic that saw Boggess off *West Side Story* can just as easily be used to insist that all future Prince Hals or Isoldes must be white. Casting can either be colour-blind or colour-obsessed, but it probably cannot be both.

The same boring fixation now affects every other area of life. There is now no occupation or pastime too serene to be taken over at any moment by a race controversy. And each time that it happens the controversy itself metastasizes, turning one incident or claim into the progenitor of a whole slew of follow-on incidents and claims which it ignites and then loses control of.

Take the controversy surrounding the tennis champion Serena Williams in September 2018. During the US Open final she was issued with a code violation and then a penalty point after she broke her racket. Williams lost her temper spectacularly with the umpire, in a way that happens but is still frowned upon in the genteel-ish sport of tennis. But Williams really went for the umpire – calling him, among other things, a 'thief'. Williams was fined $17,000, which given that the prize for winning the Open is just under four million dollars and the prize for the runner-up almost two million, is small change for Williams. But the issue could not stop there. Because Williams is a woman the Women's Tennis Association decried the referee as 'sexist'. Because she is black the matter headed straight into a full-on race dispute.

Among others the BBC alleged that criticism of Williams for her on-court outburst played into a long racial stereotype of the 'angry black woman'.[28] Nobody explained how a black woman could be angry without playing into this stereotype. *The Guardian* decided to put an even more racial spin on things. According to its contributor Carys Afoko, the criticism of Serena Williams had a larger lesson – in that it had been a demonstration of 'how hard it is to be a black woman at work'. In the opinion of Afoko, 'Black women aren't allowed a bad day at the office.

Or to be precise, if we have a bad day we can't usually risk expressing anger or sadness about it. So many of us develop a work persona that allows us to get ahead in white workplaces.' This may point just to the specific challenges of being a contributor at *The Guardian*. In any case, Afoko continued with an example of what she meant, and what she herself had had to put up with. 'A couple of years ago I disagreed with a male colleague's idea and he pulled me aside to tell me I was being aggressive. When I attempted to explain that the word aggressive is racially loaded he burst into tears.' Who knows why her colleague burst into tears? Perhaps it was yet another demonstration of racism on his part. Perhaps it was fear that an accusation of racism was about to end his career. Or perhaps he was reduced to a weeping wreck because he was beginning to feel that there was absolutely nothing he could say that his colleague would not end up interpreting as an act of racism.

Afoko at any rate drew a different lesson from her reduction of her male colleague to tears. 'It reinforced a lesson I learned throughout my 20s: most of the time it's not worth trying to explain racism or sexism at work. Just get your head down and get the job done as best you can.' Then, in order to assist any *Guardian* readers who were not yet up to speed, she added the helpful pointer, 'If you are not a black woman and are confused right now here is a two-minute video about intersectionality.'[29] This helpful video was in fact entitled 'Kids explain intersectionality' and true to the description it showed under-10s explaining how straightforward intersectionality is. With some minimal intervention from adults it explained in easy, slightly sing-song language, how intersectionality was simply 'a concept that allows us to realise that people live, like, multidimensional lives'. Despite having intersectionality explained to him by a child of First Nations origin, a white boy of five or six years old is shown still expressing some confusion about what intersectionality actually is. Eventually he is shown 'getting it' and explaining to the nice black woman who started off the short film that 'people aren't just the one picture. The whole picture basically has to need your entire personality going together to make you.' For getting it right in this fashion and overcoming his initial confusion he is congratulated, 'Thank you – that's really cool', he is told. And then he is offered a high-five by way of reward.[30]

145

CULTURAL APPROPRIATION

One obvious way to try to stop this digging down and down on race and racial characteristics would be to keep trying to blur the edges, for example by making those aspects of race which are able to be communicated and shared into an experience open to all. Aspects of a person's or a people's culture which others admire may for instance be shared so that a greater understanding can be found across any divides that do occur. That might be an ambition. But sadly a theory got there before that ambition could be fully realized. This one too started on campus and then spilt out into the real world. This concept was called 'cultural appropriation'.

It originated in post-colonial studies with the idea that colonial powers had not just imposed their own culture on other countries but had also taken back aspects of those foreign cultures to their own countries. A benign reading of this could view it as imitation, and the sincerest form of flattery. But whatever else they are known for, professors of post-colonial studies have never been known for reading things in a benign way. Instead, the least benign reading possible came into play, which was that this cultural theft was the last insult of colonialism, and that having raped a country's natural resources and subjected its people to foreign rule the colonial powers could not even leave the subject peoples with their own culture unmolested or unseized.

Perhaps it is inevitable that having originated on campuses, the greatest opposition to 'cultural appropriation' has burst out in university cities. The early wave of accusations of cultural appropriation came in reaction to inappropriate fancy-dress costumes such as the ones the Yale students had become so terrified of at Halloween 2015. The explicit fear was that there would be incidents involving people who are not themselves Native Americans being found to be wearing, for instance, a Native American headdress. This – to adopt the vernacular now used to oppose such practices – is not OK.

For some time now, Portland, Oregon, has begun to distinguish itself as the test laboratory of almost every maddening idea. In recent years the city has become especially bothered about expressions of cultural appropriation. This has included turning what one local writer described as a 'foodie paradise' into something closer to a foodie warzone.[31] In 2016 a local woman opened a bistro called Saffron Colonial. Furious mobs gathered outside the restaurant, accusing her of racism and of glorifying colonialism. Review websites like Yelp were filled with people writing negative comments about the establishment until the owner eventually gave in and changed her restaurant's name. She had been accused of setting up an establishment dedicated to bringing back empire through the back-door method of opening a restaurant in Portland. But even more egregious cases could be found. The worst, to local eyes, was that of people who had no right to be cooking the food they were cooking because their DNA was wrong.

In 2017 there was the case of a couple who opened a food truck selling burritos. According to the new local rules, this couple were guilty of cultural appropriation – specifically of 'stealing' Mexican culture by selling burritos while not being Mexican. The owners of the food truck ended up receiving death threats and had to close all social media accounts and eventually their business. To say that victories like this embolden people is to understate matters. In the aftermath of the burrito van victory a list was compiled and circulated by local Oregon activists titled 'Alternatives to white-owned appropriative restaurants in Portland'. Suggestions of restaurants owned by 'people of colour' were given instead.[32]

Like events at the universities, events in Portland might be expected to stay in Portland. But again, as with the universities, the feeling begins to grow in this interconnected age that we are all at risk of living in Portland now. In the summer of 2018, while most people were on their holidays, an outbreak of the cultural appropriation food wars broke out in Britain when a black MP called Dawn Butler denounced one of Britain's most famous television chefs. Jamie Oliver had recently released a new dish called 'punchy jerk rice'. There was swift criticism that the recipe Oliver had released was missing a number of ingredients which were traditionally used in the marinade for jerk chicken. And from criticism of missing aspects of a recipe the ruckus immediately moved on to race. Butler tweeted her disgust at the chef. She wondered whether Oliver actually knew 'what Jamaican jerk actually is? It's not just a word you put before stuff to sell products.' She went on, 'Your jerk Rice is not ok. This appropriation from Jamaica needs to stop.'[33] Fortunately

Jamie Oliver's chain of Italian restaurants – Jamie's Italian – which had branches in dozens of British cities, appeared to have gone under Dawn Butler's radar.

But one of the things about stampedes like this is that while high on moral fury the allegations can quite as easily be levelled at people who are wholly unknown as at people who are famous. In any ordinary time the end-of-year prom at a school in Utah would not cause as much consternation as a spat between an MP and a celebrity chef. But in 2018 an 18-year-old girl called Keziah shared photos online of the dress she was wearing to her prom. The red dress was in a distinctive Chinese style and the wearer was clearly hoping to get some 'likes' for looking nice. Rather than getting the praise she was looking for, Keziah instead got an immediate worldwide backlash. 'Was the theme of the prom casual racism?' asked one Twitter user. Other users poured in to accuse the non-Chinese girl of cultural appropriation for wearing a Chinese-inspired dress.[34]

In a sensible world all of this should be a tremendous gift for artists, not least satirists. But even casting a critical eye over the phenomenon seems to create another rain of accusations and another escalation in claims and sensitivity. In September 2016 the novelist Lionel Shriver gave an address at the Brisbane Writers Festival about 'fiction and identity politics'. Shriver (the author, among other novels, of *We Need To Talk About Kevin*) used the opportunity to address the issue of 'cultural appropriation'. In the weeks before the lecture the term had come up repeatedly in a variety of contexts. It had arisen over whether or not non-Mexicans should have the right to wear sombrero hats and elsewhere over whether people who were not from Thailand should be allowed to cook or eat Thai food.

Since using imagination and getting into the heads of other people might be said to be a novelist's job, Shriver felt that these movements were getting uncomfortably close to her territory. Her Brisbane address was a full-throated defence of her art, and the legitimacy of writers writing about whatever they wanted to write about. Shriver explained that thinking of a character for one of her novels, an aspect of a character such as being Armenian may be a start of a character. But 'merely being Armenian is not to have a character as I understand the word'. She went on: 'Being Asian is not an identity. Being gay is not an identity. Being deaf, blind, or wheelchair-bound is not an identity, nor is being economically deprived.'

The response was predictable. Over at the *New Republic* Lovia Gyarkye said that 'Lionel Shriver shouldn't write about minorities. The lack of nuance in her 8 September speech at the Brisbane Writers Festival proves that she mostly doesn't get it.' And Gyarkye had a question for Shriver. 'My question for Shriver is: If these labels are not identities, if being gay or disabled is not a part of who you are, then why are hundreds of people abused, shamed, and killed everyday because of them? . . . What Shriver seems to miss about cultural appropriation is its inextricable link to power.'[35] Thus catastrophism and Foucault coalesced in a single assertion.

However, Gyarkye's aggravation was superseded by Yassmin Abdel-Magied, who had actually been in the audience at Brisbane. Her first-hand account was picked up and republished in *The Guardian*. According to Abdel-Magied:

> We were 20 minutes into the speech when I turned to my mother, sitting next to me in the front row. 'Mama, I can't sit here,' I said, the corners of my mouth dragging downwards. 'I cannot legitimise this . . .'

There followed a fascinating, drawn-out account of what it feels like to stand up and leave a room.

It turned out that Shriver's speech went along different lines from Abdel-Magied's own thinking. So much so that it was barely a speech. Rather, it was 'a poisoned package wrapped up in arrogance and delivered with condescension'. Abdel-Magied tried to explain the perils of people writing in the voice of someone who they are not. By way of example she expressed her own limits:

> I can't speak for the LGBTQI community, those who are neuro-different or people with disabilities, but that's also the point. I don't speak for them, and should allow for their voices and experiences to be heard and legitimised.

After writing about colonialism for a bit Abdel-Magied concluded that:

> The kind of disrespect for others infused in Lionel Shriver's keynote is the same force that sees people vote for Pauline Hanson. It's the reason our First Peoples are still fighting for recognition, and it's the reason we continue to stomach offshore immigration prisons. It's the kind of attitude that lays the foundation for prejudice, for hate, for genocide.[36]

To its credit *The Guardian* subsequently published the full text of Shriver's speech so that its readers could discern for themselves whether her Brisbane address had been a witty assault on a fad or a foundation stone of fascism.

Shriver survived the backlash in part because she has a reputation as a no-hostages truth-teller. But still there was an obvious incentive for anyone wishing to claim to be one of her victims. Had Abdel-Magied (who subsequently left Australia under a cloud of her own) chosen to write an impersonal and thoughtful critique of Shriver's position, she would have been unlikely to draw attention to herself and have her work immediately taken up and republished in a major newspaper. Had she not felt the corners of her mouth turning down and explained to her mother that their mere presence in the hall 'legitimized' the hate, then her opinion would have been no more valid (or public) than anyone else's. This is an important cog in the crowd-maddening mechanism: the person who professes themselves most aggrieved gets the most attention. Anyone who is unbothered is ignored. In an age of shouting for attention on social media the mechanism rewards outrage over sanguinity. As for Shriver, in the years since her Brisbane speech she has been one of the few authors to publicly object to publishing houses introducing sexual and racial quota systems to decide on anything rather than literary merit, when it comes to which books and which authors they should publish.

THE CENTRAL PROBLEM

The central problem underneath all of this is a colossal confusion, a confusion caused not by a misunderstanding but by the fact that as societies we are trying to run several programmes at once. On the one hand there is the programme which declares the world to be a place where a well-lived life consists of appreciating something from every culture and indeed making it easier to access those cultures. On the other hand we are running another programme at the same time which declares that cultural boundaries may only be crossed under certain conditions. Not only has this second programme not been finished, but the job of finishing writing it appears to be open to absolutely anybody who wants to take it over. There is also a programme which recognizes that race and culture are not the same thing. And yet another – running concurrently – that says they are so much the same thing that encroaching on somebody else's culture is an act of racist aggression or 'appropriation'.

Underneath this is a matter of such explosive danger that it is perhaps no wonder it is kept deeply submerged. It is a question we do not ask because we have already decided what the answers cannot be. That question is whether race is a hardware or a software issue. In the past of which *National Geographic* and other enterprises feel some rightful shame, race was thought to be the most hardware issue of all. What race someone came from defined them. Often to the exclusion and detriment of all else. As the twentieth century progressed a more enlightened realization grew – which was that race may be important but it was not unbridgeable. Indeed, people could be as much a part of another culture or people as they liked, so long as they wanted to be and immersed themselves in it in a spirit of gratitude and love. There were caveats in the later twentieth century, such as a recognition that this path could only allow traffic to move in one direction. An Indian may become distinctly British but a white British man could not become an Indian. The boundaries of what is or is not possible here shift subtly but continuously. They shifted in recent decades around attitudes towards inter-racial adoptions, and whether or not it was beneficial or appropriate for children of one racial background to be brought up by parents of a different race. But the problem for us is that this whole territory is on the move again. And the early signals this time are not just that they could shift anywhere but that they look like they are shifting in some of the worst imaginable directions.

IS BLACK POLITICAL? THE SPEECH NOT THE SPEAKER

In 2016 when Peter Thiel endorsed Donald Trump at the Republican National Convention in Cleveland he immediately became a non-gay in the eyes of the most prominent gay magazine in America. To have gone to the right – and to the Donald Trump right at that – was such an egregious fault that *Advocate* excommunicated Thiel from the church of gay. Two years later precisely the same pattern played out among black Americans.

After almost a year of silence on Twitter, Kanye West returned to the medium in the spring of 2018. As is one of his gifts, he immediately began making news. In April he praised the black conservative commentator and activist Candace Owens. This was after a campus talk Owens had given at UCLA in which she castigated some people from the 'Black Lives Matter' movement who were protesting against her and compared them with black students sitting in the front rows listening to her talk. In a clip that went viral Owens said:

> What is happening right now in the black community . . . There is an ideological civil war happening. Black people that are focused on their past and shouting about slavery. And black people focused on their futures. What you're seeing is victim mentality versus victor mentality.

She went on to accuse the protestors of being hooked on 'oppression'.

After watching this video Kanye West tweeted out 'I love the way Candace Owens thinks'. And for a moment it was as though there had been a glitch in the matrix. Or at least a glitch in the Twitter universe. There had been plenty of black conservatives over the years, including a Supreme Court Justice and some of America's most prominent thinkers. But never before had a celebrity of the star wattage of Kanye West even implied that there was any party other than the Democratic Party for black Americans to give their political allegiance to. And here was one half of what is – for better and/or worse – one of the most famous couples on the planet willing to walk into this minefield.

It might be pointed out that Kanye West had several things going for him that allowed him to begin making this journey. The first was what used to be called F-you cash. Even if his dalliances into politics made him toxic among large segments of his audience base – both black and white – then he could always sit back on his and his wife's cash. The other thing that made Kanye West able to do this was a widespread sense, which he doesn't mind playing with: that he is slightly unhinged.

The praise of Candace Owens soon developed into open praise of Donald Trump. And by October 2018 West was in the Oval Office at a summit meeting and lunch, which was strange even by relative standards. This included West doing most of the talking, while the President sat on the opposite side of the desk, nodding carefully. West used the opportunity to talk about the black community, prison reform, how wearing a red 'MAGA' hat made him feel 'like Superman' and also about the presence of 'alternate universes'. He complained that 'People expect that if you're black you have to be Democrat.' He went on to say that he loved Trump.

From the moment that Kanye West began to go down this route a response could be predicted at some point. It was Ta-Nehisi Coates who aimed the shot of greatest length and with the greatest impact. In an essay in *The Atlantic* he wrote about his own upbringing and his fondness for Michael Jackson. He wrote about Jackson's unarguably bizarre transformation from a young black boy with an afro to the almost translucent waxwork that he became in later life. And then Coates decided to compare Kanye with Michael Jackson.

'What Kanye West seeks is what Michael Jackson sought,' he wrote. 'West calls his struggle the right to be a "free thinker", and he is, indeed, championing a kind of freedom – a white freedom, freedom without consequence, freedom without criticism, freedom to be proud and ignorant.' As the headline put it, 'I'm not black – I'm Kanye: Kanye West wants freedom – white freedom.'[37] Kanye had tripped over the same wire as Thiel. At some point minority political grievances transformed into minority political activism and from there moved into being just politics. Claiming the existence of voting blocs along minority group lines benefits certain politicians looking for voter blocs and it can benefit professional middle men who present themselves as speaking for an entire community in order to gain their own forms of preferment. But this is an exceptionally dangerous juncture, and one that each rights issue in turn has arrived at.

It suggests that you are only a member of a recognized minority group so long as you accept the specific grievances, political grievances and resulting electoral platforms that other people have worked out for you. Step outside of these lines and you are not a person with the same characteristics you had before but who happens to think differently from some prescribed norm. You have the characteristics taken away from you. So Thiel is no longer gay once he endorses Trump. And Kanye West is no longer black when he does the same thing. This suggests that 'black' isn't a skin colour, or a race – or at least not those things alone. It suggests that 'black' – like gay – is in fact a political ideology. This presumption goes so deep – and is so rarely mentioned – that it is generally simply assumed.

The London School of Economics is, as it boasts of itself, one of the world's leading universities of the social sciences: 'With an international intake and a global reach, LSE has always put engagement with the wider world at the heart of its mission.' Over at its LSE *Review of Books* page in May 2012 a review appeared of a new book by Thomas Sowell. *Intellectuals and Society* had come out two years earlier, but in the world of academia intellectual drive-by shootings often happen at a more leisurely pace than in the rest of society.

The reviewer, Aidan Byrne, was the 'Senior Lecturer in English and Media/Cultural Studies' at Wolverhampton University. In this capacity – his byline informed us – 'he specialises in masculinity in interwar Welsh and political fiction, and teaches on a wide range of modules'. A perfect authority for the LSE *Review of Books* to put in judgement over Sowell.

For his part, Byrne was 'unimpressed' by the 'highly partisan' nature of the book. And so, two years after Sowell's book had been published, Byrne took aim and attempted to fire. From his opening line he warned that '*Intellectuals and Society* consists of a series of outdated and sometimes dishonest shots at Sowell's political enemies.' Among other charges included in Byrne's review was a claim that one line in Sowell's book echoed the concerns of the Tea Party and constituted 'a thinly-disguised attack on racial integration'.

An even odder allegation against Sowell came when Byrne warned readers that Sowell's references to racial issues constituted little more than 'disordered and disturbing "dog-whistles"'. In a similar fashion, Sowell's arguments about the legacies of the past were also 'a coded intervention'. Warming to his theme, Byrne explained that 'To him [Sowell], slavery's cultural legacy means that it shouldn't be considered a moral problem, nor should amelioration be attempted.' To this charge Byrne then added the devastating rider which turned out to be an act of unbelievable self-harm.[38]

To their credit, as it now stands the LSE site has an 'amendment' at the bottom of the piece online. It is one of the great corrections. It simply notes the deletion of a line from the original piece. 'The original post contained the line "easy for a rich white man to say"', admitted the LSE site. 'This has been removed and we apologise for this error.'[39] As well they might. For of course whatever the state of his income, Thomas Sowell is not a white man. He is a black man. A very famous black man – who LSE's reviewer only thought to be white because of the nature of his politics.

It is a suggestion that has crept into an otherwise liberal debate with barely a murmur of dissent. And it has arrived from quite a range of directions. Consider for instance the reaction to the strange, and vaguely pitiful, case of Rachel Dolezal. This was the woman who became almost world famous in 2015 when, as regional head of the NAACP, she was suddenly 'outed' as white. During a television interview, Dolezal was memorably asked if she herself was black. She pretended not to understand the question. When confronted with the evidence of her birth parents the interview crashed into a buffer. For Dolezal's parents were not merely Caucasians, but Caucasians of German-Czech origin – which is very far away from the black American identity that Dolezal herself had adopted. Eventually, while admitting that her parents were indeed her parents, she insisted that – nevertheless – she was black. Her identification with the black community in America seemed to have come about through her closeness to her adopted black siblings.

Nevertheless, as her adoptive brother said, 'She grew up a white, privileged person in Montana.' She had managed to pass herself off as black by little more than the careful application of bronzer and a somewhat stereotypical frizzing up of her hair. This – and the fact that most people were clearly too terrified to say, 'But aren't you white?' – meant that Dolezal was able not only to 'pass' as black but head up the local chapter of an organization set up for black people.

The Dolezal case threw up an almost endless series of questions, and both it and the responses to it in some ways presented an opportunity to dissect a whole array of aspects of today's culture. Not least among these moments was the divide that arose among prominent black people, spokespeople and activists.

On *The View* on ABC-TV, Whoopi Goldberg defended Dolezal. 'If she wants to be black, she can be black', was Goldberg's view.[40] It seemed that 'blacking up' was not a problem on this occasion. More interesting was the reaction of Michael Eric Dyson, who stood up for Dolezal in a remarkable way. On MSNBC he declared of Dolezal, 'She's taking on the ideas, the identities, the struggles. She's identified with them. I bet a lot more black people would support Rachel Dolezal than would support, say, Clarence Thomas.'[41] All of which suggested that 'black' was not to do with skin colour, or race. But only politics. So much so that a Caucasian wearing bronzer but holding the 'right' opinions was more black than a black Supreme Court Justice if that black Supreme Court Justice happens to be a conservative.

THE SPEAKER, NOT THE SPEECH

Here then is another cause of our current crowd madness. On occasion, as in the case of Rachel Dolezal, Candace Owens and Thomas Sowell, it appears as though a consistent attitude can be located. The speaker and the speaker's own innate characteristics do not matter. What matters is the speech they utter and the ideas and sentiments that they give voice to. Then with no forewarning and no obvious means of prediction, a precisely contrary scale of values kicks in. Suddenly the content of a speech becomes of absolutely no interest or becomes of tertiary interest at the very best. On these occasions, running in tandem with those times when the speech not the speaker matters, suddenly only the speaker matters, and the speech can go hang.

This development is almost certainly connected to one of the great gifts that the social media age has brought us, which is the opportunity to publish uncharitable and disingenuous interpretations of what other people have said. When such attention is focused on someone famous the media can then seize the opportunity to give far greater attention to a handful of such interpretations than any number of honest or forgiving ones. The effects can be read in any day's news. A headline might describe someone famous being 'lambasted' for something they have said only for it to turn out – when reading down the story – that the 'lambasting' came from a couple of members of the public who the journalist has spotted on Twitter. It is the reason why politicians look so terrified when anyone tries to lead them on to any rocky terrain. Not just because the price of thinking out loud is so high, or a fear that the rules of the game may have changed since they last looked, but because even one negative response (from anybody in the world) can be turned into a storm. This fear now engulfs almost all public figures, for even when they think that they are treading deftly – or heroically – they can come off air and discover that the sound ringing in their ears was not applause but career explosion.

In January 2015 the actor Benedict Cumberbatch was interviewed on the *Tavis Smiley Show* on PBS. He used a part of his time to protest that friends of his in the UK who were actors from ethnic minority backgrounds seemed to find it easier to get work in the US than they did in the UK. It was clear from the point he made in these and all his other remarks that he was on the side of black actors rather than taking, say, the position of the Ku Klux Klan in responding to questions. Nobody had any serious reason to believe that Cumberbatch was a secret racist who was unwittingly revealing himself to Tavis Smiley. Nevertheless the actor slipped up not on an issue of intent or motive, but – as so often when there is no other evidence available – on a crime of language. In the course of his remarks Cumberbatch referred to 'coloured actors'. This is a term which would have been commonly used with no negative connotations in his home country. Until a very short time before, it was also a common enough term in the US. But shortly before Cumberbatch's interview the protocol had slightly shifted there. The new correct way to refer to 'coloured people' in January 2015 was as 'people of colour'. Linguistically this may be said to be a distinction without a meaningful difference.

Nevertheless the outcry was almost as great as if he had used the 'N' word. Indeed, the actor was forced into making an immediate and grovelling public apology. In a swiftly issued public statement after the show he announced 'I'm devastated to have caused offence by using this

157

outmoded terminology. I offer my sincere apologies. I make no excuse for my being an idiot and know the damage is done.'[42] Nevertheless headlines in the media reported that the actor was 'under fire' (*The Telegraph*) and the subject of a 'race row' (*The Independent*). Throughout this episode nobody seriously claimed that Cumberbatch was a racist. And there was no serious way in which anybody could have interpreted these or any other remarks as racist. But his name could now be linked to a 'race row'. If people had listened to the point Cumberbatch had been trying to make perhaps a small amount of good could have come from it, and more casting opportunities in the UK might have emerged for his friends. But the easier route appeared to be to pick up a few social media claims made by language patrollers and turn these into a real-life 'row'. This is the sort of thing that everybody in the public eye, and then everybody in the public, begins to learn a lesson from. And most people will never have banked the popular goodwill that comes from playing Sherlock Holmes and other popular characters that might allow them to come back from that precipice.

The difficulty of talking about race, or even mentioning it as Cumberbatch did, points to a deep procedural problem which all public discourse is struggling to find a way to speak to. Hitherto any politician, writer or other public figure could proceed fairly well along one pre-agreed line. That line was that you should attempt to speak, write and even think aloud in a manner which no reasonable person could reasonably misinterpret. If somebody did unreasonably misinterpret your words then it reflected badly on them. Anyone claiming that Benedict Cumberbatch was clearly a virulent racist who had just exposed himself could expect to be laughed off the scene and dismissed without further thought.

But in recent years – overlapping, not coincidentally, with the years of social media – this rule has changed. Today a politician, writer or other public figure is in the same position that all members of the general public are in. We can no longer trust that our listeners are honest or are searching towards similar goals. An outburst of insincere claims from members of the public may be made as eagerly as sincere ones. And so the collective ambition of public figures must become to ensure that they write, speak and think out loud in such a fashion that no dishonest critic could dishonestly misrepresent them. It should go without saying that this is an impossible, and deranging, aspiration. It cannot be done. It cannot even be attempted without going mad.

The obvious thing is to survey the options available. One would be to say nothing, or at least say nothing of any substance in public, which is a choice that many politicians have adopted – a path that leaves the door open to people who are willing to say absolutely anything. Another option is to try to work out what the game going on here really is. To do that it is worth comparing cases: cases where nothing of significance has been said but where great offence has been claimed, versus cases where truly terrible things have been said and claims of offence were dismissed. A fine example of the latter came in August 2018 with the case of Sarah Jeong.

SARAH JEONG

That was when *The New York Times* announced the appointment of a 30-year-old writer on tech issues to join the paper's editorial board. Like all such appointments, Jeong's promotion to such a position at a young age attracted a considerable amount of attention. And attention in the age of the internet obviously includes online rakings of everything the person has said. In Jeong's case the raking turned up tweets with a particular focus – which was a sustained and pretty crude abuse of white people. Jeong's tweets included 'Are white people genetically predisposed to burn faster in the sun, thus logically being only fit to live underground like grovelling goblins?'; 'I dare you to go on Wikipedia and play "Things white people can definitely take credit for", it's really hard'; 'White men are bullshit'; 'CancelWhitePeople' and in one stream of tweets 'Have you ever tried to figure out all the things that white people are allowed to do that aren't cultural appropriation? There's literally nothing. Like skiing, maybe, and also golf . . . It must be so boring to be white.'[43] It is fair to say that her Twitter feed showed an obsession with this theme. She even committed the basic error of comparing those people she didn't like with animals. 'Dumbass fucking white people marking up the internet with their opinions like dogs pissing on fire hydrants.'[44] Another tweet said, 'Oh man it's kind of sick how much joy I get out of being cruel to old white men.'[45]

Jeong was also a keen user of the phrase 'Kill all men'. But under the circumstances this took a second order of priority for her critics. It was the incessant racism expressed towards white people which drew some ire towards Jeong and against *The New York Times* for hiring her. For its part the newspaper stood beside its latest recruit. There was to be no throwing to the internet wolves on this occasion. The official statement from the paper of record said that it had hired Jeong because of her 'exceptional work' on the internet. It went straight on to claim that 'Her journalism and the fact that she is a young Asian woman have made her a subject of frequent online harassment. For a period of time she responded to that harassment by imitating the rhetoric of her harassers. She sees now that this approach only served to feed the vitriol that we too often see on social media. She regrets it, and *The Times* does not condone it.' The paper finished by saying that having learned this lesson it was confident Jeong would be 'an important voice for the editorial board moving forward'.[46]

In fact the 'period of time' during which Jeong had engaged in her more controversial tweeting activities was from 2014 until just a year before *The New York Times* hired her. But her new employer's defence worked. The use of Jeong's gender, youth and race along with the modern reprieve which comes from claiming victimhood got her off. Again, if Jeong had said that she had never been particularly insulted online, or didn't check Twitter with enough care to know what people were saying about her, or (most implausible of all if a round needs to be won) claimed that online insults didn't remotely bother her, then her alibi would have been less useful.

But the Jeong case revealed one other fascinating insight. A writer at the website *Vox* called Zack Beauchamp had come to Jeong's defence by tweeting 'A lot of people on the internet today confusing the expressive way anti-racists and minorities talk about "white people" with actual race-based hatred, for some unfathomable reason.'[47] There was no elaboration about what is or is not 'expressive' in racial epithet terms, nor any guide for how to judge the difference between 'actual race-based hatred' and these 'expressive' forms of language. But an even more interesting defence of Jeong was mounted by another writer at *Vox*. Ezra Klein opened his defence of Jeong by dismissing the furore as being 'about actually racist alt-right trolls weaponizing old tweets in bad faith to get an Asian woman fired'. This brought in not just the racial identity of Jeong that *The New York Times* had also deployed but also the alleged political motivations of any (and perhaps all) people who had found anything to object to in her tweets.

But it was the defence Ezra Klein made from there that was most interesting because it precisely mirrored the argument that Salma El-Wardany had deployed in defence of people tweeting that 'All men are trash' and the argument Klein had made that '#KillAllMen' was just another way of saying 'it would be nice if the world sucked less for women'. In defence of Sarah Jeong making repeated racial slurs against white people, Klein similarly explained that when Jeong uses the term 'white people' in her 'jokes' it does not mean what it says. As Klein put it, 'On social justice Twitter, the term means something closer to "the dominant power structure and culture" than it does to actual white people.'[48]

Here is a magnificent spur for madness. If Benedict Cumberbatch and Sarah Jeong can both end up in 'race rows' it would ordinarily mean that they would have been guilty of similar provocations. And yet they were not. Cumberbatch got into a 'race row' because he used an outmoded term. Jeong got into a race row because over a period of years she had repeatedly used the same racial epithets in a derogatory way, and appeared to have enjoyed doing so. What is worse is that motive can be assigned without reference to the severity of the words. Whereas a term that one person may use unwittingly can in some cases be levelled against them (Cumberbatch), in other cases extreme terms which people are using knowingly do not in fact count as being the words they have used. This is the explanation that Klein, El-Wardany and others have given. Whereas some people unwittingly use the wrong term and can be castigated for it, other people use terms that are so wrong and so extreme and yet no especial castigation is due. Because of something.

There are really only a couple of possibilities for what that 'something' might be. The first is that there is a scrambling device over all public pronouncements in relation to sex, race and much else and that an unscrambling device is required, but that not everybody has it. Klein and El-Wardany obviously do, but it is not clear how many others have the correct unscrambling equipment to work out what words are meant and what are not. Do we always have to rely on them to tell us which words mean what we hear and which ones we are mishearing? How exactly will this work?

The other explanation for this is that there is a far simpler scramble going on. Which is that it has nothing to do with words and nothing to do with intent, but solely to do with the innate characteristics of a particular speaker. So Cumberbatch is starting off from a place of the greatest unsafety. He is white, heterosexual and male. It probably seemed like a good idea at the time to stress his anti-racist credentials on Tavis Smiley. On the other hand, somebody making disparaging comments for years about another ethnic group might ordinarily be thought to be in serious trouble. Unless their identity happens to be correct. Had Cumberbatch spent years tweeting about Asian people living in holes like goblins and how much he enjoyed making elderly Asian people cry he might not have got away with it. Jeong did but only because of her own racial identity (although Asian privilege is currently being weighed up in the social justice scales) and because of the race she was attacking.

It is impossible to unscramble the different standards being applied simultaneously by the content of speech because speech itself has become unimportant. What matters above everything is the racial and other identity of the speaker. Their identity can either condemn them or get them off. This means that if words and their contents do still matter then they have become deeply secondary orders of business. It also means that rather than managing to ignore the issue of race we are going to have to spend the foreseeable future constantly focused on it, because only by concentrating on people's race can we work out who we ought to allow ourselves to listen to.

THE RAISING OF THE RHETORIC

Some of it will be in the form of shouting. For there is something in the pitch of what has been happening in recent years in the discussion on race that is strikingly close to the move that occurred in feminism around the same time. A similar acceleration of rhetoric and accusations appears to have revved up just around the point which might have been regarded as victory. As with the debate within feminism, this is not to say that racial disparities and racist opinions do not exist – any more than it could be claimed that no women are ever held back anywhere because of their gender. But it is a curiosity of the age that, after the situation appears at the very least to be better than it ever was, it is presented as though it has never been worse.

Movements that have become political or are in the process of becoming political need thinkers to ignite them rather than just represent them. And just as Marilyn French and others became celebrated for the extremity of their claims, so in recent years the prize for being regarded as the most celebrated writer on race has not fallen to the most ameliorating or pacifying voice, but to the writer who more than perhaps any other has presented race in America in particular as being at a stage of unprecedented awfulness.

A lot can be surmised about the cultural expectations of publishers when they sign up authors whose first book is a memoir. Such an honour was afforded to Ta-Nehisi Coates, whose first book, *The Beautiful Struggle* (2008), describes with admirable honesty not just his upbringing in Baltimore but his own attitude towards every aspect of it. In the book he admits that when he sees white people in the Baltimore Arena he views their caps and clothes and junk food with disdain: 'I thought they looked dirty, and this made me racist and proud.'[49] He describes how his father – a member of the Black Panthers – had seven children by four different women. It is a world of gun violence, of rival groups of blacks threatening other groups of blacks. And while Coates admits that he talked through his Latin classes and threw away much of the chance of learning, his mother taught him about slavery and the slave revolts. He describes his disdain for what mainstream civic nationalism that his father at one stage felt. His son dismisses his father as being 'of that era, an acolyte of that peculiar black faith that makes us patriots despite the yoke. So he worshipped JFK, got amped off old war movies.'[50]

Later his father comes 'to consciousness'. The 'years of slumber pass' and Coates senior 'stood with those who had come to believe that our condition, the worst of this country's condition – poor, diseased, illiterate, crippled, dumb – was not just a tumor to be burrowed out but proof that this whole body was a tumor, that America was not a victim of great rot but rot itself'.[51] Coates has an English teacher ('a small man with a small voice') about whom he writes, 'I accorded him all the esteem of an anthill and expected great deference in return'. The young Coates ends up in a fight with this teacher one day because he has been yelled at 'and I could not back down' and he finishes by 'mushing the teacher in the face'. Later he describes, with no remorse, his role in a racist attack on a white boy.[52] Yet it is only ever Coates and members of his community who are the fated ones.

'We know how we will die,' he says. 'We are the walking lowest rung, and all that stands between us and beast, between us and the local zoo, is respect, the respect you take as natural as sugar and shit. We know what we are, that we walk like we are not long for this world, that this world has never longed for us.'[53] The book was a huge success, highly praised and superlatively puffed. In its wake Coates received a 'genius' grant from the MacArthur Foundation, and having broken through with a memoir, in 2015 he wrote his second book (*Between the World and Me*), in the form of a letter to his then 15-year-old son. Two memoirs before the age of 40.

In *Between the World and Me* Coates describes his own reactions to the events of 11 September 2001. Coates had arrived in New York only a couple of months before, but he is admirably honest about his own reactions to 9/11. He records that as he was standing with his family on the roof of an apartment building watching the smoke billowing across Manhattan Island 'my heart was cold'. He reflects that 'I would never consider any American citizen pure. I was out of sync with the city.' A year earlier a schoolmate of his had been killed by a Maryland police officer who had mistakenly thought that the man – Prince Jones – was a drug dealer. What this leads Coates to write about, the firemen in another state risking – and giving – their lives to save the lives of Americans of all races and backgrounds, is shocking. 'They were not human to me,' writes Coates. 'Black, white, or whatever, they were the menaces of nature; they were the fire.'[54]

So seamless has Coates's career been that even the mildest criticism of him has been either withheld or – when it has come – been responded to with shock. When *Between the World and Me* was published, Toni Morrison wrote in the blurb that Coates had filled 'the intellectual void' that had plagued her since the death of James Baldwin. At least one person – Dr Cornel West – took exception to this, though West's reasons for doing so were typically, and admirably, idiosyncratic. 'Baldwin was a great writer of profound courage who spoke truth to power,' wrote West. 'Coates is a clever wordsmith with journalistic talent who avoids any critique of the Black president in power.'[55] Coates reacted badly to this, because he was wounded that somebody could be saying that he was not the equal of James Baldwin. But aside from the privilege that it demonstrates there is also a useful reminder of something.

For aside from being one of the great writers and moral forces of the late twentieth century, Baldwin grew up at a time where a rage against the injustices in America was not just justifiable but necessary. Aside from the grave injustices that the communities he grew up in were still living through, Baldwin had also experienced those injustices first hand. As he recounts in *The Fire Next Time*, at the age of ten he had been beaten by two police officers. His grievances were if anything understated. And yet Baldwin always wrote to find a way to communicate the divides that existed in America, never to widen them. Coates, by contrast, has made a career enlarging the differences and widening the wounds.[56] In matters big and small he is willing to perform this task: willing to demand that America make reparation payments, even after all these centuries, to Americans today who are black; and willing always to wield the biggest tool against the smallest sin. In 2018 when *The Atlantic* magazine (for which Coates is 'national correspondent') announced that they were hiring the conservative writer Kevin Williamson, a raking of Williamson's past articles began. He was found to have had very anti-abortion views, which already riled many of his critics, but an article of his from *National Review* on Illinois was dishonestly claimed to contain a reference to a young black boy which was derogatory.

Williamson was relieved of his new position at *The Atlantic* less than a fortnight after his hiring had been announced. But after the hiring and firing there was a staff meeting at which the editor – Jeff Goldberg – sat on stage with Coates. Although no one demanded that Goldberg adopt the hand postures demanded of the President of Evergreen, it was clear that he was fighting for his professional life and that Coates was his life raft. At one point Goldberg pleads, 'Look, it's very hard for me to disaggregate the professional Ta-Nehisi from the personal Ta-Nehisi because . . . I mean, I want to say that. I just feel the need to say this. I mean he's one of the dearest people in my life. I'd die for him.'

Many contributors to such a magazine would consider this fealty enough, and reason to perhaps spread around a certain amount of the love. Coates did no such thing

In discussing Williamson, Coates managed to do what he had done in each of his memoirs to date: to put the worst possible gloss on a situation from the great height at which he had himself been placed. Coates used the meeting to say that he had no expectations of Williamson beyond some flowery prose. No expectations other than the certain knowledge that Williamson – and here is an extraordinary claim – was not capable of 'seeing me or, frankly, a lot of you as fully realized human beings'.[57] The idea that Williamson did not view Coates – and indeed did not view any black person – as 'fully realized human beings', and that this was simply a sad reality, was a terrible statement by Coates and says a lot about what he has been allowed to get away with throughout his career. James Baldwin never spoke about white people as though they were as a whole unredeemable. Nor did he have any need to exaggerate offence. Coates not only exaggerates hurt, but does so knowing that all of the weaponry is now on his side. There is a gun loaded on the stage, but it is not the white men who are holding it, it is him. When students starting out on campuses across the US wonder whether making insincere claims and catastrophizing minute events can be rewarding, they can look to Coates and know that it is.

Nor in the modern information age is the heightening of race awareness in one country confined to that country. Coates's success in the US was mirrored by Reni Eddo-Lodge in a country with a very different history of race relations. When her book *Why I'm no Longer Talking to White People about Race* was first published in 2017 it immediately raised not only the same issues as Coates's but received a comparable amount of plaudits and awards. Eddo-Lodge mainstreamed into British public discourse concepts like 'white privilege', but she had to go looking harder than Coates for her complaints. The opening of Eddo-Lodge's book recounts a number of terrible incidents from Britain's past such as the racist murder of a black seaman called Charles Wooton in the docks of Liverpool in 1919.[58] Eddo-Lodge recounts such unusual events as though they are not merely emblematic of a country but a hidden history. Crucially they are a history for which she needs to go searching, returning from her endeavours to tell us how much worse the past was than we had imagined and how much worse white people must be now as a result.

How are individuals meant to react to people in the present when they have returned from scouring the past in this retributive mood? One consequence would appear to be the normalization of vengefulness – a vengefulness which has spent recent years seeping into everyday language. So at the 'Women's March' in London in January 2018 one of the placards waved by a young woman with pink hair read 'No Country for Old White Men'.[59] One irony was that one of the Socialist Worker banners beside her read 'No to racism'. The sadness was that the young woman was waving her placard just beside the Cenotaph, which admittedly commemorates a lot of white men, but white men who never had a chance to grow old.

In this new era of retribution it has become perfectly acceptable to accuse white people in general – even white women in particular – of crimes which other people would not be guilty of. So *The Guardian* sees fit to publish a piece titled 'How white women use strategic tears to avoid accountability', in which the author complains that 'Often, when I have attempted to speak to or confront a white woman about something she has said or done that has impacted me adversely, I am met with tearful denials and indignant accusations that I am hurting her.'[60] 'WhiteTears' is a popular hashtag. And then there is the mainstreaming of the term 'gammon', a term that has become the *mot juste* for people of enlightened opinion online to refer to people with white skin which can flush pink. The term came into use around 2012 and by 2018 was being used freely on television shows as well as online to highlight not just the amusing skin tone of white people and their porcine appearance, but to imply that the flushedness masked some barely repressed outrage and likely xenophobia. So once again in pursuit of anti-racism the anti-racists resorted to racism. And what might be the negative consequences of such a posture?

IQ

Of all the foundations on which to base a diverse and civilized society, human equality must be the most important of all. Equality is the stated objective of every Western government, the stated aim of all mainstream civic organizations and the aspiration of anybody wishing to find a place in a polite society. But beneath this aspiration, presumption or hope, lies one of the most painful and unexploded bombs of all – and one of the best reasons why we need to be treading far more carefully than we are doing in the era of Twitter hashtaggery. That is the question of what equality means and whether it even exists.

Equality in the eyes of God is a core tenet of the Christian tradition. But it has translated in the era of secular humanism not into equality in the eyes of God but equality in the eyes of man. And here there is a problem, which is that many people realize, fear or intuit that people are not entirely equal. People are not equally beautiful, equally gifted, equally strong or equally sensible. They are certainly not equally wealthy. They are not even equally lovable. And while the political left talks constantly of the need for equality and even equity (arguing, as Eduardo Bonilla-Silva and others do, that equality of outcome is not just desirable but possible), the political right responds with a call for equality of opportunity, not equality of outcome. In fact both claims are almost certainly impossible locally and nationally, let alone globally.

A child of rich parents will have opportunities that a child of poor parents will not have, and this will almost certainly give that child advantages at the start of its life if not throughout it. Although everybody could go to better schools, not everybody will be able to go to the best schools, and though a lot of people may wish to go to Harvard not everybody in the world can do so. Around 40,000 people a year try to get in to Harvard but not all of them can. As it happens this is where the most recent and most devastating landmine of all was recently glimpsed and from where it may yet go off.

As we saw earlier, it was Harvard that gave the world the 'Implicit Bias' test. Or as one web headline puts it, 'Are you a racist? This Harvard racism test will tell you.'[61] If that is the case then it would appear that America's oldest university ought to take the test itself. And if the implicit bias test was in fact accurate it would come back with the result that Harvard itself is very racist indeed.

In 2014 a group called 'Students for Fair Admissions' filed a lawsuit against Harvard. The group represented Asian-Americans who argued that the university's admissions policies had shown a pattern of discrimination going back decades. Specifically they alleged that in the name of 'affirmative action' Harvard had been routinely and systematically biased against Asian-American applicants. The university fought hard to prevent the release of documents revealing information on its application criteria, arguing that these were effectively Harvard's trade secrets. But the university – which claimed not to discriminate against applicants 'from any group' in its admissions process – was eventually forced to reveal these secrets.[62] It is no wonder that they had tried to keep them hidden.

Since Harvard is only able to accept around 4.6 per cent of each year's applicants, it is perhaps inevitable that some form of vetting was needed. But the vetting procedure that Harvard allowed itself could hardly have been more unpalatable. Like most other universities in America (and spreading out from there), Harvard wanted to eradicate the idea of racial bias in its selection process. But it turned out that if you attempt to eradicate the idea of racial bias you do not get a completely ethnically representative hierarchy, but a hierarchy which disproportionately favours certain groups. Harvard – being smart – realized this, and had to find some way to get around the problem, specifically in order to try to increase the number of African-Americans who were attending the university. And so it decided to find ways to bias its ostensibly colour-blind entrance policy against one of the groups which was dramatically over-performing. Harvard turned a process that presented itself as intended to be race-blind, but which was actually set up to improve the chances for some, into a process that was race-obsessed.

Although the university denied the allegations in court, its own records showed that over a period of years Harvard had been routinely downgrading Asian-American applicants. In particular it was downgrading them on personality traits including 'positive personality', kindness and likeability. Unfortunately for Harvard, during the disclosure stage it transpired that the downgrading of Asian-American students was happening without Harvard having necessarily had any interview or meeting with the applicants. It looked like a deliberate policy of downgrading Asian-Americans on their character scores without even meeting them. And why might Harvard or any other educational institution of excellence need to do that? For two reasons.

The first is that Harvard like all other similar elite institutions has committed itself to presenting to the world not simply the best possible people, but the best possible people after they have been put through the selection strainer that is the institution's commitment to diversity. The second is that if Harvard did not deliberately disadvantage certain groups and advantage others in its commitment to 'affirmative action' policies and diversity criteria in general, the products of Harvard might be worryingly non-diverse. Specifically they might have a student body which disproportionately or even largely consisted not of white Americans or black Americans, but of Asian-Americans and Ashkenazi Jews. Here we get a glimpse of the world's ugliest landmine.

Research into IQ and genetics is among much competition probably the most dangerous and cordoned-off subject of all. When Charles Murray and Richard J. Herrnstein published *The Bell Curve* in 1994 they were believed to be setting off precisely this landmine. Even though few of their critics read the book, criticisms of its investigation into the hereditary aspect of genetics were widely attacked. A few publications realized that the subject was of such significance that it had to at least be discussed. But in the main the reaction to *The Bell Curve* was to try to shut it and its author down ('author' because Herrnstein had the misfortune, or luck, to die shortly before the book's publication). Almost all publications that reviewed the book noted that its findings were 'explosive'.[63] But most critics decided to do a very specific job with those explosive findings. That was to cover them with as much soil as could be found and then pat it down as tightly as possible. One extreme, but not uncommon, piece about the book by a fellow academic was headlined 'Academic Nazism' and claimed that the book was 'A vehicle of Nazi propaganda, wrapped in a cover of pseudoscientific respectability, an academic version of Adolf Hitler's *Mein Kampf*.[64] Not just any old *Mein Kampf*, but Adolf Hitler's one.

The criticism of *The Bell Curve* demonstrated why almost nobody wanted to go over the evidence that suggests that intelligence test scores vary with ethnic group and that just as some groups score higher on intelligence tests, others must score lower. This of course is not to say that everybody in such groups does. As Murray and Herrnstein were at pains to point out repeatedly, the differences within racial groups were larger than the differences between them. Yet those who have surveyed the academic literature on IQ differentials across racial groups appreciate better than anyone that the literature in the area is – as Jordan Peterson has said – 'an ethical nightmare'.[65] And it was a nightmare which almost everybody seemed very keen to steer clear of.

They did it through a variety of methods. The first was simply to dismiss the authors as racists and, having covered them with sufficient ordure, rely on the resulting smell to do the rest. This worked so well that in 2017 when Charles Murray was invited to speak about a more recent book at Middlebury College in Vermont, students barracked him, prevented Murray from giving his speech in the hall and then chased him off the campus, in the process hospitalizing the female academic who was attempting to escort Murray out. Other techniques for pushing the *Bell Curve* controversy away included casting doubt on IQ predictors in general, or claiming that they favour certain racial groups over others because of inbuilt bias. These counter-claims have themselves been persuasively refuted, but after a quarter of a century it is perfectly clear that the *Bell Curve* controversy will never be fought on the basis of the facts. These are too uncomfortable to be allowed to roam freely in the intellectual air. And so the fall-back position for refusing to engage with the evidence on IQ differentials is to say that even if the facts are there, and even if they are very clear, it is morally suspicious to want to look into them and that they in any case present us with ethical and moral problems so vast and complex that there is nothing at all that can be done with them.

This retreat from 'the facts are wrong' to 'the facts are unhelpful' has become the signature retreat of opinion in the face of the growing literature on the subject. In 2018 one of the world's leading experts in the field – David Reich of Harvard – published a piece to coincide with his new book on genetics. Among much else he charted the way in which the claim had been made of race (as with sex) that it was merely a 'social construct' with no basis in genetics. Reich explained how this view had become the orthodoxy, and why it had no hope of holding up against the evidence now flooding towards it. Reich knew the pitfalls, admitting in his piece that he had 'deep sympathy for the concern that genetic discoveries could be misused to justify racism'. But he added that 'As a geneticist I also know that it is simply no longer possible to ignore average genetic differences among "races".[66] However, no amount of caveating works in the area, and the race and IQ debate flared up again. A fairly typical attack on him was to say 'Did Reich really not see how racists and sexists could twist his thinking? Or does he in fact on some level share their prejudices?'[67]

Even today, just being seen to have communicated fairly with Murray is cause for this same manoeuvre to be played. The neuroscientist Sam Harris had, by his own admission, avoided any even remote contact either with Murray or his most famous book because of the slurry poured around the area. On reading the literature he said that he had come to realize that Murray was 'perhaps the intellectual who was treated most unfairly in my lifetime'.[68] Just for having him on his podcast and for having a respectful and insightful conversation (titled 'Forbidden Knowledge') about Murray's work, various media attempted to tar Harris with the same brush. *Vox* declared that such enquiry was not 'forbidden knowledge' but merely 'America's most ancient justification for bigotry and racial inequality'.[69] This ignores – among other troubling things – the possibility that it could be both.

For now this is where the enquiry and debate on IQ have stalled. Because the knowledge could be used by bad people the enquiry cannot proceed or it must be denied. And as Murray said in his conversation with Harris there is one possible obvious reason for all the fury that surrounds it. This is that from the top of government and through almost every institution in our societies today a commitment to a particular idea of 'diversity' and 'equality' is all-encompassing and all-consuming. It is written into all employment law and employment policies and embedded into all social policies that everybody is 'the same above the neck'. Indeed, this assumption is so widespread that any subject which could be said to undermine it or run counter to it must be quashed with as much force as the Church at the height of its power was able to bring down on anybody who ran counter to its teachings. The teachings of our day are that everybody is equal and that race and gender and much else besides are mere social constructs; that given the right encouragement and opportunity everybody can be whatever they want to be; that life is entirely about environment, opportunity and privilege. This is why when even the tiniest fragment of the argument crops up – as with Asian admissions at Harvard – it causes such extraordinary pain, confusion, denial and rage. In general the denial is systemic, but occasionally it fixes its gaze on a particular object or person, and then everything that can be thrown is thrown against the person who has even raised (or threatens to raise) the heresy. The truth is that there are people (and they may well grow in number) who do welcome research into this area with a deeply unpalatable glee. It is not hard to recognize the difference between those who look into this dark area with concern and those who look into it with positive delight.

In any case this is the worst hardware-software question of all. For a long and disreputable period race was believed to be a hardware issue – the most hardware issue of the lot. And then in the wake of World War II, and far from unconnected with the horrors of that conflict, the consensus ran the other way. Race became, perhaps out of necessity, a social construct like everything else. Because if it is a hardware issue then we may at some point be in serious trouble.

In March 2019 Professor Robin DiAngelo of the University of Washington gave a speech at Boston University. DiAngelo specialises in 'whiteness studies' and has written a book, *White Fragility*. Since DiAngelo is herself white she has to do a certain amount of self-abasement to earn the trust of her audiences. She does so by assuring them that she is aware that just by standing on a stage and speaking she is 'reinforcing whiteness and the centrality of the white view'. She asks for forgiveness by stating, for instance, that, 'I'd like to be a little less white, which means a little less oppressive, oblivious, defensive, ignorant and arrogant.' To her audience in Boston she also explained how white people who see people as individuals rather than by their skin colour are in fact 'dangerous'.[70] Meaning that it took only half a century for Martin Luther King's vision to be exactly inverted.

Today there appears to be a return to a heightened level of rhetoric on race and a great crescendo of claims about racial differences – just when most of us hoped that any such differences might be fading away. Some people in a spirit of resentment, others in a spirit of glee, are jumping up and down on this quietly ticking ground. They can have no idea what lies beneath them.

INTERLUDE

On Forgiveness

The arrival of the age of social media has done things we have still barely begun to understand and presented problems with which we have hardly started to grapple. The collapse of the barrier between private and public language is one. But bigger even than that (though partly resulting from it) is the deepest problem of all: that we have allowed ourselves no mechanisms for getting out of the situation technology has landed us in. It appears able to cause catastrophes but not to heal them, to wound but not to remedy. Consider the phenomenon now known as 'public shaming'.

In February 2018, only a few months before Sarah Jeong's appointment to *The New York Times* editorial board, the paper had announced another recruitment, that of a 44-year-old tech journalist called Quinn Norton. The internet immediately went to work, and – as they later would with Sarah Jeong – analysed her Twitter feed. Again they found tweets which were, in the language of social justice campaigners, 'not good'. Among the things that were found were a number of tweets from 2013 in which Norton had used the word 'fag'. As in 'Look, fag' and (on one occasion with another Twitter user with whom she was rowing) 'you shit eating, hypersensitive little crybaby fag'.[1] On another occasion – back in 2009 – Norton was found to have used the most unacceptable word of all. In 2009, in a row with another Twitter user, she had replied, 'If God had meant a nigger to talk to our schoolchildren, He would have would have [*sic*] made him president. Oh, but wait . . . Um.'[2] Just seven hours after *The New York Times* had announced its new hire it backpedalled by saying Norton would not in fact be joining the paper.

In a subsequent piece in *The Atlantic* Norton explained what she thought had happened. She acknowledged that many things she had written and tweeted in the past had been ignorant and embarrassing. She also explained what it felt like to, in her words, have a 'doppelganger' version of herself swiftly emerge online. In common with other people who had been the subject of online shaming this version of her that people were railing against was not 'who she was' but a hideous, simplified, out-of-context version of tiny parts of herself.

She explained that she believed herself to have been the victim of what she referred to as 'context collapse'. This is another term for the collapse of the divide between private and public language, where a conversation meant for an in-group becomes known to an out-group with no knowledge of the original context of the discussion. Norton said that her use of the 'n' word had been in the context of an online row in which she was 'in support of [President] Obama'. Since Norton had been in friendly as well as unfriendly rows with various white racists it was possible that she was using vile language to mirror back at someone who was also using vile language. Elsewhere her engagement with 'Anons' (members of the activist collective 'Anonymous') was explained to be the reason for her use of the word 'fags'.[3] Such language gets used in such groups, but clearly does not transfer well to the world of *The New York Times*. The two worlds met, Norton was history there, and the world stampeded on.

But these cases deserve some reflection. First because cases like Norton's and Jeong's invite the question: 'What is a fair representation of a person in the internet age?' What is a fair way to describe somebody? Norton, for instance, might henceforth be summed up as 'The racist, homophobic tech journalist fired by *The New York Times*'. She might think a fairer version of her life would be 'Writer and mother'. But then Jeong presumably does not think of herself as a racist either. So who gets to call it? If it is the mob then we are in trouble.

Indeed, only the worst version of someone's life contains the information that makes the internet stop and look. It is pure gold for a network addicted to shaming and schadenfreude. We all know the glee at watching someone fall from grace; the righteous feeling that can come with joining in the punishment of a transgressor. Even (perhaps especially) if their transgression is for a sin we ourselves have committed. And we know from the work of the anthropologist and philosopher René Girard of the societal release that can come from the identification of such a scapegoat. So the inclination is to go for the account of a life which is least understanding and least nuanced: most appalling and most appalled.

Here lies an additional quagmire. There is little enough recourse when old school journalism tramples across someone's life. But on the internet there is not even a regulatory body to appeal to if your life has been raked over in this way. Thousands – perhaps millions – of people have been involved, and there is no mechanism to reach all of them and get them to admit that they raked over your life in an unfair manner. Nobody has the time, few people are deemed important enough. There are other people to move onto. And unlike the pool of people the old media might trample over, tech can pick on almost anyone on the planet and spin them around in the tornado.

The second thing that is important about stories like those of Norton, Jeong and others is the question that the internet age has still not begun to contend with: how, if ever, is our age able to forgive? Since everybody errs in the course of their life there must be – in any healthy person or society – some capacity to be forgiven. Part of forgiveness is the ability to forget. And yet the internet will never forget. Everything can always be summoned up afresh by new people. A future employer will always see Norton's use of the 'n' word and wonder, context aside, whether this is the sort of person they would really want to hire.

The controversial tweets of Norton and Jeong have been erased from their Twitter pages, but they have been captured for posterity by multiple other users. To see them online today can prompt a reaction as great as though they appeared not a few years ago, or a decade ago, but yesterday or today.

Until very recently a slip-up or error made even by a very famous person would be whittled away by time. There are some things so big that they will never be forgotten. Someone being tried in a courtroom or going to prison keeps that on their record. But living in a world where non-crimes have the same effect is especially deranging. What court can be appealed to? Especially when the nature of the crimes, or what constitutes a crime, can vary almost from day to day. What is the correct way to refer to somebody who is trans today? Did you use this word as a joke or an insult? How will what we are doing now look like in 20 years? Who will be the next Joy Reid, held to account for the 'wrong' view expressed at a time when everybody else was also expressing the 'wrong' view? If we do not know the answer to these questions then we have to try to ensure that we can predict the crowd-turns not just of the next year but of the rest of our lives. Good luck with that.

It is wholly unsurprising that studies show an increase in anxiety, depression and mental illness in young people today. Rather than being a demonstration of 'snowflake'-ism it is a wholly understandable reaction to a world whose complexities have squared in their lifetimes. A perfectly reasonable response to a society propelled by tools that can provide endless problems but no answers. And yet there are answers.

In November 1964 Hannah Arendt delivered a lecture at the University of Chicago titled 'Labour, Work, Action', part of a conference on 'Christianity and Economic Man: Moral Decisions in an Affluent Society'. The main subject of her lecture was the question of what an 'active' life consists of. What do we do when we are 'active'? But towards the close of her lecture Arendt reflected on some of the consequences of being active in the world. Every human being's life is able to be told as a story because it has a beginning and an end. But the actions between those two fixed points – what we do when we are 'acting' in the world – have consequences that are unbounded and limitless. The 'frailty and unreliability of human affairs' means that we are constantly acting into a 'web of relationships' in which 'every action touches off not only a reaction but a chain reaction'. This means that 'every process is the cause of unpredictable new processes'. A single word or deed could change everything. As a consequence, says Arendt, 'we can never really know what we are doing'.

What makes the 'frailty and unreliability of human action' worse is the fact that, as Arendt says:

> Though we don't know what we are doing when we are acting, we have no possibility ever to undo what we have done. Action processes are not only unpredictable, they are also irreversible; there is no author or maker who can undo what he has done if he does not like it or when the consequences prove disastrous.

Just as the only tool to protect against unpredictability is some ability to make and keep promises, so Arendt says only one tool exists to ameliorate the irreversibility of our actions. That is 'the faculty of forgiving'. These two things necessarily go together – the ability to bind together through promises and the ability to stay bound through forgiveness. Of the latter Arendt writes:

> Without being forgiven, released from the consequences of what we have done, our capacity to act would, as it were, be confined to one single deed from which we could never recover; we would remain the victim of its consequences forever, not unlike the sorcerer's apprentice who lacked the magic formula to break the spell.[4]

This was a truth before the rise of the internet, but how much truer it has become since.

One key to addressing this lies in historical rather than personal forgetting. And historical rather than personal forgiveness. Forgetting is not the same thing as forgiving, but it often accompanies it and certainly always encourages it. Terrible things are done, by a person or a people, but over time the memory fades. People gradually forget the exact details or nature of a scandal. A cloud surrounds a person or an action and then that too dissipates among a mass of new discoveries and experiences. In the case of the worst historical wrongs the victims and perpetrators die out – the one who gave offence and the person to whom offence was done. Some descendants may remember for a time. But as the insult and grievance fade from generation to generation those who hold on to this grievance are often regarded as displaying not sensitivity or honour but belligerence.

As well as helping people to remember, the internet helps make people approach the past from a strange, all-knowing angle. This makes the past hostage – like everything else – to any archaeologist with a vendetta. Events that were scandals long ago but which have not been for generations can be brought to the surface again. How could we have forgotten about this crime committed over a hundred years ago? Should we not all know about it? Should we not feel shame? What does not knowing about it say about us now?

Even things that seemed settled can be unsettled again. In his poem 'In Memory of W. B. Yeats', W. H. Auden famously wrote of literary reputations: 'Time that with this strange excuse / Pardoned Kipling and his views, / And will pardon Paul Claudel, / Pardons him for writing well.'[5] Except that now we learn that if Kipling was ever pardoned then he can also later be unpardoned. Perhaps such writers always could to some degree, but today this can be done far away, remotely, fast and fanatically.

In July 2018 students at the University of Manchester painted over a mural of Kipling's 'If' – a poem which has previously been voted Britain's favourite. But however moving or inspiring many people find that poem, these students decided to erase it. Perhaps inevitably, they wrote a poem by Maya Angelou over the top of it. The 'liberation and access' officer at the university's student union justified the action by explaining that Kipling was guilty of having 'sought to legitimate the British empire's presence in India' and of 'dehumanising people of colour'.[6]

Before the advent of the internet, people's mistakes could be remembered within their communities or circles. Then being able to start a new life somewhere else in the world was at least a possibility. Today, people may be followed by their doppelgänger wherever they go in the world. And even after death the excavation and tomb-raiding will go on, not in a spirit of enquiry or forgiveness but in one of retribution and vengeance. At the heart of which attitude lies the strange retributive instinct of our time towards the past which suggests that we know ourselves to be better than people in history because we know how they behaved and we know that we would have behaved better. There is a gigantic modern fallacy at work here. For of course people only think that they would have acted better in history because they know how history ended up. People in history didn't – and don't – have that luxury. They made good or bad choices in the times and places they were in, given the situations and shibboleths that they found themselves with.

To view the past with some degree of forgiveness is among other things an early request to be forgiven – or at least understood – in turn. Because not everything we are doing or intend to do now will necessarily survive this whirlwind of retribution and judgement. Can such an attitude of forgiveness be applied to the personal as well as the historical? To the people going through history with us?

Over New Year's Eve 2017/18 the British government slipped out news of a new government appointment: the journalist and schools founder Toby Young had been appointed as one member of a government advisory board on higher education which was being set up by the Department of Education. For some years Young had been best known as a prominent advocate of the government's 'free schools' programme and had dedicated his time to opening a new school in London and heading up the New Schools Network. Before taking this route Young had been the author of, among other things *How to Lose Friends and Alienate People* – an account (also made into a film) of his failure to crack America. It was a rumbustious, self-lacerating and revealing book, and like many of Young's journalistic columns it relied to some extent on shocking readers. Perhaps a Damascene conversion from one phase of his life to the next could have led to some forgiveness, but for a period Young was certainly riding two horses: funny and shocking journalist plus person helping children from poorer families get a better education. It was at the crossroads that the online mob caught him.

In the hours and days after his appointment was announced Young's Twitter account – and back articles – provided a treasure trove for offence archaeologists searching for errors. Indeed, for anyone unfamiliar with his work it must have been the online shaming equivalent of finding Tutankhamun's tomb.

It was discovered that in 2009 Young had expressed an interest in women's breasts on a number of occasions and was willing to talk about them on Twitter to his followers. He talked about one friend's 'massive boobs'. Watching Prime Minister's Questions on television he asked his followers on Twitter: 'Serious cleavage behind Ed Miliband's head. Anyone know who it belongs to?'[7] As he later said, none of these comments was among his proudest moments. But the excavation would not stop. In a piece in *The Spectator* from 2001 he had written about a new television programme on the 'Men and Motors' channel called 'The glamour game' which he said was basically pornography and that he liked it. A sub-editor gave the piece the headline 'Confessions of a porn addict'.[8] Almost two decades later this became one of the principal charges against him. Labour and Conservative MPs criticized him. *The Times* of London headlined its piece, '"Porn addict" Toby Young fights to keep role as student watchdog'.[9]

London's commuter paper *The Evening Standard* ran with 'New pressure on Theresa May to sack "porn addict" Toby Young from watchdog role.'[10]

He was found to have once used the term 'queer as a coot' to describe a gay celebrity and once sat at the back of the audience of a conference on IQ and genetics that took place at a London university. Essentially, he was found to have nicked every single tripwire of the era. Nine days after the announcement of his new position, as the potential for examining Young's back catalogue looked like it could go on all year, he withdrew from the appointment. Within a few more weeks he had lost every other job and position he had tried to hold onto, including the job of running the New Schools Network, which was his principal source of income and the passion of this second phase of his life.

Nobody would defend Young's tweets about women's breasts. Plenty of people would question the judgement of anyone tweeting out self-confessedly 'sophomoric' humour as an adult.[11] But what the Young case, like all the other cases of public shaming, raises is the most important question of all. Is there any route to forgiveness? Could Young's years of voluntary work helping disadvantaged children ever have the possibility of eradicating the sin of the boob tweets? If so, how many would be needed on each side, how many children helped in order to eradicate how many boobs? And what is a decent interval of time between an error and forgiveness? Does anybody know? Is anybody interested in working it out?

It is time we at least tried. After all we have now entered some of the most perilous territory of all. We now have cross-generational shaming. In August 2018 Lilly Diabetes announced that they were withdrawing from their sponsorship arrangement with the professional racecar driver Conor Daly just before the 26-year-old was about to make his NASCAR racing debut. This time the scandal was not about something Daly himself had said. The sponsors withdrew their support because a story surfaced from the 1980s. That decade – before Conor was born – his father had given an interview to a radio station in which he had used a derogatory term to refer to African-Americans. Daly senior declared himself 'mortified' and said that the term had a different meaning and connotation in his native Ireland and that he had only just moved to the US at the time. He expressed shame and regret and asked for forgiveness for the offence. But his son still lost the sponsorship deal.[12]

In some manner with which we still haven't even begun to wrestle, we have created a world in which forgiveness has become almost impossible, in which the sins of the father can certainly be visited upon the son. And we remain remarkably unconcerned to create any mechanisms or consensus over how to address the resulting conundrum.

The consensus for centuries was that only God could forgive the ultimate sins. But on a day-to-day level the Christian tradition, among others, also stressed the desirability – if not the necessity – of forgiveness. Even to the point of infinite forgiveness.[13] As one of the consequences of the death of God, Friedrich Nietzsche foresaw that people could find themselves stuck in cycles of Christian theology with no way out. Specifically that people would inherit the concepts of guilt, sin and shame but would be without the means of redemption which the Christian religion also offered. Today we do seem to live in a world where actions can have consequences we could never have imagined, where guilt and shame are more at hand than ever, and where we have no means whatsoever of redemption. We do not know who could offer it, who could accept it, and whether it is a desirable quality compared to an endless cycle of fiery certainty and denunciation.

So we live in this world where everyone is at risk – like Professor Tim Hunt – of having to spend the rest of their lives living with our worst joke. And where the incentives lie not in acting in the world but in reacting to other people: specifically to audition in the role of a victim or judge for a piece of the moral virtue that suffering is mistakenly believed to endow. A world where nobody knows who is allowed to give alleviation for offence but where everybody has a reputational incentive to take it and run with it. A world in which one of the greatest exertions of 'power' is constantly exerted – the power to stand in judgement over, and potentially ruin, the life of another human being for reasons which may or may not be sincere.

To date there are only two weak, temporary answers to this conundrum. The first is that we forgive the people we like, or the person whose tribe or views most closely fit our own, or at least aggravate our enemies. So if Ezra Klein likes Sarah Jeong he will forgive her. If you dislike Toby Young you will not forgive him. This is one of the surest ways imaginable to embed every tribal difference that already exists.

A second temporary route that has been found is the route that another racing driver – Lewis Hamilton – recently took. At Christmas 2017 he released a video on his Instagram account. It showed Hamilton saying 'I'm so sad right now. Look at my nephew.' The 32-year-old then turned the camera-phone to show his young nephew wearing a pink and purple dress and waving a magic wand. 'Why are you wearing a princess dress?' Hamilton asks him. 'Boys don't wear princess dresses,' he adds. The boy laughs during this.

But this soon all turned deadly serious for Hamilton and his career. An anti-bullying charity condemned him for using his social media platform to 'undermine a small child'. Across the internet Hamilton was slammed for being transphobic and for embedding dated gender stereotypes. The media picked up on the story and made it a headline news item. An anti-rape charity which campaigns to help rape survivors called for the driver to be stripped of his MBE. Hamilton himself swiftly went on social media to apologize for his 'inappropriate' comments and tell everyone how much he loved his nephew. 'I love that my nephew feels free to express himself as we all should,' he said in one message. In another he said, 'I have always been in support of anyone living their life exactly how they wish and I hope I can be forgiven for this lapse in judgement.'[14]

This clearly wasn't enough. Some months later, in August 2018, readers of the men's magazine *GQ* would find a picture of Lewis Hamilton on the cover, with a large interview and photo shoot inside. All of this – including the cover shot – was done in a skirt. As well as showing off his rippling abs and pecs in a lurid open multi-tartan top, he was also prominently wearing the kilt-like garment of many lurid patches and colours. The front-cover headline accompanying this image read: '"I want to make amends." Lewis Hamilton refuses to skirt the issue.'[15] So this is the only other currently available mode for forgiveness. If you are rich enough and famous enough, you can use PR people and the front cover of a men's magazine to dress in a skirt and prostrate yourself before the swiftly moving dogmas of the age. Perhaps it is no wonder that an increasing number of people are persuaded that they should simply go along with those same dogmas. No questions allowed. No questions asked.

4

Trans

Every age before this one has performed or permitted acts that to us are morally stupefying. So unless we have any reason to think we are more reasonable, morally better or wiser than at any time in the past, it is reasonable to assume there will be some things we are presently doing – possibly while flushed with moral virtue – that our descendants will whistle through their teeth at, and say 'What the hell were they thinking?' It is worth wondering what the blind spots of our age might be. What might we be doing that will be regarded by succeeding generations in the same way we now look down on the slave trade or using Victorian children as chimney sweeps?

Take the case of Nathan Verhelst, who died in Belgium in September 2013. Nathan had been born a girl and was given the name Nancy by her parents. She grew up in a family of boys and always felt that her parents preferred her three brothers to her. There was certainly plenty that was strange about the family. After Verhelst's death his mother gave an interview to the local media in which she said, 'When I saw "Nancy" for the first time, my dream was shattered. She was so ugly. I had a phantom birth. Her death does not bother me. I feel no sorrow, no doubt or remorse. We never had a bond.'[1]

For reasons that this and other comments make clear, Nancy grew up feeling rejected by her parents and at some stage settled on the idea that things might be better if she was a man. In 2009, in her late thirties, she began taking hormone therapy. Shortly after this, she had a double mastectomy and then a set of surgeries to try to construct a penis.

In total she had three major sex-change operations between 2009 and 2012. At the end of this process 'Nathan', as he then was, reacted to the results. 'I was ready to celebrate my new birth. But when I looked in the mirror I was disgusted with myself. My new breasts did not match my expectations and my new penis had symptoms of rejection.' There was significant scarring from all the surgery Verhelst had undergone, and he was clearly deeply unhappy in his new body. There is a photograph of Verhelst as 'Nathan' on a sparsely populated Belgian beach. He is squinting from the sunlight as he looks into the camera. Despite the tattoos covering part of his chest the scarring from the mastectomy is still visible. In a photo from another occasion he is lying on a bed in shoes and a suit, looking uncomfortable in his body.

The life that Nathan had clearly hoped for had not come about, and depression soon followed. So in September 2013, at the age of 44 – only a year after the last sex-change procedure – Verhelst was euthanized by the state. In his country of birth euthanasia is legal and the relevant medical authorities in Belgium agreed that Verhelst could be euthanized due to 'unbearable psychological suffering'. A week before the end he held a small party for some friends. Guests reportedly danced and laughed and raised glasses of champagne with the toast 'To life'. A week later Verhelst made the journey to a university hospital in Brussels and was killed by lethal injection. 'I do not want to be a monster,' he said just before he died.[2]

It is not hard to imagine future generations reading such a story in a spirit of amazement. 'So the Belgian health service tried to turn a woman into a man, failed and then killed her?' Hardest of all to comprehend might be the fact that the killing, like the operations that preceded it, was performed not in a spirit of malice or of cruelty, but solely in the spirit of kindness.

Of course the case of Verhelst is unusual in all sorts of ways. But it is worth focusing on precisely because some of the lessons it raises are reflected upon so little. What is trans? Who is trans? What makes someone trans? Are we sure that it exists as a category? And if so, are we certain that attempting to turn somebody physically from one sex to another is always possible? Or even the best way to deal with the conundrum this presents?

Among all the subjects in this book and all the complex issues of our age, none is so radical in the confusion and assumptions it elicits, and so virulent in the demands it makes, as the subject of trans. There is no other issue (let alone one affecting relatively few people) that has so swiftly reached the stage whereby whole pages of newspapers are devoted to its latest developments, and where there is a never-ending demand not just to change the language but to make up the science around it.[3] The debate around gay rights moved too swiftly for some people, but it still took decades to go from acceptance that homosexuality existed and might need to be accommodated to the position where gay marriage was legalized. By contrast trans has become something close to a dogma in record time. Conservative ministers in the British government are campaigning to make it easier for people to change their birth certificates and alter their sex at birth.[4] A local authority has issued educational guidelines suggesting that in order to make transgender children feel more accepted, teachers in primary schools should tell children that 'all genders', including boys, can have periods.[5] And in the US a Federal bill was passed in May 2019 which redefines sex to include 'gender identity'.[6]

Everywhere the feeling is the same. Among the crowd madnesses we are going through at the moment, trans has become like a battering ram – as though perhaps it is the last thing needed to break down some great patriarchal wall. The British gay rights group Stonewall is back with a new version of its old gay rights T-shirt. This one says, 'Some people are trans. Get over it.' But are they? And should we?

WHAT ISN'T STRANGE

It should be said that there is nothing very strange about where the 'trans' phenomenon started from. Today a great many things have got caught up together under this label. Trans has – just in recent decades – been used to describe a range of individuals, from people who occasionally dress as a member of the opposite sex to those who have undergone full-blown gender-reassignment surgery. And just one early confusion about all of this is that some aspects of trans are far more familiar than others.

Not only is some type of gender-ambiguity or gender-fluidity common across most cultures, it is hard to think of a culture in the world that does not include – and allow for – some variety of gender-ambiguity. It is not an invention of late modernity. As we have seen, Ovid wrote of a shifter between the sexes in the story of Tiresias. In India there are the Hijras – a class of intersex and transvestite – knowledge and acceptance of whom dates back centuries. In Thailand the *Kathoey* is a type of effeminate male who is widely accepted to be neither male nor female. And on the island of Samoa there are *fa'afafine*, men who live and dress as women.

Even parts of the world most hostile to male homosexuality have allowed for some category of person either between the sexes or who crosses the sexes. In Afghanistan there is the tradition of the *Bacha posh* in which parents who do not have a male heir select a daughter to become like a man. And in the early 1960s, long before the revolution, the Ayatollah Khomeini published a ruling on the permissibility of sex-change operations. Indeed, since the 1979 revolution the Iranian state has disturbingly as a consequence become a leader in the region in sex-realignment surgery, in large part because undergoing it is one of the only ways in which people who are found to be gay can avoid punishments worse even than unwanted surgery.

So awareness of some blurring between the sexes exists in almost every culture and ranges from transvestitism (people dressing up as members of the opposite sex) all the way through to transsexualism (going through with a range of procedures in order to 'become' the opposite sex). Whatever the evolutionary factors behind this, a considerable range of cultures has adapted to the idea that some people may be born in one body but desire to live in another.

But who are these people, and what are the different lines, not just between them and other people, but within this loosely aligned group of individuals? This whole subject has become so emotive and incendiary that dealing with it requires a forensic approach, though even that will never be accurate enough to satisfy everyone. Still, it has to start somewhere. And perhaps the best place to begin is with the part of the trans debate that is the most fixed. Because once the most settled aspects of the debate are agreed upon then the least settled – which not coincidentally are the most bitterly fought over – can be seen more clearly.

INTERSEX

If we place our trust in scientists, rather than social scientists, and if we agree that it is easier to respond to what people are than what they claim to be, then the aspect of the trans debate which becomes the least problematic to discuss is the whole question of intersex.

Intersex is the natural phenomenon known to the medical profession for centuries but necessarily obscure to everyone else. It is the fact that a small percentile of human beings are born either with ambiguous genitalia or turn out to have other biological attributes (for instance an unusually large clitoris, or an unusually small penis) which suggest that they may lie somewhere between the sexes. Not all of these symptoms are outwardly visible. In rare cases people may show outwardly the traits of one sex but also contain hidden traces of the organs of the other sex. For instance, Persistent Mullerian Duct Syndrome (PMDS) is the term for people born with male genitalia but who also turn out to have female reproductive organs such as fallopian tubes and even a uterus.

Medical professionals have been aware of these phenomena for centuries and there has been some very limited public awareness of it, though this tends to focus on the freakish. Circuses featured the 'bearded woman' as a freak of nature, while historical references to 'hermaphrodites' showed that a recognition of non-transvestite dwellers between the sexes existed. Although pushed to the margins of discussion, there was always some awareness that biology throws up certain complex and often cruel challenges.

Yet even today there is little understanding of how relatively common intersex is. It has been estimated that in America today around one in every two thousand children is born with sexual organs that are indeterminate, and around one in every three hundred will need to be referred to a specialist.[7] Of course the more awareness there has been about intersex, the greater the debate over what to do with those born with this extra challenge in their lives. In the second half of the last century Johns Hopkins University in Baltimore developed a standard model whereby experts would examine a child referred to them, consider which sex was more prevalent or easier to fit the child into and then treat them accordingly, with surgery and hormones.

After a considerable amount of bad practice was uncovered, a different way of approaching the issue began to emerge. Over the last 30 years one of the great campaigners for advancing the rights of intersex people has been the American bioethics professor Alice Dreger. Although not intersex herself she has been one of a small number of people who have argued against the early surgery model (often done to satisfy the parents) and for a greater understanding of the phenomenon among the public as well as professionals. Some daylight would certainly help those confronted with this challenge. In her book on the subject – *Galileo's Middle Finger* – Dreger recalls a senior surgeon telling her in the late 1990s that she just didn't understand the dynamics at play. According to him the parents of children born with ambiguous genitalia were presented with a problem they just could not cope with. 'The mother cries, and the father gets drunk,' he told her. 'If you let a child with ambiguous genitalia grow up without surgery . . . the kid will commit suicide at puberty.'[8]

But from the mid-1990s and the invention of the internet all of this changed. As Dreger notes, something happened that 'the Victorian doctors would never have imagined: People who had been born with various sex anomalies had started to find each other, and they had started to organize as an identity rights movement.'[9] The Intersex Society of North America (ISNA) was founded in 1993 and similar groupings eventually followed. Jeffrey Eugenides's bestselling 2002 novel *Middlesex* brought the outlines of the story to wider attention. A few brave individuals made themselves and their stories public. But the question of what medical intervention might be suitable and when, and the question of what best practice looks like, still remain matters of serious contention.

Nevertheless, through the advocacy of groups like ISNA a number of things have become clear. One is that intersex people exist and should not be held responsible for a situation over which they have absolutely no control. A considerable amount of sympathy and understanding can be felt for anybody who is born intersex. What else should people feel about fellow human beings who have found themselves born with a set of cards which are – to say the least – sub-optimal? If anything in the world is undoubtedly a hardware issue then it is this.

Intersex is a perfectly legitimate, sensible and compassionate cause for anyone to take up. Indeed, it should be taken up by anyone concerned with human rights. Yet it is striking how rarely the cause of intersex people is taken up on its own and how rarely, even today when trans is in every day's news, intersex is addressed. The reason seems to be that intersex has come to what public attention it has at the exact same moment that a whole set of ostensibly similar but in fact very different causes have emerged.

TRANSSEXUALISM

In the post-war period in Europe and America a small number of high-profile cases emerged of people who had tried to change from one sex to the other. The transition from male to female of Roberta (formerly Robert) Cowell in Britain and Christine (formerly George) Jorgensen in the US made headlines around the world. People still alive today remember their parents hiding the newspapers when the news of these first 'sex changes' were reported. For the stories were not just salacious and highly sexualized in the telling, but seemed to strike at the most basic societal norms. Could someone change sex? If so did that mean that anyone could? Did it mean that perhaps – if encouraged – everyone and anyone would?

Looking back it isn't hard to see why these earliest cases caused deeper confusions. After World War I the idea of feminine men and masculine women became something of an *idée fixe* for people criticizing the younger generation. One hit song of the 1920s went 'Masculine women! Feminine men! Which is the rooster? Which is the hen? It's hard to tell 'em apart today.'[10]

At the time homosexuality and transvestitism seemed to be at least very considerably linked: perhaps these were very committed transvestites or especially effeminate gay men. But the first public trans figures bucked any prevailing expectations. Early in his career Cowell had been a fighter pilot, and after that became famous as a motorcar racing driver. If not a knock-out argument, this certainly made the claim of an ultra-wild form of effeminacy harder – though not impossible – to sustain. And then there were the claims made by the individuals themselves. For example, Cowell wanted people to believe that she had been born intersex and that her vaginoplasty and other procedures were merely correcting a glitch of birth. So the more visible that all these categories became – homosexuality, intersex, transvestitism, transsexualism – the more they became intertwined.

It took time, some individual courage and descriptive skill to even begin to extract what we now know as the 'trans' element from this mix. Anybody in doubt about whether this category of individual exists should explore the work of the trans people who have not only thought deeply, but expressed themselves deeply, about this issue. One of the most successful attempts to communicate what many trans people claim is incommunicable was by the British writer Jan (formerly James) Morris. Like Roberta Cowell, Morris's story introduced layers of confusion and curiosity which still preoccupy audiences and interviewers to this day.

Morris had served in the army in the last days of World War II. Afterwards he had worked as a journalist for *The Times* and *The Guardian*. Like his war service, Morris's work as a foreign correspondent across the Middle East, Africa and behind the Iron Curtain did not fit into existing expectations of what a man who wanted to become a woman might be – any more than did the fact that he was happily married to a woman and had fathered five children.

James's transition into Jan began in the 1960s and culminated in a sex-change operation in 1972. Already renowned as an author, this soon made her one of the most famous trans people in the world. Morris's memoir of that transition, *Conundrum* (1974), remains one of the most persuasive and certainly the best-written accounts to date of why some people feel a need to transition across the sexes. Indeed, it is hard to read Morris's book and come away thinking that something like trans doesn't exist or is 'merely' a trick of the imagination. Morris describes her earliest memory as being a young boy sitting under his mother's piano – at the age of three or four – and realizing that he had been 'born in the wrong body'.[11] In the years that followed – through the military, marriage and fatherhood – the conviction never left him. It was only on meeting the famous New York-based endocrinologist Dr Harry Benjamin that some solution to the problem presented itself. These were the very earliest stages of trying to understand trans. A few doctors like Benjamin had satisfied themselves from their study that a certain minority of people felt that they were born in the body of the wrong sex. Nevertheless, all questions of what to do about this still lay before them. Some professionals like Benjamin came to the conclusion that something could be done. And as he once put it, 'I ask myself, in mercy, or in common sense, if we cannot alter the conviction to fit the body, should we not, in certain circumstances, alter the body to fit the conviction?' To alter the body, or as Morris put it 'to expunge these superfluities . . . to scour myself of that mistake, to start again', was not just what he had wanted, but what he had dreamed of and indeed prayed for.[12]

In *Conundrum* Morris describes how the desire to become a woman became stronger with every passing year. Each year his male body 'seemed to grow harder around me'. Morris was on a form of hormone therapy from 1954 until 1972 and describes accurately the strange effects of feeling younger and softer that female hormones have on men when they take them. The hormones not merely stripped away the layers of maleness that Morris had felt accumulating around him but stripped away too the 'unseen layer of accumulated resilience, which provides a shield for the male of the species, but at the same time deadens the sensations of the body'. The result over time was that Morris became a 'somewhat equivocal' figure. Some people thought he was a male homosexual, others something in between the sexes. On occasion, men would open doors for him and otherwise mistake him for a woman. All this was before the surgery.

In those days very few surgeons in Europe or America were willing to carry out procedures which were still at such an experimental stage. But equally nobody was sure of what it was that led some individuals to want to change from one sex to another. Did it represent a form of mental illness? If not always, then might it on occasion? And if so, how could anybody tell the two states of mind apart? How could this urge to remove a part of one's body be distinguished from a patient telling a doctor that they believed themselves to be Admiral Nelson and in pursuit of this belief wanted their right arm removed? Could somebody wanting their penis removed be any more sane?

In the 1960s and 1970s the few surgeons willing to carry out such procedures needed a number of assurances. One was that the patient must in no way be psychotic. Secondly, by changing sex the patient must not be abandoning anybody who depended on them in the sex they were currently in. Thirdly, the patient should have been undergoing hormone treatment for a length of time. And finally, the patient must have lived in the role of the gender they were adopting for a number of years. These basic principles have not changed much in the decades since.

In the end, after years of hormone treatment, Morris chose to go for his surgery in Morocco with Dr Georges Burou (referred to in *Conundrum* as 'Dr B - '). This doctor had already performed gender reassignment surgery on another famous British male to female transsexual, April Ashley and, though he kept a low profile, by this stage Dr Burou was famous in certain circles. So much so that 'Visiting Casablanca' became a fairly well-known euphemism for changing sex. For his patients, visiting Dr Burou in his surgery and recuperation centre in the back streets of Casablanca was – as Morris said – 'like a visit to a wizard.'[13]

Anyone who doubts that there are some people completely persuaded of the need to change sex should consider Morris's description of what he was willing to go through. Two nurses entered his room at Dr Burou's clinic, one French and one Arab. James is told that he will be operated on later but that they need to shave his privates. Since he has a razor he shaves himself while the two nurses sit on the table swinging their legs. He uses the cold water and the Moroccan soap to shave his pubic region and then goes back to the bed to be injected. The nurses tell him to go to sleep and that the operation will take place later. But Morris gives a moving description of what happens next. After the two nurses have left the room he gets out of bed, rather shakily, because the drug was starting to work, and 'went to say goodbye to myself in the mirror. We would never meet again, and I wanted to give that other self a long last look in the eye and a wink for luck.'[14]

Morris spent two weeks in the clinic, wrapped and bandaged, and described the feeling after the operation as one of being 'deliciously *clean*. The protuberances I had grown increasingly to detest had been scoured from me. I was made, by my own light, normal.'[15] Morris described the period following the operation, including after the return home, as the experience of a constant feeling of 'euphoria'. This went along with an absolutely certainty that 'I had done the right thing.'[16] Nor did the feeling of happiness wear off. At the time of writing *Conundrum*, Morris was aware that what had happened in the process of James becoming Jan was 'one of the most fascinating experiences that ever befell a human being'. There can be little doubting it.

This Tiresias had a view not only on the movement between the sexes but of the distinctive ways in which society looks – or at any rate looked – at men and women. The cab driver who sidles up to her and places a not unwanted kiss on her lips. The things people say to men but not to women. The things people say to women but not to men. And also that greater secret: not how the world views men and women, but how men and women differently view the world. Not much of this would satisfy a modern feminist.

For instance, Morris described the fundamentally different viewpoints and attitudes between the sexes. So, as a man, James was far more interested in the 'great affairs' of his time, whereas as a woman Jan acquired a new concern 'for small' affairs. After becoming a woman Jan writes, 'my scale of vision seemed to contract, and I looked less for the grand sweep than for the telling detail. The emphasis changed in my writing, from places to people.'[17]

She is willing to admit what problems it caused. It had been a tragedy in some ways, and it had certainly put severe strains on all those around her. Before her operation in 1972 she had to divorce her wife, Elizabeth, though she subsequently remarried her in 2008 after same-sex civil partnerships had become legal in the UK. The four surviving children who she fathered obviously did not have the easiest time adapting to the change in circumstances, though they seem to have been as adaptive as anyone could be. But by her own admission the whole process caused bewilderment among many, and culminated in a process by which a 'fine body' was 'deformed with chemicals and slashed by the knife in a distant city!' All this to reach what she sums up as reaching 'Identity', with a capital 'I'.[18] As she says, 'Of course one would not do it for fun, and of course if I had been given the choice of a life without such complications, I would have taken it.'[19] Nothing, she says, could have shaken her conviction that the person born as a he was in fact a she. And in search of a fulfilment of that realization there is, she says, absolutely nothing she would not have done. If she were trapped in that cage again, she says at one point, 'nothing would keep me from my goal . . . I would search the earth for surgeons, I would bribe barbers or abortionists, I would take a knife and do it myself, without fear, without qualms, without a second thought.'[20]

It is perfectly easy to recognize that there are people who are born intersex. After reading the account of someone like Morris it is possible to understand there may be some people born as one sex who sincerely believe that they should be in the body of the other sex. What is exceptionally hard – and what we currently have few means of knowing – is how to navigate the leap beyond biology into testimony. Intersex is biologically provable. Trans may in the years to come turn out to be psychologically or biologically provable. But we don't even have much idea which field it might ever come under. And if this seems like a needlessly nit-picking way to look at what is some people's entire sense of 'identity', then consider the difficulty of just one part of this delicate terrain.

AUTOGYNEPHILIA

If we start by recognizing that at one end of the spectrum there are people who are born intersex, and if we acknowledge that this is one of the clearest hardware issues of all, then the rest of the trans issue is clearly on a spectrum going inwards from there – from people who have visible, biological justification for being described as between the sexes to those with no proof of difference other than testimony. Where the provable hardware part of trans ends and where the 'software' part begins is one of the most dangerous speculative exercises of all. So let's begin.

Somewhere along the spectrum from people who are born intersex are those who have been born with conventional XX or XY chromosomes, the resulting genitalia and everything else that comes along with it, but who believe – for reasons that we are still almost nowhere near understanding – that they inhabit the wrong body. Their brain tells them they are a man, but their body is that of a woman. Or vice versa. As well as not knowing what, if anything, might cause this, we still have relatively little idea of how common it is. No meaningful physiological differences have been shown to exist between trans and non-trans people. And though there has been some study of differences in brain function, nothing to date has shown that there is a clear hardware reason why some people want to change from the body of one sex into that of another.

Yet there is still a push – as with homosexuality – to move the issue from software to hardware. In the world of trans this move has focused on a number of areas. One of them arises from an obvious reason for anyone to want to change sex: for a sexual thrill. A man may like to dress in ladies' underwear or even full female attire because it gives him a performative 'kick': the stockings; the feel of the lacy material; the transgression; the naughtiness. All of these have long been recognized as a sexual kink that some people yearn after. Among the technical terms for this instinct is the unlovely term 'autogynephilia'.

Autogynephilia is the arousal that comes from imagining yourself in the role of the opposite sex. But – nobody will be surprised to learn – there are divisions even within this 'community' and concerns and disputes over one type of autogynephilia versus another. For the different varieties of autogynephilia may range from a man's arousal at the idea of wearing an item of women's clothing all the way to arousal at the idea of actually having the body of a woman.

One of the most striking trends as the trans debate has picked up in recent years is that autogynephilia has come to be severely out of favour. Or to put it another way, the suggestion that people who identify as trans are in actual fact merely going through the ultimate extreme of a sexual kink has become so hateful to many trans individuals that it is one of a number of things now decried as hate speech.

In 2003 J. Michael Bailey, professor of psychology at Northwestern University, published his long-researched book *The Man Who Would Be Queen: The Science of Gender-Bending and Transsexualism*. In it Bailey looked at a different idea of transsexualism to the dominant one of a brain of one sex being trapped in the body of another. Specifically he looked at the possibility that trans was propelled by the object and nature of desire. Building on work carried out by Ray Blanchard at Canada's Centre for Addiction and Mental Health, he argued that a desire to change sex might be especially prevalent among a certain type of feminine gay man. As biological males attracted to other biological males it made sense for a particular type of gay man who could not attract straight men (due to being a man) or gay men (due to being too feminine) to pass as a woman, thus leading to more opportunities to attract the men who were the real object of desire. Blanchard used the term 'homosexual transsexuals' to describe this category of person.

In his book Bailey also explored another type of person who identifies as trans. This is a man who has always been heterosexual and may even have married and had children: men who when they announce that they wish to become a woman shock everyone around them. While they may never have shown any hint of femininity in their outer life, such people have in private found themselves sexually aroused by the idea of presenting as, or actually becoming, a woman. Bailey marshals a considerable amount of evidence to show that, of the two types of transgenderism he identifies, the first is more prevalent around the world. In many cultures it has been some sort of 'answer' to the conundrums presented by very feminine – most often gay – men. And although Bailey, like Blanchard, recognizes a difference between this and people propelled by autogynephilic impulses, neither in any way condemns or criticizes either group. Indeed, both argue for absolutely equal human rights, care and support. Nevertheless, Bailey was on top of the landmine.

In the years before his book was published there had been a concerted effort by trans campaigners to desexualize their cause. This had been one reason for the move away from talking about 'transsex' to 'transgender'. As Alice Dreger wrote in her book on this subject, 'Before Bailey, many trans advocates had spent a long time working to *de*sexualize and *de*pathologize their public representations in an effort to reduce stigma, improve access to care, and establish basic human rights for trans people.'[21] Dreger compares this with the successful effort by gay rights campaigners to achieve equal rights by taking the focus away from what gay people do in the bedroom and onto what they do in the other rooms of their house.

Bailey's book risked setting this campaign back, and so a campaign against it ensued, with fellow academics and trans campaigners immediately embarking on an effort not just to critique and dismiss Bailey's work but to get him sacked from his position at Northwestern

University. Among the more extreme of his critics was the Los Angeles-based transgender consultant Andrea James. She chose to retaliate against Bailey by posting pictures of his children (taken when they were in elementary and middle school) on her own website and juxtaposing these with sexually explicit captions.[22] Among other seemingly coordinated attacks, several people came forward to claim that they had been misrepresented in the book, only for it to transpire that they did not even feature in it. The book's nomination for an award from the gay literary organization LAMBDA was swiftly retracted. According to one friend of Bailey's, he had been so 'terrorized' by the extreme response to his book that he almost became a different person after its publication.[23]

All this happened simply because Bailey had performed detailed research to get to the root of a crucial question and come back with an answer that had just become unpopular. Because for the best part of this century so far the idea that trans is in any way about sexual enjoyment has become an outrage and sexualizing slur.

The correct idea for people to currently hold is that trans people get absolutely no sexual thrill from the idea of being trans. They positively hate it. Nothing could be more boring. So in November 2018 Andrea Long Chu wrote in *The New York Times* about the next phase of her gender reassignment surgery. As the headline for the piece by the Brooklyn-based 'essayist and critic' put it: 'My new vagina won't make me happy. And it shouldn't have to.' As Chu outlined in the piece: 'Next Thursday, I will get a vagina. The procedure will last around six hours, and I will be in recovery for at least three months. Until the day I die, my body will regard the vagina as a wound; as a result, it will require regular, painful attention to maintain. This is what I want, but there is no guarantee it will make me happier. In fact, I don't expect it to. That shouldn't disqualify me from getting it.'[24]

Although there has been some pushback in the work of Anne A. Lawrence (a self-declared autogynephilic[25]) and others, the idea that transsexualism is any way propelled by autogynephilia has become a considerable source of aggravation to trans campaigners. The reason for this sharp U-turn is obvious. And it takes us back to the hardware-software issue. If people have a particular sexual kink then it may be due either to hardware or to software. But it is hard to persuade society that it should change nearly all of its social and linguistic norms in order to accommodate those sexual kinks. Society may tolerate you. It may wish you well. But your desire to dress in lady's knickers is no reason to force everyone to use entirely new pronouns. Or to alter every public bathroom. Or to bring up children with the belief that there is no difference between the sexes and that gender is a social construct.

If trans were largely, mainly or solely about erotic stimulation then it should no more be a cause to change any societal fundamentals than it would be to change them for people who get a sexual thrill from wearing rubber. Autogynephilia risks presenting trans as a software issue. And that is the cause of the turn against it. For – as with homosexuals – there is a drive to prove that trans people are 'born this way'.

What makes all of this even more complex is the fact that built into the actions of many trans people is something that surely demonstrates (as in the case of Jan Morris) that their desire to be in the body of the opposite sex surely cannot be a mere fantasy or kink. After all, it is hard to think of anything which demands more commitment from a person than the decision to have irreversible surgery that permanently transforms their body. Any man willing to have his penis cut off or flayed and then turned inside out can hardly be said to be taking matters lightly. Such a procedure might be considered the precise opposite of a hobby or lifestyle choice. Yet even this does not 'prove' that trans is a hardware issue. For there are almost no extremes that some people will not go to in order to satisfy something they believe to be true. The question becomes about whether what one person or even a lot of people believe to be true about themselves has to be accepted as true by other people or not.

THE TRANS BREAKTHROUGH

This lack of evidence is one reason why some people believe that the whole trans issue is a delusion. And this undertow of suspicion exists even while society as a whole is being encouraged to accept trans people's claims on their own terms.

In April 2015 the former Olympic athlete and reality television star Bruce Jenner came out as a trans and revealed his new identity as Caitlyn Jenner. She immediately became perhaps the highest-profile trans person in the world. Within weeks she was on the front cover of *Vanity Fair* with the headline 'Call me Caitlyn'. The Annie Leibovitz photo shoot showed Jenner in a slinky corset-set, showing off the top of her breasts, while the bottom part rode up to what the world would learn were her yet to be removed male genitalia. Leibovitz's shoot cleverly got around the most visibly male parts of Jenner's anatomy. Not just with the crossed legs getting around the bulge issue, but with her arms tucked behind the body so as to reduce the former Olympian's shoulders and biceps. One year earlier *Time* magazine had put the trans actress Laverne Cox on its cover with the headline 'The Transgender Tipping Point: America's Next Civil Rights Frontier'.[26] That feeling of a new frontier needing to be broken through was in the air. As Ruth Hunt of Stonewall said when the group added transgender campaigning to their work, 'It's their turn now.'[27] Gay had essentially been done. And everybody seemed to know the contours of racial and women's advancement. Some people – perhaps especially legacy magazines with falling circulations – seemed ripe for a new civil rights battle. Caitlyn Jenner's timing turned out to be perfect.

The year 2015 was the one in which trans rights, visibility and demands went mainstream and Jenner was everywhere. Aside from the ubiquitous Leibovitz shoot, there were months when it seemed Jenner had made a clean sweep through every awards ceremony in America. *Glamour* magazine named her one of its 'women of the year'. At the ESPYs (Excellence in Sports Performance Yearly award) Jenner was awarded the Courage Award and was given a standing ovation by the arena full of sports men and women. Like everything else in the growing trans story, every fragment and splinter of it had the potential to take out anybody who even hesitated before the stampede. Or in the ovation.

During and after the ESPYs the American Football quarterback Brett Favre was lambasted first on social media and then in the rest of the media for not clapping Jenner enthusiastically enough. Although Favre joined the standing ovation for Jenner he controversially took his seat again before everyone else in the audience had taken theirs, and this was caught on camera. For this behaviour the *New York Post* denounced the culprit's insufficient enthusiasm with a piece headlined 'Brett Favre makes the ESPYs uncomfortable for everyone'.[28] Nobody seemed certain precisely how many seconds of standing ovation it was correct to give a trans woman receiving an award for courage. Some attention to the etiquette in the Soviet Politburo might have helped. The only lesson unarguably imparted was that if everyone is applauding a trans person you should make sure that you are the last person to resume your seat.

Other shards from the Jenner controversy struck with equally unpredictable regularity. In July 2015 the then 31-year-old conservative commentator Ben Shapiro was among a number of guests invited onto *Dr Drew On Call* on HLN to discuss Jenner's courage award. One of the other guests, seated beside Shapiro in the studio, was Zoey Tur, who was introduced as a 'Transgender reporter'. Some way into the discussion Tur was asked by Dr Drew whether Jenner was really 'brave'. Tur expressed the view that 'being brave is being yourself', and being transgender is 'about the bravest thing you can do'.

At this point Shapiro expressed his view that by celebrating Jenner people were 'mainstreaming delusion'. 'Why would you call it "delusion"?' asked another, outraged, female guest. Shapiro continued and in passing referred to Jenner as 'him' rather than 'her'. Although Jenner had been Bruce for 66 years and had only identified as Caitlyn for three months, everybody else in the studio immediately turned on Shapiro, criticizing him for being rude. 'It's her,' the same outraged woman insisted. 'You're not being polite to the pronouns. It's disrespectful.'

Ignoring how you can be polite or otherwise to pronouns, Shapiro dug in. 'Forget about the disrespect,' he said. 'Facts don't care about your feelings. It turns out that every chromosome, every cell in Caitlyn Jenner's body, is male, with the exception of some of his sperm cells. It turns out that he still has all of his male appendages. How he feels on the inside is irrelevant to the question of his biological self.' At which point the only other guest in the studio who had expressed mild criticism of Jenner getting the award (on the basis that Jenner was rich and white and had not been sufficiently outspoken in the past on LGBT issues) swiftly announced that he was not 'on board' with what had just been said. Perhaps the distancing was necessary given what followed.

The host tried to calm things down and invited Tur to tell everyone about the science of gender dysphoria. Tur announced, 'We both know chromosomes don't necessarily mean you're male or female.' She then put a patronizing hand on Shapiro's shoulder and told him, 'So you don't know what you're talking about. You're not educated in genetics.' Shapiro tried to ask whether or not they were allowed to discuss genetics but was interrupted again. And so he then said to Tur, 'What are your genetics, sir?' At which point Tur put her hand on the back of Shapiro's neck and said menacingly, 'You cut that out now, or you'll go home in an ambulance.'

A fairly unfazed Shapiro said, 'That seems mildly inappropriate for a political discussion.' And while it would ordinarily be assumed that other guests might frown at a threat of violence in the studio, the present dynamics were such that everyone instead turned on Shapiro. 'But to be fair, you're actually being kind of rude, and that's not fair,' one of the other male guests proclaimed. Another male guest denounced Shapiro, saying that he must have known that saying 'sir' would be 'egregiously insulting'. After all of which Tur was allowed to tell Shapiro, unchallenged, 'You're consumed with hatred. That is who you are. You're a little man.'

Shapiro had not lost his temper during any of this. He had not 'trolled' Tur. After she had threatened to send him home in an ambulance he had not said, 'That's not very ladylike behaviour.' He had not waited for her to punch him and then told her 'Gosh you punch like a man.' He had not even pointed out how strange it was for somebody who had done what Tur had done to their body to now be trying to emasculate him by denigrating his size. Shapiro had simply stuck to a point about the significance of biology that would have been uncontroversial even a few years earlier but which was now held with such widespread opprobrium among the media and celebrity classes that they would rather defend a threat of physical assault than someone who had not been 'polite to the pronouns'.

The swiftness and near-completeness of the stampede in one direction may have had several causes. One (exemplified in the *Time* magazine cover) was the fear, suspicion or hope that trans is the new gay, women's or civil rights and that anybody caught on the wrong side of the trans fence in this decade will look back as regretfully – and be looked upon as negatively – as society looks back on those who argued against those movements. And in some sense the similarity is there. If there is nothing genetically different about gay people then the only thing that signifies a difference is their behaviour. Gay people are gay when they say they are and when they do the things that show them to be gay. Likewise, perhaps, people are trans when they say they are, and no outward sign – or any biological signifier – need be there in the trans case any more than it is expected (or demanded) in the case of being gay.

But there is one very significant difference. If a gay woman falls in love with a man or a gay man suddenly falls in love with a woman, or a straight man or woman suddenly falls in love with a member of their own sex, all of their existing biological hardware is still in place. A gay person who goes straight or a straight person who goes gay is doing nothing that is permanent or irreversible. Whereas the end-point of trans advocates is irreversible and life-altering. People expressing concern or urging caution in regard to transsexualism may not be 'denying the existence of trans people' or claiming that they should be treated as second-class citizens, let alone (the most catastrophizing claim of all) causing trans people to commit suicide. They may simply be urging caution about something which has not remotely been worked out yet – and which is irreversible.

A concern which many people stifle in public arises precisely from this concern about irreversibility. News of an increase in the number of children claiming to be gender-dysphoric, and the growing evidence of a 'cluster effect' when such claims begin to be made (that is, that once a number of children in a school claim to be in the wrong body similar claims expand exponentially), means that parents and others are not wrong to be wondering and worrying about where this is all leading. Questions about the age at which people who believe they are in the wrong body should be allowed to access drugs or surgery are worth contesting deeply. Not least because there is growing awareness of children who may have identified as having gender dysphoria but who then grow out of it – many of them to become gay. This heaps problem upon problem. Nobody likes recalling the time when gay people were told 'it's just a phase', but what if trans is (even on occasion) just a phase? And what if that phase is realized only too late? These questions are not primarily 'transphobic' but rather child-centric, and the attempt to pathologize such concern has made this tripwire far uglier than it needs to be.

ONE YOUNG MAN'S STORY

Naturally this is a sensitive subject and for that reason I am going to change the name of the person I am about to describe. Let us call him 'James'. But the person is real, his case is not uncommon and he is the sort of person whose story should at least be in the mix in the societal discussion now under way.

Now in his twenties, James was born and brought up in the UK. In his mid-teens he found himself attracted to the gay scene and to the drag scene in particular. He had a lot of gay friends and from the age of about 16 began to spend a lot of time in drag clubs. He liked the people, he liked the scene and its closeness. The people he found there seemed to him almost like a 'lost generation of people' who huddled together in this world because they were worried their parents would disown them if they knew they were gay or liked doing drag. As a result these people didn't just have fun together, they became 'like a family'. Eventually James himself started doing a bit of drag. Around this time he also became very close friends with someone in their early twenties who had transitioned from male to female – a person who seemed to James to be completely fabulous.

At around the age of 18 James went to his family doctor and plucked up the courage to tell him, 'I think I'm in the wrong body. I think I might be a woman.' For the year and a half or so after this he started travelling around seeing different doctors, trying to find one who had a better sense than his family doctor had about what he was actually going through. Finally at the age of 19 he got a referral to a psycho-sexual service in Manchester and sat for three and a half hours of psychoanalysis. He was asked about his sex life, his relationship with his parents and much more. In fact he was slightly taken aback by how intimate the questions were. But the counsellor's conclusion in Manchester was clear. 'You're trans,' he was told. And so he was referred to the gender identity clinic at Charing Cross in London.

The waiting room there was colourful, with everyone from 'the very feminine to Bob the Builder in a wig'. Six months later a workshop of around 20 of them were brought together. The consultant gave them the National Health Service's best understanding of what had brought them to that room. They were told (as Dr Benjamin had told Morris),

'We know it is a problem with the brain. We can't operate on the brain so we do our best to make the body match the brain.' And this then became the NHS's role in dealing with the case of James and others. Six months after that workshop he had his first one-on-one interview, which went into considerable detail. There were questions about relationships and work. The all-round stability of the person was obviously important. James saw endocrinologists and had a testosterone reading. The fact that the reading was low on one occasion (in fact it varied at other readings) was taken as proof that there was indeed a trans issue that needed addressing. Looking back, James is struck by a number of things. One is that he was never offered any counselling. How he said he thought he felt was just accepted. And there was another thing. 'It was all a bit too nice,' he says now. There was 'never any pressure'. Never any 'grilling'.

Two years of living as a member of the opposite sex is taken as proof that the person can go to the next stage. And since the NHS meetings were all six months apart, James came up to his two-year mark after only a few of them. At this stage the issue of hormone replacement therapy came up. As James says, 'If you're patient and play the game it is ridiculously easy to get hormones. You just turn up twice a year and wait.' And of course people in the groups as well as friends on the scene swop stories of how to get to this next stage.

James went on oestrogen, which included daily doses as well as injections. Accounts from him and from others about the nature of this process hits – among much else – right at the heart of claims that there are no essential differences between the sexes. Indeed, in any other context the descriptions of the effects of oestrogen on the male body would be considered wildly sexist. James's experience was much like that of others who start taking oestrogen and anti-androgens (testosterone blockers). Among the things that happened was that he became more emotional than he had been before. 'I cried a lot.' His skin began to soften and his body fat began to redistribute. But he noticed other things. The movies and even the music he liked began to change – as did what he liked in bed.

James took the oestrogen for more than a year. He had been a late developer and there was speculation over whether he had in fact still got a small amount of puberty to go through when he had begun taking hormones. He also had two meetings – one by Skype and one in person – about the possibility of moving to the next stage. He knew that the backlog of cases meant the NHS couldn't be hurried to this part of the process, but he says that he raised with them the possibility of going for private treatment abroad for gender reassignment surgery. A place in Marbella on the Costa del Sol had been recommended by a number of people and he says that the NHS neither tried to endorse nor stop him when he mentioned that he was thinking of taking this route. He got information on the costs of procedures, drugs and even flights. 'I came very close to doing it,' he says. 'I am very glad now that I didn't.'

Even during the time that he had been on hormones and had been looking to going to the next stage of transitioning, a number of things had begun to preoccupy him. So far James had only really heard one side of the argument. His friends on the trans scene had shown him a path down which he might go too. And the NHS had not seriously questioned the wisdom of his going down this path. They had treated him as someone with a condition that needed fixing. But online James sought – and found – contrary points of view. Through alternative media he discovered YouTube stars and others who were questioning the wisdom of his decision, including younger and hipper people than he had expected. He was also struggling with his faith. Brought up as a liberal Christian, he went around and around questions of God and design. On the one hand, 'If God doesn't exist then my body isn't designed.' But he also came to think that people who said that they had been born in the wrong body took a very egocentric view of things, as though this was 'a challenge that had been given to them'. If the whole universe was a coincidence, 'Why do so much so drastically for the sake of changing myself?' He began to wonder whether the answer to some of his questions didn't lie in psychology rather than surgery. Specifically he began to look at 'what I need to do to be content with my body, not change my body'. Of all the consultants he had spoken to, none had engaged him in questions like these. 'I was never encouraged to look into it too deeply.'

There was something else which made James begin to wonder whether this was really something that he wanted. As he and others in his circle were well aware, anyone who takes hormones for a period of years will eventually notice effects which are irreversible. These happen after around two years of anti-androgen treatment. And as James approached his second year on anti-androgens he began to feel nervous. The NHS had no emergency appointments for him to consult with a doctor because they were so overwhelmed with people coming to them to consult on gender reassignment. He would have to wait another six months. But James felt he couldn't wait that long. He faced not only physical changes that risked becoming permanent, but also biological facts. After more than two years on anti-androgens most men will become infertile and so incapable of ever being able to father a child. James was wondering not only whether he really wanted to become a woman, but also whether he might not one day want to be a father. He had a boyfriend and the boyfriend was not convinced that James was actually a woman. His boyfriend just thought that James was gay like him. James himself felt that the hormones were bringing him to 'the point of being permanent'.

And so after considering all of these things, unilaterally, and without any support or advice from the doctors who had put him on the hormones, James decided to come off them. He described coming off them as 'very intense'. The changes it brought about were 'much more severe' than when he started on the hormones. He suffered terrible mood swings. And while taking oestrogen made him cry more and change his taste in movies, when testosterone came back into his body it had an equally 'sexist' set of effects. He noticed a lot of common behaviours. He became more angry, more aggressive and – yes – far more horny.

Today he has been off hormones for more than two years. But the effects of his time 'transitioning' across the sexes is still with him. He thinks he may be 'just about alright' but he may also be permanently sterile. More immediate is the fact that he still has breasts, or what he refers to as 'breast tissue'. When asked about this he shyly pulls aside one side of the top of his T-shirt. There is a strap visible. It is a compression vest that he wears at all times in order to try to hide the fact that he has this breast tissue. His clothes are noticeably baggy and he obviously avoids anything that might be figure-hugging. He thinks he will probably have to have surgery to remove the remaining breast tissue.

With some of the perspective afforded by time he is able to think about his changes over recent years. 'I do believe transgenderism exists,' he says. The sheer volume of people who are moving in this direction at the moment is one thing that suggests this to him. But he says the whole area hasn't been looked at or thought about with nearly enough rigour. The whole idea remains fixed on things, as he puts it, like 'So you don't like rugby. Interesting.' When he told the psychoanalyst in Manchester that he didn't get on with all the boys at his primary school, the response was, he says, 'Aha'. As it was when he told them that as a boy he sometimes dressed in his sister's Pocahontas dress.

'I've always thought it was curious that the NHS didn't look at wider options,' he says. And from the moment that he went to consult the experts he 'felt like I was on a conveyor belt'. The NHS was overstretched, with only two doctors in the UK doing gender reassignment surgery, one full time, one part time. But the doctors were always promising that with around 3,000 people already in treatment and another 5,000 reportedly on the waiting list in the UK, the NHS was busily training up lots more people to deal with the demand. Maybe some patients will hesitate, as James did, when the conveyor belt brings them up to the point of surgery. But even then, as James's baggy clothes attest, the process is not in any way cost-free.

James is gay – 'very gay' as he puts it at one stage. And he feels that he has always been 'a bit of a social chameleon. Probably the people I was spending time with had an effect.' But he says, 'I don't want to be one of those people who says that trans makes more trans.' It is too close, in his opinion, to the old claim that gay people cause more gay people. 'But there is something in it,' he adds: 'The thing of "My really cool trans friend"'. He is confused, like everyone else, about what trans may or may not be. 'If anything, we just need to know more,' he says. For instance, why is it the case that suicide rates don't change between pre- and post-op trans? 'We're running too quickly,' he says. 'It's like a knee jerk. We're terrified of being on the wrong side of history.' But he knows it could have been worse. Looking back at how close he came to surgery, James reflects, 'I dread to think what position I'd be in now. I don't know if I would be here now.'

Listening to James's story – which resembles those of many others – one of the things that stands out is how much we pretend to know, but how little we know. How fast we appear to be to landing on solutions to questions we haven't answered yet. But another thing that stands out is the way in which trans just keeps invading so many of the other controversy-laden subjects of our time.

Gay rights campaigners have argued for years that anybody can be gay and that the historical view of gay people being effeminate men and masculine women is not just outmoded and ignorant, but prejudiced and homophobic. And then along comes another rights claim which is so close that it even gets to share an acronym with 'gay'. But this one suggests something infinitely more undermining than the idea that certain behavioural characteristics are typical of gay people. The trans claim keeps suggesting that people who are slightly effeminate or don't like the right sports are not merely gay but potentially inhabiting the wrong body and are in fact men, or women, inside. Given the number of connotations it is surprising that so few gay men and women have objected to some of the claims that have become embedded in the trans movement. Gay groups have generally agreed that trans rights exist within their orbit, forming part of the same continuum and acronym. Yet many of the claims made by trans do not simply run in contravention to the claims of the gay movement: they profoundly undermine them. 'Some people are gay. Or possibly trans. Or the other way round. Get over it.'

But it isn't just gay that trans runs against. Rather than 'unlocking' the intersections of oppression, as the intersectionalists had claimed, trans simultaneously throw their own movement's aims into the starkest possible relief and produce a veritable pile-up of logical contradictions.

At Wellesley College in 2014 there was a fascinating case where a student arriving at the all-female college announced that she was a 'masculine of centre genderqueer person' who wanted to be known as 'Timothy' and expected people to use male pronouns. Despite having applied to Hillary Clinton's *alma mater* as a girl, the other students reportedly had no problem in particular with their male-identifying contemporary. That is, until Timothy announced that he wanted to run for the position of multicultural affairs coordinator: the purpose of this role being to promote a 'culture of diversity' on the university campus. It might have been expected that a 'masculine of centre genderqueer person' might have the perfect scorecard for the position. Except that students at Wellesley reportedly felt that having Timothy in such a position would perpetuate the patriarchy at the college. A campaign got under way to abstain in the election. One student behind the 'campaign to abstain' said, 'I thought he'd do a perfectly fine job, but it just felt inappropriate to have a white man there.'[29]

In one way Timothy had gone all the way around the oppression cycle. From woman, to trans, to white man and therefore to the personification of the white patriarchy. From minority to oppressor. Where female to male transitioners can create one pile-up, male to female transitioners produce another of their own – most obviously with people who have been born as women. And on this occasion, unlike the 'G' bit of LGBT, the women who feel their turf being trodden over have not all been silent. Indeed, it is this portion of the new intersectional rights alliance that has gone south fastest.

THE FEMINIST TRIPWIRE

The women who have tripped on the trans tripwire over recent years have a number of things in common, but one is that they have all been at the forefront of every women's issue. And this makes perfect sense. For if a significant amount of modern rights campaigning is based on people wishing to prove that their cause is a hardware issue, then trans forces other movements to go in precisely the opposite direction. Trans campaigners intent on arguing that trans is hardware can only win their argument if they persuade people that being a woman is a matter of software. And not all feminists are willing to concede that one.

The British journalist Julie Bindel has been one of the most consistent and hard-fighting feminists in Britain or anywhere else in the world. As one of the founders of Justice for Women she has campaigned since 1991 to help women who have been imprisoned or threatened with imprisonment for killing their violent male partners. As an out lesbian and a lifelong feminist of the pre-third- and fourth-wave variety, Bindel has never kept any of her views to herself. And in the early part of this century she started to notice that people who had been born men and were now demanding to be regarded, and treated, as women (whether they had had any surgery or not) were all over what had been her area – including the most understandably sensitive parts.

In 2002 Bindel was specially incensed by news from Canada where a Vancouver Human Rights Tribunal had ruled that a male-to-female transsexual named Kimberley Nixon should be allowed to train as a counsellor for female rape victims. Indeed, the tribunal had ruled that Vancouver Rape Relief's refusal to allow Nixon to train for this role had breached her human rights. The tribunal awarded Nixon $7,500 for injury to 'her dignity', the highest such amount it had ever awarded. The decision was later overturned by the British Columbia Supreme Court in Vancouver. But for a feminist of Bindel's generation the idea that even in rape-counselling a woman could not be certain that the female helping them was actually female was a Rubicon that could not be crossed. She let rip, in the pages of *The Guardian*, defending the Rape Relief sisters who 'do not believe a surgically constructed vagina and hormonally grown breasts make you a woman'. She warmed up, 'For now at least, the law says that to suffer discrimination as a woman you have to be, er, a woman.' Perhaps Bindel knew the world of pain she was getting into, perhaps not. But in the early 2000s it was easier to tread on this landmine than it soon would be. In any case, she rounded off her tirade with a flourish. 'I don't have a problem with men disposing of their genitals, but it does not make them women, in the same way that shoving a bit of vacuum hose down your 501s does not make you a man.'[30]

For this phrase in particular, and for the article as a whole, Bindel was going to suffer for the rest of her life. In the first phase the newspaper was flooded with letters of complaint. Bindel herself swiftly apologized for the tone of the article. But in the years that followed she found it hard to speak in public without efforts to cancel her speeches or her appearance on panels. When she was allowed to speak, aggressive protests and pickets were often arranged to stop her. Even a decade later she was forced to cancel an appearance on a panel at the University of Manchester after dozens of rape and death threats against her were reported to the police.

Bindel may have been one of the first left-wing feminists to trip the trans wire and suffer the consequences, but she was certainly not the last. In January 2013 Suzanne Moore fired a column off to the left-wing *New Statesman* magazine about the power of female anger. The column addressed many of the injustices against women that Moore could see, from the patronizing of female members of parliament to attitudes towards abortion and her claim that 65 per cent of cutbacks in the public sector affected women. Unfortunately for Moore, amid this blizzard of points she included the claim about women themselves that 'We are angry with ourselves for not being happier, not being loved properly and not having the ideal body shape – that of a Brazilian transsexual.'[31] If an article could have a puff of smoke over it, then Moore's was it.

In the real world and the virtual one it was clear that Moore had made a serious error. Among the more printable accusations against her was that she was a 'transphobe'. Moore did not help matters by responding that, among other things, she did not care for the word. People who were used to beating women down with the accusation were even more furious that their weapon had not worked. Nevertheless, so vociferous and furious was the backlash that within hours Moore was having to 'clarify' her views and assure readers that she was not the hate-filled figure she was now called.[32] A day earlier she had been a progressive left-wing feminist. Now she was a reactionary hate-filled right-wing bigot. After being hounded by trans people and others accusing her of the most base bigotry, Moore announced that to avoid the 'bullies' and 'trolls' she was leaving social media.

One of the people who took all this least well was Julie Burchill. The *enfant terrible* of 1980s journalism, Burchill had developed her reputation not just as a literary stylist but as a literary pugilist. In her own description, the sight of her friend Suzanne Moore being bullied, at risk of losing her job and livelihood for one passing trans reference, was too much for her.

In Burchill's reckoning Moore was not just a friend but one of the very few other women like her from a working-class background who had made it in journalism. Burchill was not going to allow her 'homey' to go down without someone fighting more nastily for her at her side. And so in that Sunday's *Observer* Burchill decided to hide Moore's puff of smoke by producing a mushroom cloud.

Among much else Burchill attacked Moore's critics for attacking a woman. As Burchill put it, women like her and Moore had had to go through their whole lives as women. They had suffered through period pains, batting off sexual advances from male strangers, gone through childbirth, had stared the menopause in the face and now had the delights of hormone replacement therapy. Women like Moore and her were damned if they were now going to be lectured at or called names by 'dicks in chicks' clothing' and 'a bunch of bed-wetters in bad wigs'.

The response was instantaneous. The British Home Office minister in charge of 'Equalities', Lynne Featherstone, immediately declared that Burchill's 'rant against the transgender community' was not merely 'disgusting' and 'a bigoted vomit' but something 'for which the *Observer* should sack her'. The minister also called for the editor of the paper to lose his job. Duly cowed, the *Observer* issued an apology for the column and swiftly unpublished it from its website. In the apology issued by the paper's editor explaining why the paper had chosen to 'withdraw' the piece from publication, John Mulholland wrote, 'We got it wrong and in light of the hurt and offence caused I apologise and have made the decision to withdraw the piece.' Something which is very nearly unheard of in British journalism. Five years later Burchill herself blamed this episode as one of the reasons why her own career in journalism had ended up, as she put it, 'up the creek'.[33] Meanwhile, though the woman who had called for her sacking, Lynne Featherstone, soon lost her seat in Parliament, she was immediately given a lifetime sinecure in the House of Lords.

The next person to go up the same creek as Bindel and Burchill was perhaps the most famous modern feminist of all. The author of *The Female Eunuch* had only dealt with trans issues in depth once in her career. In her 1999 book *The Whole Woman* Germaine Greer devoted a ten-page chapter ('Pantomime Dames') to her contention that people who were born men could not be classed as women. Although it wasn't the main point she was making, she referred in passing to the 'mutilation' that 'transsexuals opt for'. She decried the fact that so many male-to-female transsexuals chose the 'profoundly conservative' body shape that she believed reinforced stereotypes. And she was alive to the fact that none of the surgical procedures often talked about so blithely was remotely straightforward. In 1977 the gender clinic at Stanford University had said that its two-stage sex-change procedure in fact required an average of three and a half operations, and that at least 50 per cent of the patients experienced some form of complication, often making the relationship between surgeons and patient lifelong.[34] Greer also put her finger on something that very few other people noticed, but which parents of children claiming to suffer from gender dysphoria soon began to worry about: the fact that the transsexual 'is identified as such solely on his/her own script, which can be as learned as any sex-typed behaviour and as editorialized as autobiographies usually are'.[35]

Greer had not pursued the subject in the years that followed. But it took only a decade and a half for her views to become firmly outside the acceptable norm. In late 2015 Greer was due to deliver a lecture at Cardiff University on the subject 'Women and Power: The Lessons of the 20th Century'. However, a significant number of students didn't want to hear from the most significant feminist of the late twentieth century. Instead, they lobbied their university with the excommunicating words of their time.

Greer's views on trans issues were, they said, 'problematic'. She had demonstrated 'time and time again her misogynistic views towards trans women'. Only years earlier it would have been deemed the height of insanity to dismiss Greer as a misogynist. Yet here they were, with the anti-Greer petition organizer describing herself as into 'lefty queer feminist politics'. These students claimed that among Greer's crimes was 'continually misgendering trans women and denying the existence of transphobia altogether'. Whilst acknowledging that 'debate in a university should be encouraged', the petitioners warned that 'hosting a speaker with such problematic and hateful views towards marginalized and vulnerable groups is dangerous'.[36]

In a subsequent BBC interview about the controversy Greer said, 'Apparently people have decided that because I don't think that post-operative transgender men are women, I'm not to be allowed to talk. I'm not saying that people should not be allowed to go through that procedure. What I'm saying is it doesn't make them a woman. It happens to be an opinion, it's not a prohibition.' What is more, as Greer explained, trans issues weren't even something she talked about much. 'They're not my issue. I haven't published anything about transgender for years.' But for the trouble of even touching this rail, she said, 'I've had things thrown at me, I've been accused of things I have never done or said, people seem to have no concern about evidence or indeed, even about libel.' Asked whether she would still bother to turn up at Cardiff University she responded: 'I'm getting a bit old for all this. I'm 76. I don't want to go down there and be screamed at and have things thrown at me. Bugger it. It's not that interesting or rewarding.'[37]

But insulting Greer, and indeed excommunicating her from the latest version of feminism, became a rite of passage for a generation of women who had – whether they knew it or not – benefited from her trailblazing. In *Varsity* magazine at Cambridge University (Greer's own alma mater in the 1960s) Eve Hodgson wrote an article headlined 'Germaine Greer can no longer be called a feminist.' According to its author, 'Greer is now just an old, white woman who has forced herself into exile. Her comments are irreparably damaging, reflecting a total lack of regard for trans lives. Thinking what she thinks, she cannot be a prominent feminist any longer. She no longer stands for the same things we do.'[38] Just as Peter Thiel was no longer gay and Kanye West no longer black, so Germaine Greer was no longer a feminist.

As the years went on it became clear that this attitude of contempt for one's forebears was not limited to the universities, but had spilled out everywhere. And the presumption that feminists of Greer's generation were to be vilified for their attitudes on trans became completely normalized. In September 2018 a stay-at-home mum in the north of England called Kellie-Jay Keen-Minshull paid £700 to hire a billboard in Liverpool. The poster she had put up consisted simply of a dictionary definition. In full the poster read: 'woman: women, noun, adult human female'. Keen-Minshull said that she had paid for the poster because of her concern that 'woman' was a word that was 'being appropriated to mean anything'. But the dictionary definition did not stay up for long. An academic and self-proclaimed 'ally of the transgender community' called Dr Adrian Harrop complained to the police that the billboard was a 'symbol that makes transgender people feel unsafe'.[39] In a subsequent television discussion a Sky presenter accused Keen-Minshull of being 'transphobic' for putting up the poster. And after Harrop had told off Keen-Minshull for not using his full title of 'Dr' when referring to him, he then explained that excluding trans women from a definition of women 'is not something that is appropriate in a modern and progressive society'.[40] Even right-wing and conservative news sites ran stories about Keen-Minshull's TV appearances, headlining that she had been 'branded "disgraceful"' by viewers for 'insisting' that trans women are not the same as women.[41]

Women who tried to hold the boundary of womanhood around women started inviting the same vitriol everywhere. At the 'London Pride' event in 2018 a group of lesbian campaigners spoilt the LGBT party by protesting at what they saw as the transgender takeover of the celebrations. The UK gay press accused these women ('TERFS') of bigotry and hate speech, and a few weeks later at Manchester Pride there were reportedly 'loud cheers' when a gay male MC announced that the protestors in London should have been dragged off by their 'saggy tits'.[42]

Amid the no-platforming, threats and silencing, one question which is rarely asked is why feminists of a particular tradition should not object to elements – at least – of the emerging trans argument. The more women get chased away for treading on this terrain the clearer the point of contention becomes. Feminists like Bindel, Greer and Burchill come from the schools of feminism which remain concerned with matters of women's reproductive rights, the rights of women to escape violent and abusive relationships and much more. They are also women who believed in breaking down the stereotypes over what a woman should be or could be. Perhaps the most obvious point of non-overlap with the trans movement is that in many ways trans does not challenge social constructs about gender, but reinforces them.

Consider a prominent male-to-female transsexual YouTuber like Blaire White, who on becoming a woman (prior to announcing a de-transition late in 2018, in order to father children) adopted the body type of a sort of teenage male fantasy pin-up woman: all prominent breasts, flicking hair and pouting lips. Or consider the other end of the female archetype spectrum. In December 2015 Julie Bindel was finally allowed to speak at the University of Manchester where she appeared on a panel with the trans writer and activist Jane Fae. During Bindel's speech and at other points in the event Fae sat knitting a purpley-pink garment of some kind. She had brought her knitting with her. Or consider April Ashley, who in one documentary film celebrating her 80th birthday in 2015 was shown going back to her childhood haunts in Liverpool, where she was receiving the keys to the city. Throughout the film it is impossible to throw off a sense that Ashley is auditioning as a stand-in body-double for HM the Queen.[43] Despite the vilification that a particular generation of feminists has received for not getting on the trans train, it is never explained why they should. Their language may be colourful when they attack this target – as when they attack other targets – but the accusations of being hateful, dangerous, encouraging violence and even of not being feminists sidestep the legitimate questions they raise. Why should certain feminists feel entirely fine about men who become women only then to either flaunt their perfect breasts, ape the royal family or take up knitting?

THE PARENTS

The late Robert Conquest once adumbrated three rules of politics, the first of which was that 'everybody is conservative about what he knows best'. And parents, it might be said, know about their children best. One explanation for a recent upsurge in critical questions being asked about the nature of trans is that parents in countries like America and Britain are beginning to worry about what the next generation is being taught. They are also worried about what, in some cases, is already being done.

Parents worry when they hear the San Francisco-based developmental psychologist Diane Ehrensaft claim that a one-year-old 'assigned male' baby who unsnaps a onesie and waves it in a particular way is in fact giving a 'pre-verbal communication about gender'.[44] Unlike parts of the media, parents do not rejoice in a nine-year-old drag queen being given a modelling contract with an LGBT fashion company and telling other children in a viral YouTube video, 'If you wanna be a drag queen and your parents don't let you, you need new parents.'[45] And they worry when their child's school allows anyone who says they are the opposite gender to be recognized and treated as such. One parent from the north of England recently described how her 16-year-old daughter came out first as a lesbian and then as trans. When her mother and father attended a parents' evening they discovered that the school had already been using their daughter's chosen male name and were using male pronouns to describe her. 'The school was "full on affirming".'[46]

Advice to schools from the Scottish government is that the parents of a child should not be told if their child wishes to change gender. Elsewhere the Scottish government's document 'Supporting Transgender Young People' suggests that pupils should be able to compete in sports in the gender that they feel comfortable with and that parents should not be informed if their child wants to share rooms with members of the opposite sex on school trips. In other parts of Britain parents have told of going to parents' evenings where a teacher called their child by the 'wrong' gender, only to be told by the teacher, 'Oh didn't you know, your son/daughter identifies as a girl/boy.' This happens at schools which have to get parental permission to issue their child with an aspirin during the school day.

Parents are also becoming familiar with the phenomenon known as 'clustering'. For example, in 2018 the 'equality information report' at one school in Brighton known for its 'liberal vibe' had 40 pupils between the ages of 11 and 16 who 'do not identify as [the] gender presented at birth'. A further 36 pupils said they were gender fluid, meaning that they did not identify with their assigned gender at birth 'all the time'. One effect of all this is that the UK has seen a 700 per cent rise in child referrals to gender clinics in just five years.[47]

Of course trans campaigners like the group Mermaids suggest that the clustering and the increase in referrals is happening because some people are simply more aware of the possibility that they are trans than they would have been even a few years ago. But other explanations are at least equally possible. One is the way that trans is portrayed in popular culture – especially online. Another is the increasing number of concessions to any and all trans demands by figures in authority.

In online culture it is not at all unusual for the taking of hormones to be turned into an absurdly easy and consequence-free exercise. On YouTube, Instagram and other sites there are countless people who say that they are trans and who push the idea that you might be too. A single video by Jade Boggess (a female-to-male transsexual) called 'One year on testosterone' has more than half a million views on YouTube alone. Another by Ryan Jacobs Flores about the same subject has more than three million views. In such videos testosterone injections become known as 'T' or 'man juice'. Some of these people who are transitioning in real time become celebrities in their own right. Not older figures like Caitlyn Jenner, but bright, bubbly new YouTube stars like Jazz Jennings.

Born a boy in 2000, Jennings began to appear on the media talking about being transgender at the age of six. At the age of seven the child was interviewed by Barbara Walters, who among her other questions asked who the child was attracted to. The promotion of Jennings was unabated. At the age of 11 the Oprah Winfrey Network broadcast a documentary on her called *I am Jazz*. As a teenager Jennings has received numerous media awards and been put in 'Most Influential' lists. There have also been product promotion deals, and the other advantages of fame. The documentary series *I am Jazz* on TLC is now in its fifth season and continues to make her, her parents and siblings (who all appear on the show) both famous and rich. Season 5 follows Jazz turning 18 and going into her 'gender confirmation surgery'. On the trolley she clicks her fingers sassily and says 'Let's do this.' The YouTube excerpts alone of 'I am Jazz' have received millions of views.

But it is not just the element of popular culture in this that is likely to be having an effect. There is also the willing agreement of medical professionals. On series like *I am Jazz* it is clear that there are medical professionals perfectly happy to do everything they can to help turn somebody who was born a boy into a girl. It is all part of a slide of acceptance which led the NHS in England to sign an agreement that NHS professionals will never 'suppress an individual's expression of gender identity'.[48] But despite some healthcare professionals warning about the potential for 'overdiagnosis and overtreatment' the assumptions all continue to go in just one direction.

ONE FAMILY'S STORY

This is the experience of just one American parent whose family has had to navigate the trans journey in recent years. To protect the identity of the child I will be deliberately vague about locations and some specifics. But the family were living in one of the big cities of America and have only fairly recently moved to a more rural location. This is where they are when I speak with the child's mother, who I will call Sarah.

Sarah is, in every way, an average middle-class mom. She cares for her children and like her husband works to support them. She describes her politics as 'slightly left of centre'. Four years ago, at the age of 13, her daughter announced that she was trans and that she was actually a boy. The daughter had already been diagnosed with a mild form of autism, and had had trouble being accepted by some of her peers. She had trouble picking up on conversational signals. Invitations to play weren't reciprocated, and her fashion choices weren't deemed quite right by all of her peers. In time Sarah's daughter found that boys in her school were slightly more amenable to her than girls. But even then she couldn't quite get the degree of social acceptance which she wanted. 'Why doesn't anyone like me?' she used to intermittently ask her mother. Trying to make sense of why she was 'not fitting in with girls' in particular, she was also trying to work out why she wasn't fitting in with her peers in general.

Then one day she announced to her mother that she was in fact a boy and that this was the cause of her problems. Sarah asked her what had given her the idea that she was trans. After all, for her family it had all seemed to come on very suddenly. Her daughter said that she had got the idea after a presentation at her school. At this point it emerged that around 5 per cent of the children at her daughter's school now identified as transgender. They included a remarkably similar range of children, including children who had been diagnosed as having forms of autism and a history of being unpopular or poor at connecting with their peers. Of course her mother wanted to know more. If there had not been any other children at her school who identified as trans, would she have decided that she was a boy? Sarah's daughter said that no, she wouldn't have done so because she 'wouldn't have known that it was an option'. It was not that she thought she was a boy, but that she was a boy. And what is more, her mother would not be able to understand this, because she was 'cis'. Sarah had never heard the word 'cis' before, let alone been described as it. Sarah's daughter repeatedly told her mother that 'trans children know who they are'.

But Sarah was supportive. She agreed to call her daughter by her new, preferred, male name and began to address her using male pronouns. She even introduced her daughter to her friends as her son. Trying to be as supportive as possible, mother and daughter even went on a 'trans pride' march together and danced along to Lady Gaga's 'Born this way'. Sarah was so supportive that she bought the first binder her daughter needed to conceal her developing breasts. It is hard to see what more a mother could have done.

At the same time, quite understandably, Sarah started to read up online about the whole trans business. It was new to her family's life and she wanted to get a range of views in order to arrive at some understanding of her own. By Sarah's own admission, her first impressions of the online debate were not good. A lot of the critical reading online was, she thought, marked by a strain of 'anti-LBGT' sentiment. The people who wrote about it often seemed to be what she describes as 'bigoted or religious'. She had never explored any of this deeply before. She was 'just concerned about my daughter'. And so Sarah went to speak to some professionals – starting with some gender clinicians.

The first of these told her something which echoes what many other people in her position have heard. The clinician told her that 'parental acceptance was the first step to prevent suicide'. As with any parent, this was a threat of the worst nightmare imaginable. The doctor clinician also told Sarah that since her daughter had been 'insistent, persistent and consistent' in her claims this meant that her daughter was indeed a boy.

Sarah was not only worried by the words of the professionals but also by some of what her daughter was saying. Whenever Sarah's daughter described her feelings of gender dysphoria her mother noticed that the words seemed 'rather scripted'. And to say that the script was manipulative is an understatement. At one stage her daughter issued a list of demands which included blackmail and threats unless these demands were met.

Sarah's daughter was 13 and a half when she announced that she was trans. At 14 and a half she went to the therapist. And at 15 she was told that she should start taking the puberty blocker Lupron. At each stage it was stressed that it was 'insulting' for the mother to question the feelings of her daughter and that as with trans people so with autistic people: 'Autistic people know who they are', she was reassured. Even to question this was to be 'able-ist'. A number of different therapists were approached and eventually mother and child returned to the first one. When Sarah expressed some concerns over the choices being offered to her daughter by the profession, and specifically the idea of her daughter going on puberty blockers, she was told, 'You have a choice between puberty blockers and the hospital.' And so at 17 and a half Sarah's daughter announced that she wanted to transition.

Of course Sarah asked her daughter about whether she really wanted to do this. She stressed the irreversibility of the path down which her daughter was going. Even more irreversible than the hormones was the irreversibility of transitioning. What if – Sarah asked her daughter – after choosing to transition she then felt the need to de-transition? What if having made this change she decided she didn't want it? Her daughter's response was, 'So. I'll kill myself.' While no parent should ever take such a threat lightly there does seem to be a pattern to it, as Germaine Greer had claimed much earlier. And not only from the young people, but from some of the medical professionals who are pushing their case.

For instance, in 2015 Michelle Forcier, MD, professor at Brown University Medical School and Director of Gender and Sexual Health Services at the Lifespan Physician Group in Providence, Rhode Island, was interviewed on NBC. Asked about whether children as young as three or four could possibly know what they want, Forcier replied, 'To say three- and four-year-olds don't understand gender doesn't give our kids a lot of credit.' When asked what harm could be done by waiting before transitioning she said, 'The biggest harm is not to do anything.' But what was the risk of waiting, she was asked. Her reply: 'The risk of waiting is suicide. The risk of waiting is running away. The risk of waiting is substance abuse. The risk of waiting is bullying and violence. The risk of waiting is depression and anxiety.'[49] Joel Baum, who is Senior Director at the campaign group Gender Spectrum, has put this even more starkly. To parents worried about consenting to their children going on hormones he has said, 'You can either have grandchildren or not have a kid any more, either because they've ended the relationship with you or in some cases because they have chosen a more dangerous path for themselves.'[50]

The problem with the choice being presented this way – in the most catastrophizing light possible – is that it leaves no room for discussion or dissent. Instead, the moment that a child says they think they may be of the opposite sex, they must be greeted only with acceptance and from then on only with a set of life-changing steps which an increasing body of professionals appear to want to encourage with as little pushback as possible.

Yet stories like James's and also that of Sarah's daughter are filled with suggestive turns. Just as James says he might never have considered trying to become a woman if he hadn't been in a milieu in which drag and trans were common, so Sarah's daughter admits that she might never have considered the possibility that she was actually a boy if there had not been other pupils at the same school who were making the same claims. All of which brings us to the crux of the issue. Even if there are some people who actually suffer from gender dysphoria, and even if for some of them life-changing surgery is the best possible option, how might they be differentiated from people who have such ideas suggested to them but who later turn out to have made the wrong decision for themselves?

Among the most hard-nosed but likely arguments for an eventual slowing of the current trans stampede is the growing possibility of an avalanche of lawsuits. Although the UK, including the NHS, has opened itself up to this eventuality, the potential in Britain for successful future legal actions is nothing compared to the US. Whereas Britain's health service is struggling to satisfy the increased demand for gender reassignment surgery, in the US there is not merely a movement but a business incentive for pushing this. Just one of the signs that trans is an area where social demands are starting to attract business opportunities lies in the extraordinary levity with which trans activists – including some surgeons – are now talking about life-changing surgery. Some of this requires a strong stomach.

THE PROFESSION

Take for example Dr Johanna Olson-Kennedy. Regarded as a leader in her field, she is at present the medical director of the Center for Transyouth Health and Development at the Children's Hospital Los Angeles. This is the largest transgender youth clinic in the US and is one of four recipients of a taxpayer-funded National Institutes of Health grant for a five-year study on the impact of puberty blockers and hormones on children. A study for which, as it happens, there is no control group.

In her career Dr Olson-Kennedy has, by her own admission, regularly issued hormones to children as young as 12. And in an article in the *Journal of the American Medical Association* titled 'Chest Reconstruction and Chest Dysphoria in Transmasculine Minors and Young Adults: Comparisons of Nonsurgical and Postsurgical Cohorts'[51] she says that a number of girls as young as 13 had been put on cross-sex hormones for fewer than six months before they were given surgery. This means that girls as young as 12 have been given these life-changing drugs. Furthermore, progress reports show that as of 2017 children as young as eight have become eligible for such treatments.

Dr Olson-Kennedy's public statements are remarkable in their insistence, assurance and, one might say, dogmatism. She has been publicly critical of the idea of mental-health assessments for children who say that they want to change sex. In comparing children who say they want to change sex with children suffering from diabetes she has in the past said, 'I don't send someone to a therapist when I'm going to start them on insulin.'[52] She is a leading proponent of the idea that any challenge to the decision that a child has arrived at risks jeopardizing the relationship between the professional and the patient. As she has written: 'Establishing a therapeutic relationship entails honesty and a sense of safety that can be compromised if young people believe that what they need and deserve (potentially blockers, hormones, or surgery) can be denied them according to the information they provide to the therapist.'[53] Olson-Kennedy is sceptical about the idea that some 12- or 13-year-olds might not be in a position to make an informed and irreversible decision. She has said that 'I have never had anyone who was put on blockers that did not want to pursue cross-sex hormone transition at a later point.' In making this point she has emphasized that:

> When we make a decision to move forward with medical intervention, either puberty suppressants, or cross-sex hormones, the most important person we consider in that decision making is the child – the young person. There are some centers that use much more technical, psychometric testing, that looks at various and assorted factors in children's psychiatric development. We don't practice that model in our clinic.[54]

Yet elsewhere she has said that she has seen a small number of patients who have stopped treatment or have come to regret transitioning, but added that this should not influence attitudes to other people who wish to transition. One problem – in her view – is that such important decisions have sometimes been taken by 'professionals (usually cisgender) who determine if the young people are ready or not'. Olson-Kennedy believes that this is 'a broken model'.[55]

Despite the fact that the guidelines of the Endocrine Society (the world's oldest and leading organization in the field of endocrinology and the study of metabolism) state that there is 'minimal published experience' about hormone treatment for people 'prior to 13.5 to 14 years of age',[56] Olson-Kennedy and other colleagues seem extraordinarily confident about what they are doing, for example in her extraordinary dismissal not just of her opponents but of the irreversibility of the actions she is encouraging children to take. In one presentation, recorded undercover, she rails about something which she says she feels she's 'just got to say'. This is an answer to any critics who think that children do not have the ability to make such fundamental and life-altering choices. Waving her arms and losing her temper with such intransigent points of view, Olson-Kennedy points out that people get married when they are under 20 and choose colleges to go to, and that these are also 'life-altering choices' made in adolescence that mostly work out. We spend too much time focusing on the bad stuff, she says. 'What we do know is that adolescents actually have the capacity to make a reasoned logical decision.' So far so indisputable. But it is the casualness with which she makes the follow-on point that is vaguely staggering. 'Here's the thing about chest surgery,' she says. 'If you want breasts at a later point in your life you can go and get them.'[57]

Really? Where? How? Are people like blocks of Lego onto which new pieces can be stuck, taken off and replaced again at will? Is surgery so painless, bloodless, seamless and scarless today that anyone can just have breasts stuck on them at any point and live happily ever after, enjoying their new acquisitions? A fairly typical male-to-female transformation does not only involve operations to change the genitals and breasts but also operations to shave bone off the chin, nose and forehead which involves procedures where the skin is peeled off the face. And then there are the hair implants, speech therapy and much more.[58] A woman who seeks to become a man must have an approximation of a penis constructed from skin elsewhere on the body. The subject's arms are often flayed to build this, with no assurance of success. And all at the cost of tens – often hundreds – of thousands of dollars. It requires a specific level of mendacity to describe all this as an absolute doozy.

It gets worse. In February 2017 an organization called WPATH held its inaugural USPATH conference in Los Angeles. WPATH stands for 'World Professional Association for Transgender Health'. But this was the 'Inaugural United States Professional Association for Transgender Health Scientific Conference'.[59] One part of the symposium was called 'Outside of the binary – care for non-binary adolescents and young adults'. In this session Dr Olson-Kennedy addressed a room full of people who clearly already agreed with her. But as well as some of her presumptions that they obviously agreed with, it also became clear just how young the 'adolescents and young adults' of the title actually are.

For example, Olson-Kennedy described how she once had to deal with an eight-year-old child who had (clearly laughably to her) been 'assigned female at birth'. As Olson-Kennedy describes it, 'So this kid comes into my practice' and her parents were confused. Their daughter was 'completely presenting male', which means, 'short haircut, boy's clothes. But what was happening is this kid went to a very religious school. And in the girls' bathroom – which was where this kid was going – people were like "Why is there a boy in the girls' bathroom, that's a real problem." So this kid was like "So that's not super working for me, so I want to figure out like, I think I wanna enrol in school as a boy."' Olson-Kennedy rattles on with this story in the style of a hilarious anecdote, including impressions of the confused parents and the crazy attitudes of those around them, who clearly don't understand what the doctor and her audience on this occasion see as the bleeding obvious.

Some 'kids' who come to her apparently have great 'clarity' and 'great articulation' about their gender and are just 'endorsing it'. This 'kid' had apparently not 'really organized or thought about all these different possibilities'. Although Olson-Kennedy tells the story of a three-year-old girl apparently telling her mother how she felt like a boy, which the doctor now says the child didn't say, the crowd all laughs along knowingly. At one point Olson-Kennedy recounts how when she asked the 'kid' (from the previous example) whether she was a boy or a girl and saw 'confusion' on the kid's face, the kid replied, 'I'm a girl cos I have this body.' To which Olson-Kennedy adds, 'This is how this kid had learned to talk about their gender, based on their body.' She then recounts a brilliant idea, 'completely made this up on the spot, by the way'. She asks the child whether she likes pop tarts. The eight-year-old says yes. And so Olson-Kennedy recounts that she asked the child what she would do if she came across a strawberry pop tart in a foil packet in a box that contained 'cinnamon pop tarts'. Is it a strawberry pop tart or a cinnamon pop tart? 'The kid's like "Duh, it's a strawberry pop tart." And I was like, sooooo . . '. At which point the audience all laugh knowingly and begin to clap. Olson-Kennedy continues, 'And the kid turned to the mom and said "I think I'm a boy and the girl's covering me up."' At this the audience all 'coo' and 'aww' with appreciation for the moment. As Olson-Kennedy concludes, 'The best thing was that the mum was like "Awww" and just got up and gave the kid this big hug. It was an amazing experience.' Before other members of the audience can get up and recount their own heart-warming stories, she goes on: 'I worry about when we say things like "I am a" versus "I wish I were a" because I think that there's so many things that contextually happen for people around the way they understand and language gender. So, I don't think I made this kid a boy.' At which the audience laugh appreciatively at the very idea of such a thing. 'I think that giving this kid the language to talk about his gender was really important.'[60]

Just one of the strange things about all of this, from the audience reaction at the USPATH conference, is that Olson-Kennedy is not speaking at a meeting of 'professionals' but to a congregation. A fixed set of ideas are being discussed. A fixed set of virtues are being celebrated. And a fixed set of propositions are being set up, laughed at and dismissed. The audience does not sit, listen and then ask questions as at an academic or professional conference. They cheer, laugh, snort and applaud in a manner which more than anything else resembles a Christian revival meeting.

Or some kind of comedy club. The next person up to the microphone gets asked by Olson-Kennedy, 'Are you a medical provider?' There is an 'Uh-huh'. 'OK,' she says, apparently unwilling to give up the mike: 'here's something I learned from being married to a mental-health person.' At which point the medical provider says in a husky voice, 'Tell me more about that.' There is a wild burst of applause, whoops and appreciative laughter at what appears to be some kind of hilarious innuendo. After this has finally died down the medical provider (who turns out to be from Iowa) says, 'So I was just going to share that in my practice what I do when I first meet someone is just tell them – if you had a magic wand or one of those *Star Trek* things that you can do whatever you want, what would you like to see happen? What can I do? So that way I know where they want to go and see what the tools might be.' Ordinarily if a child says that they would like to wave a wand and change something they then open their eyes to realize that the wand, and whatever spell they have intoned, does not work. Only in the world of trans ideology do the adults tell the children that the wand can be waved, the wishes can be granted and that if they want to be something enough then the adults can make the magic happen.

As it turns out, the joke that this participant took part in with Dr Olson-Kennedy isn't even as funny as the USPATH conference participants seemed to think. Because the 'mental-health person' to whom she is married has some pretty extraordinary practices of his own.

Aydin Olson-Kennedy works at the Los Angeles Gender Center. His biography there explains that as well as being a 'licensed clinical social worker', a 'mental health professional', and also somebody involved in 'advocacy work', Aydin Olson-Kennedy has transitioned himself. And as the centre says, he 'brings a unique perspective to his career as a transgender man who at one time needed similar mental health and medical services for himself'. In such a situation the question of where medicine, care, social work and advocacy cross over is a very pertinent one.

As part of her transition to a 'him', Aydin underwent a double mastectomy – an operation which very rarely leaves no scarring at all. But perhaps Aydin's choice to undergo this operation is one reason why he seems happy to recommend it to others. The known cases include that of a 14-year-old girl with a history of psychological problems. More shocking still is the case of an American child who suffered from Down's Syndrome. This girl – who was known as Melissa – suffered from a range of physical and mental-health problems and had reportedly also suffered from leukaemia. For complicated reasons the mother of the child appeared to be shopping around for other diagnoses for her daughter. One conclusion that she came to – with help – was that her daughter was in fact trans. Among those who supported this claim and the resulting call for the girl to transition was Aydin Olson-Kennedy. Indeed, he asked for other trans people to donate funds in order that the Down's Syndrome child could have a double mastectomy.[61] As though the whole business could not get any more complex, both Olson-Kennedys are also registered consultants with Endo Pharmaceuticals, which – among other things – are makers of testosterone.

WHERE DOES THIS GO?

If L and G and B are uncertain elements in the LGBT alphabet, then the last of those letters is the least certain and most destabilizing of all. If gay, lesbian and bi are unclear, trans is still very close to a mystery and the one with the most extreme consequences. It is not that there are demands for equal rights – few people think anyone should be denied equal rights. Instead, the preconceptions and assumptions are what cause the problems. The demand that everyone should agree to use new gender pronouns and get used to people of the opposite sex being in the same bathrooms is at the relatively frivolous end of the spectrum of demands. Far more serious is the demand that children be encouraged towards medical intervention over a matter that is so incredibly unclear – and the age at which such children will be encouraged in this way will only keep going down. At the end of 2018 a private gender clinician in Wales was convicted in court of illegally providing healthcare services. Her clinic was providing sex-change hormones to children as young as 12.[62]

Moreover, why would their ages not keep going down, when the claims being made are backed up by so much threatening rhetoric, blackmail and catastrophism? Anyone mentioning the drawbacks or concerns about going trans is said to be hateful and either encouraging violence against trans people or encouraging them to do themselves harm. This suggests that the only thing that non-trans people can do is stay silent on the issue and never speak about it unless what they have to say is affirming. This stance has already led to the invention of new concepts which flow out from parts of the feminist and trans movements – such as the idea that some people are 'non-binary' and 'gender-fluid'. A BBC film called *Things Not to Say to a Non-Binary Person* features some young people talking about how 'restrictive' the idea of being male and female is – and simplistic. As one of them says, 'I mean, what is a man and what is a woman?'[63] The overwhelming feeling from watching the young people in the film, and others who make the same claims, is that what they are actually saying is 'Look at me!'

Is that also the case with some young people who say they are trans? Almost certainly. Yet there is no clear way of knowing to whom this applies and to whom it may not – or who should be encouraged to gravitate towards medical intervention and who should be strongly urged to stay clear of it. Even Johanna Olson-Kennedy has conceded that most individuals who identify as transgender do not have any sex development disorder.

The move to present the answers of hormones and surgery in a radically simplistic light will certainly persuade a number of people that the problems in their lives can easily be solved by addressing this one fundamental misunderstanding. It may have worked for Jazz Jennings so far, and it may have worked for Caitlyn Jenner. But it did not remedy the troubles of Nathan Verhelst, if anything could have done. The problem at present is not the disparity, but the certainty – the spurious certainty with which an unbelievably unclear issue is presented as though it was the clearest and best understood thing imaginable.

Conclusion

The advocates of social justice, identity politics and intersectionality suggest that we live in societies which are racist, sexist, homophobic and transphobic. They suggest that these oppressions are interlocked and that if we can learn to see through this web, and unweave it, we can then finally unlock the interlocking oppressions of our time. After which something will happen. Precisely what that thing is remains unclear. Perhaps social justice is a state which once arrived at remains in place. Perhaps it requires constant attention. We are unlikely to find out.

Firstly, because the interlocking oppressions do not all lock neatly together, but grind hideously and noisily both against each other and within themselves. They produce friction rather than diminish it, and increase tensions and crowd madnesses more than they produce peace of mind. This book has focused on four of the most consistently raised issues in our societies: issues which have become not just a staple of every day's news, but the basis of a whole new societal morality. To raise the plight of women, gays, people of different racial backgrounds and those who are trans has become not just a way to demonstrate compassion but a demonstration of a form of morality. It is how to practise this new religion. To 'fight' for these issues and to extol their cause has become a way of showing that you are a good person.

Of course there is something in this. Allowing people to live their lives the way they wish is an idea which reveals some of the most cherished attainments of our societies – attainments which are still disturbingly rare worldwide. There remain 73 countries in the world where it is illegal to be gay, and eight in which being gay is punishable by death.[1] In countries across the Middle East and Africa women are denied some of the most basic rights of all. Outbursts of inter-racial violence occur in country after country. In 2008, 20,000 people fled back to Mozambique from South Africa after riots by South Africans against Mozambicans in the black townships left dozens dead and thousands homeless. Nowhere in the world are the rights of trans people to attempt to live their lives the way they wish more protected in law than in the developed West. All of these things can be celebrated as achievements that have come about because of the system of law and the culture of rights. But there is a paradox here: that the countries which are most advanced in all of these attainments are the ones now presented as among the worst. Perhaps it is just a version of Daniel Patrick Moynihan's dictum on human rights: that claims of human rights violations happen in exactly inverse proportion to the numbers of human rights violations in a country. You do not hear of such violations in unfree countries. Only a very free society would permit – and even encourage – such endless claims about its own iniquities. Likewise, somebody can only present a liberal arts college in America or a dining experience in Portland as verging on the fascist if the people complaining are as far away from fascism as it is possible to be.

But this spirit of accusation, claim and grudge has spread with a swiftness that is remarkable. And it has not only to do with the arrival of new technologies, even though we are only one decade into the era of the smartphone and Twitter. Even before this, something had been going wrong in the language of human rights and the practice of liberalism. It is as though the enquiring aspect of liberalism was at some stage replaced with a liberal dogmatism: a dogmatism that insists questions are settled which are unsettled, that matters are known which are unknown and that we have a very good idea of how to structure a society along inadequately argued lines. This is why the products of rights are now presented as the bases of rights even though these bases form such unstable entities. If only this liberalism could allow a dose of humility to be injected where the certainty has prevailed. For this form of dogmatic, vengeful liberalism may, among other things, at some stage risk undermining and even bringing down the whole liberal era. After all it is not clear that majority populations will continue to accept the claims they are being told to accept and continue to be cowed by the names that are thrown at them if they do not.

The flaws in this new theory of, and justification for, existence require identification because the pain that is going to continue to be caused if this intersectional train keeps on running is immeasurable. The metaphysics that a new generation is imbibing and everyone else is being force-fed has many points of instability, is grounded in a desire to express certainty about things we do not know, and to be wildly dismissive and relativistic about things that we actually do know. The foundations are that anyone might become gay, women might be better than men, people can become white but not black and anyone can change sex. That anyone who doesn't fit into this is an oppressor. And that absolutely everything should be made political.

There are enough contradictions and confusions here to last a lifetime. Not just at certain points, but from their absolute fundamentals. What are gay or straight men and women to make of the claims of those who would attribute different genders to children other than those assigned at birth? Why should a young woman who displays tomboyish characteristics be viewed as a pre-op female-to-male transsexual? Why should a little boy who likes to dress up as a princess be a male-to-female transsexual in waiting? The claims of gender experts about those who are pop tarts in the wrong packaging may themselves be the ones whose packet-reading abilities are all wrong. It has been estimated that roughly 80 per cent of children diagnosed with what is now called gender dysphoria will find that this problem resolves itself during puberty. That is, they will come to feel at ease with the biological sex they were identified as being at birth. A majority of these children will grow up to become gay or lesbian as adults.[2] How should lesbian women and gay men feel about the fact that decades after they came to be accepted for who they were a new generation of children who would grow up to be gay or lesbian are being told that their feminine traits make them women and their masculine traits make them men? And what are women to make of this? After years of establishing what their rights were as women, to be told what their rights are – including their right to speak – by people who were born male?

THESE CLAIMS DO NOT INTERSECT, THEY DERANGE

Contrary to the claims of the advocates of social justice, these categories do not in fact interact well with each other. The oppression matrix is not a great Rubik's cube waiting for every square to be lined up by social scientists. It consists of a set of demands which do not work together, and certainly not at this pitch.

In 2008 *Advocate* magazine was campaigning against Proposition 8, which would overturn the possibility of gay marriage in the state of California. In its quest to continue campaigning for same-sex marriage the front page of America's most prominent gay magazine in November 2008 read: 'Gay is the new black'. The claim did not go down well among black Americans. Any more than did the front-page story's sub-heading: 'The last great civil rights struggle'. Even the addition of that old journalistic get-out, the after-the-fact added question mark, did not dampen the criticism.[3] As one critic put it, the 'gay is the new black' argument was offensive for – among many other listed reasons – 'the complete disconnect between same-sex "marriage" and anti-miscegenation laws'.[4] Whenever it looks as though such controversies and comparisons may be superseded, and all the rights demands and achievements may all exist in harmony, similar rows break out.

Sometimes this is because someone asks the wrong question. In the aftermath of the Rachel Dolezal affair the feminist philosophy journal *Hypatia* ran a piece by an untenured academic called Rebecca Tuvel. She raised a most interesting question. Comparing the treatment of Rachel Dolezal with the treatment of Caitlyn Jenner, she questioned whether if we 'accept transgender individuals' decision to change sexes, we should also accept transracial individuals' decisions to change races'. This argument did not go down well. In terms of logical consistency Tuvel had a very good point: if people should be allowed to self-identify why should that right stop at the borders of race and not at the borders of sex? But in terms of the current mores she could not have been in a worse place. Black activists, among others, mobilized against the piece. A petition was organized against Tuvel, an open letter was signed, and one of *Hypatia*'s associate editors was among those denouncing her. The publication was accused of allowing 'white cis scholars' to take part in arguments which exacerbated 'transphobia and racism'.[5]

The fall-out in the world of this little-known feminist journal was such that within a very short space of time *Hypatia* apologized for ever publishing the piece, the editor resigned and the directors of the magazine were all replaced. Tuvel herself begged that she had written her piece 'from a place of support for those with non-normative identities, and frustration about the ways individuals who inhabit them are so often excoriated, body-shamed, and silenced'.[6] But the 'extension of thinking' which she pleaded was her sole aim was clearly not welcome. If Rebecca Tuvel had watched Rachel Dolezal on *The Real* in 2015 she would have had an answer to her question. The women of colour on that show made it clear to Dolezal that trans-racialism was not acceptable because a person who had grown up white could not understand what a person who had grown up black could feel like. They could not have had the same experiences.[7] This was the point that the second-wave feminists were making at the same time about the transsexuals. But an argument that had worked with race had not worked for women.

Sometimes the problem develops because somebody has asked the wrong, or awkward, question. And at other times it is because the person who is being lined up to make matters nice and neat turns out to be a messy and complex human being.

In October 2017 the British magazine *Gay Times* announced its first BME editor, Josh Rivers (this was in a month when BME [Black and Minority Ethnic] had not yet been replaced by the longer, now more acceptable, acronym: BAME [Black Asian and Minority Ethnic]). Rivers lasted three weeks. Shortly after the announcement *Buzzfeed* chose to do a trawl of his Twitter history and found yet another person with a long online trail of hostages to fortune. From 2010 to 2015 Rivers had made a number of comments to his two thousand followers that *Buzzfeed* warned 'would shock many readers'.

Rivers was not very anti-racist. In fact he seemed to have a particular issue about Jews and did not like Asians very much. Others – including Africans and particularly Egyptians – came in for worse. He called Egyptian men 'fat, smelly, hairy, cunty-face, backward rapists'. He disliked people who were fat, people who were working class and people who he called 'retards'. Lesbians were another object of his considerable ire. And his views on transsexuals was especially unenlightened. In 2010 he had told one person 'Look here tranny. 1) You look like a crackhead 2) YOU'RE A TRANNY & 3) your wig doesn't deserve a mention. Avert your eyes, honey.'[8] This tweet was given a health warning by another gay publication which was un-gleefully writing up the whole affair. This tweet was, they warned readers, 'particularly horrific'.[9]

Gay Times carried out a swift 'investigation' of their own and within 24 hours announced that their first BME editor's employment had been terminated with immediate effect and that all his previous articles had been removed from the website. The magazine 'does not tolerate such views and will continue to strive to honour and promote inclusivity', they promised.[10] Some weeks later Rivers apologized for the content of his earlier tweets, and also explained his own interpretation of these events in an interview. The feedback to his tweets had, he said, been 'racialized'. He continued, 'White feedback has been: Ha ha! Ha! Ah ha! And it's so – it's actually that cut-and-dry. Black and white, as it were!'[11] For him, criticism over his racist tweets was itself in fact racism.

Similar disappointments mount in all directions. When male-to-female transsexuals are allowed to participate in women's sports the results often go dead against the idea of parity between the sexes. In October 2018 the women's world championship at the UCI Masters Track World Championship in California was won by male-to-female transsexual Rachel McKinnon. The woman McKinnon beat into third place, Jen Wagner-Assali, called McKinnon's victory 'unfair' and demanded a rule change from cycling's international body. But the idea that male-to-female transsexuals in any way threatened the participation of women in sports was dismissed by the winner as 'transphobic'.[12]

This row rumbles along. When Hannah Mouncey had trouble getting nominated in the Australian women's handball team she said it sent a terrible message to women and girls about their bodies. According to Mouncey it said 'If you're too big, you can't play. That is incredibly dangerous and backward.' Mouncey was the only transgender woman in the squad and the disparity in her size was not slight. The team photo of the Australian women's handball team with Mouncey in it looked like a team of handball players with one very large male rugby player at the back. Was this more size-ism? Is it backwards to notice it? As it is to comment on the advantage somebody born a man – like Laurel (born Gavin) Hubbard – has in women's +90KG weight-lifting competitions?

In 2018 an 18-year-old called Mack Beggs won the Texas girls' Class 6A 110lbs division wrestling title for the second year in a row. Beggs is transitioning from female to male and is taking doses of testosterone. Press write-ups of Beggs' victories have tended to focus on the boos from some members of the crowd as another female opponent is beaten, as though bigotry and small-mindedness are the real problem here. But a remarkable self-deception is being sustained. After all, in the sporting world, being discovered to have taken testosterone is ordinarily grounds to prevent someone from competing – unless, it turns out, the person is taking testosterone to transition to the opposite sex. In which case sensitivity overrides science. As always, it gets worse.

One precept not just of feminism but of any decent, civilized society, is that men should not hit or beat up women. And then the world turns its face away from the discovery that in a variety of contact sports people who were born men are now regularly beating women to the ground. In Mixed Martial Arts (MMA) fighting this controversy has been building for several years. The case of Fallon Fox is the most famous. Having been born a man, married, fathered a child and joined the Navy, Fox came out as trans in 2013, at the start of her time competing as a woman. As one board-certified endocrinologist (Dr Ramona Krutzik) explained it, Fox's advantages included the bone density she had accrued from her time as a man, the muscle mass she will have accrued from those years and the testosterone imprint on the brain which does not go away through taking androgens or having surgery. All this could give Fox not just a physical edge but also a potential aggression edge.[13]

As MMA expert and podcaster Joe Rogan pointed out, 'there is a giant difference between the amount of power that a man and a woman can generate . . . There's a difference in the shape of the hips, the size of the shoulders, the density of the bones, the size of the fists.' And this is a sport where, as Rogan put it, the objective is very clear: 'Beat the fuck out of the other person in front of you.' Yet even questioning whether someone with the physical advantages of having been born male should be allowed to floor women in front of a live audience produces the strongest possible objections. As Rogan later put it, 'People came down on me harder than anything that I've ever stood up for in my life. Never in my life did I think there was going to be a situation where I said "Hey,

I don't think a guy should be able to get his penis removed and beat the shit out of women" and then people were like "You're out of line". But that's literally what happened.'[14]

If a growing awareness of people's differences was meant to unlock some grand system of justice, or allow interlocking prejudices to free everyone up, then even at this fairly early stage the process has produced more problems than it has solutions, and more exacerbation than healing. The casting wars continue to turn colour-blindness on its head and make everybody colour-obsessed, while ignoring other characteristics has become a part of the problem. Everywhere the custom grows that people have no right to portray someone they are not. Having survived the attacks for playing an Asian woman's consciousness inside a white android in *Ghost in the Shell* (2017), Scarlett Johansson had the bad luck to be cast the following year as a 1970s crime boss in *Rub & Tug*. But the real-life character she was to portray had been trans and the actress Johansson would only have been impersonating a trans woman, so after criticism she withdrew from the role. Even those places which raised questions about this direction of travel found themselves in the line of fire. The financial news website Business Insider originally published an opinion piece defending Johansson from being 'unfairly criticised for doing her job', but it swiftly unpublished the article once the backlash against Johansson got under way.[15] That same year there were calls to boycott a film starring the gay actor Matt Bomer. The calls for a boycott came not from some fringe church but from people complaining that a 'cis white actor' – even a gay one like Bomer – playing a trans woman was an 'affront' to 'the dignity of trans women'.[16]

While on some occasions an affront was claimed, on others it was suppressed when it might well have been voiced. In February 2018, when Prime Minister Justin Trudeau was addressing students and answering questions at MacEwan University in Edmonton, a young woman politely asked a question in which she referred in passing to 'mankind'. The Canadian Prime Minister interrupted her, waving his hand dismissively. 'We like to say people-kind, not necessarily mankind, because it's more inclusive,' he explained, getting a roar of applause from his audience. But nobody subsequently pointed out why a powerful white male embarrassing a young woman in this way was not 'mansplaining'.

The identity groups that some people form don't even work within themselves. In 2017 a student group at Cornell University calling themselves 'Black Students United' chose to issue the college authorities with a six-page list of demands. This included the obvious demands, namely that all faculty members should be trained in 'systems of power and privilege' and that black people who had been 'affected directly by the African Holocaust in America' and by 'American fascism' should be invested in to a greater degree. But one demand was that their university should pay more attention to 'Black Americans who have several generations (more than two) in this country'. This was to make them distinct from first-generation students from Africa or the Caribbean.[17] The Black Students United group later apologized under pressure for making this demand. But the message was clear. There is a hierarchy of oppression and victimhood which exists even within each identifiable group. Not only are the rules unclear, but the prejudices that underly them aren't always clear either and can break out in extraordinary places and ways.

THE IMPOSSIBILITY PROBLEM

As a culture we have entered an area which is now mined with impossibility problems. From some of the most famous women on the planet we have heard the demand that women have the right to be sexy without being sexualized. Some of the most prominent cultural figures in the world have shown us that to oppose racism we must become a bit racist. Now a whole set of similar impossibilities are being demanded in an equally non-conciliatory manner.

There was a fine example on the BBC's *This Week* in October 2017 when an artist and writer going by the mononym 'Scottee' appeared on the programme to discuss a short political film he had made. As a self-described 'big fat queer fem' he complained that he was a 'victim of masculinity in a way because of the aggressions I put up with on a day-to-day basis'. Although he had no answers to this problem, he insisted that 'queer, trans, non-binary people' shouldn't have to be the ones who have to disable "toxic masculinity"'. It has to come from within, he argued. Men 'have got to acknowledge their privilege, and I want them to hand over power, and also I want them to hand over some platform. I'm really up for like trying a matriarchy. We've done patriarchy for a long time. Hasn't really worked.'[18] Avoiding the nuclear presumption of 'hasn't really worked' for a moment, there was one even larger fact staring any viewer in the face. This was that one of the main complaints that this flamboyantly dressed self-declared 'big fat queer fem' had made about the society he lived in was that he found himself so often ridiculed. So here is another paradoxical, impossible demand. A person who chooses to be ridiculous without being ridiculed.

Other impossible demands can be found everywhere – such as the one that was on display at Evergreen State College and Yale University and was highlighted by Mark Lilla on the panel at Rutgers (where the audience member insisted to Kmele Foster that he 'didn't need no facts'). On that occasion Lilla provided an insight into one of the other central conundrums of our time. He said, 'You cannot tell people simultaneously "You must understand me" and "You cannot understand me".' Evidently a whole lot of people can make those demands simultaneously. But they shouldn't, and if they do then they should realize that their contradictory demands cannot be granted.

Then of course there is the question of how the hierarchy of oppression is meant to be ordered, prioritized and then sorted out. Laith Ashley is one of the most prominent transgender models in the world today. The female-to-male transsexual has received prominent coverage and done prestigious fashion shoots for leading brands and magazines. In a 2016 television interview he was asked by Channel 4's Cathy Newman if in the two years he had been transitioning from a woman to a man he had encountered any discrimination. Ashley said that in fact he had not, but then alleviated his interviewer's disappointment by adding that transgender activists and others he knew from transgender rights movements had 'told' him that he had in fact gained some male privilege. As he said, breaking it down for the viewers, 'I have gained some male privilege. And although I am a person of colour I am fair skinned and I adhere to society's standard of aesthetic beauty in a sense. And for that reason I have not necessarily faced much discrimination.'[19] So he had taken a couple of steps further into the hierarchy by becoming a man, had taken a couple of steps back by being a person of colour, but a step forward by being a light-skinned person of colour. And then he had hit the negative of being attractive. How can anyone work out where they are meant to be in the oppressor/oppressed stakes when they have so many competing privileges in their biography? No wonder Ashley looked concerned and self-effacing when going through this list. This is enough constant self-analysis to knock anybody's confidence. But a version of that impossible self-analysis is being suggested for many people today, when in fact there is no way of knowing how to perform this task fairly on another person let alone on yourself. What is the point of an exercise that cannot be done?

And where to next? One of the pleasures in recent years has been watching people who think they are being a good liberal boundary keeper discover that one of their feet has nicked one of the tripwires. One Saturday evening in 2018 *Vox*'s David Roberts was spending his time happily auditioning for the committee for public virtue on Twitter. In one tweet he wrote, 'Sometimes I think about America's sedentary, heart-diseased, fast-food gobbling, car-addicted suburbanites, sitting watching TV in their suburban castles, casually passing judgement on refugees who have walked 1000s of miles to escape oppression, and . . . well, it makes me mad.' As he sent it off he must have thought 'Sounds good. Attack Americans, defend migrants, what could go wrong?' A more cautious member of the new media might have wondered whether it was wise to sound quite so disdainful of people who live in the suburbs. But in fact it was not Roberts's suburbo-phobia that caused him to spend the rest of his Saturday evening frantically trying to save his career in dozens of remedy tweets. The thing that caused an instant backlash from the very crowd he was hoping to impress was that he had been 'fat-shaming' and this was 'problematic'.

By his 17th tweet attempting to mop up his crime Roberts was reduced to begging: 'Fat-shaming is real, it's everywhere, it's unjust & unkind, and I want no part of it.' Soon he was apologizing sincerely for only being 'half woke', and blaming his upbringing.[20] The potential for claims of offence, allegations of shaming and new positions in the grievance hierarchy based on ever-evolving criteria could go on indefinitely. But how would they be arranged? Is a fat white person equal to a skinny person of colour? Or are there different scales of oppression which everyone should know even if no one has explained the rules because the rules are made not by rational people but by mob stampedes.

Perhaps rather than derange ourselves by working out a puzzle that cannot be solved, we should instead try to find ways out of this impossible maze.

WHAT IF PEOPLE AREN'T OPPRESSED?

Perhaps instead of seeking out oppression and seeing oppression everywhere, we could start to exit the maze by noting the various 'victim groups' that aren't oppressed or are even advantaged. For instance, studies have shown that gay men and lesbian women consistently earn more on average than their heterosexual counterparts.[21] There are a variety of possible reasons, not least the fact that most of them won't have children and can put in the extra hours at the office which benefits both them and their employer. Is this a gay advantage? At what stage can heterosexuals claim that they are unfairly disadvantaged in the workplace? Should there be a 'stepping back' by gay people to allow their straight contemporaries a better run at work opportunities?

In recent years earning disparities between racial groups have consistently been weaponized. While it is often cited that the median income of Hispanic Americans is less than that of black Americans, and the earnings of black Americans lower than that of white Americans, there is never as much focus on the group which out-earns everybody.[22] The median income of Asian men in America is consistently higher than any other group, including white Americans. Should there be some attempt to level this figure out by bringing Asian men down a few earning percentiles? Perhaps we could get out of this mania by treating people as individuals based on their abilities and not trying to impose equity quotas on every company and institution?

Because the most extreme claims keep getting heard, there is a tendency for people to believe them and their worst-case scenarios. For example, a poll carried out in 2018 for Sky found that most British people (seven in ten) believed that women are paid less than men for performing exactly the same job. The 'gender pay gap' that does exist is between average earnings across a lifespan, taking into account differences in career, child-rearing and lifestyle choices made by men and women. But 'the pay gap' has become such a staple of discussion on the news and on social media that most people have interpreted it as evidence of a gap that does not exist as they have been led to believe it does. It has been illegal to pay women less for performing the same task as a man since 1970 in the UK, and since 1963 in the US. Just one result of this confusion is that even though seven in ten people in the poll thought women were paid less than men for performing precisely the same job, almost exactly the same percentage of the public (67 per cent) thought that feminism had either gone too far or as far as it should go.[23] This finding might epitomize the confusion of our time. We see oppression where it doesn't exist and have no idea how to respond to it.

THE IMPORTANT DISCUSSIONS WE AVOID

Just one of the negatives of portraying life as this endless zero-sum game, between different groups vying for oppressed status, is that it robs us of time and energy for the conversations and thinking that we do need to do. For example, why is it, after all these decades, that feminists and others have been unable to more fully address the role of motherhood in feminism? As the feminist author Camille Paglia has been typically honest enough to admit, motherhood remains one of the big unresolved questions for feminists. And that isn't a small subject to miss or gloss over. As Paglia herself has written, 'Feminist ideology has never dealt honestly with the role of the mother in human life. Its portrayal of history as male oppression and female victimage is a gross distortion of the facts.'[24]

If asked to name her three great heroes of twentieth-century womanhood, Paglia says that she would select Amelia Earhart, Katharine Hepburn and Germaine Greer: three women who Paglia says 'would symbolize the new twentieth-century woman'. Yet as she points out, 'All these women were childless. Here is one of the great dilemmas facing women at the end of the century. Second-wave feminist rhetoric placed blame for the female condition entirely on men, or specifically on "patriarchy" . . . The exclusive focus of feminism was on an external social mechanism that had to be smashed or reformed. It failed to take into account women's intricate connection with nature – that is, with procreation.' Or why, 'in this era of the career woman, there has been a denigration, or devaluing of the role of motherhood.'[25]

The ongoing dishonesty about this leads to presumption being piled on dishonesty, and ugly, misanthropic notions of the purpose of women becoming embedded in the culture. In January 2019 CNBC ran a piece flagged with the heading, 'You can save half a million dollars if you don't have kids'.[26] As the piece went on: 'Your friends may tell you having kids made them happier. They're probably lying.' It then referenced all the outweighing problems of 'extra responsibilities, housework and, of course, the costs'.[27] Or here is how *The Economist* recently chose to write about what it called 'the roots of the gender pay gap', a gap which the magazine claimed has its roots in childhood. One of the main factors which is responsible for women on average earning less than men during the course of their working life is the fact that women are the ones who bear children. As *The Economist* put it, 'Having children lowers women's lifetime earnings, an outcome known as the "child penalty".[28] It is hard to imagine who could read that phrase, let alone write it, without a shudder. If it is assumed that the primary purpose in life is to make as much money as possible, then it is indeed possible that having a child will constitute a 'penalty' for a woman and thereby prevent her from having a larger sum of money in her bank account when she dies. On the other hand, if she chooses to pay that 'penalty' she might be fortunate enough to engage in the most important and fulfilling role that a human being can have.

There is in that *Economist* viewpoint something which is widely shared and which has been spreading for decades. On the one hand women have – largely – been relieved of the need to have children if they do not want them, the better to pursue other forms of meaning and purpose in their lives. But it is not hard for this reorientation of purpose to make it look as though that original, defining human purpose is no purpose at all. The American agrarian writer Wendell Berry put his finger on this almost 40 years ago when there were already, as he put it, 'bad times for motherhood'. The whole concept of motherhood had come to be viewed in a negative way: 'A kind of biological drudgery, some say, using up women who could do better things.' But then Berry hit on the central truth:

We all have to be used up by something. And though I will never be a mother, I am glad to be used up by motherhood and what it leads to, just as – most of the time – I gladly belong to my wife, my children, and several head of cattle, sheep, and horses. What better way to be used up?[29]

Is this not a better way to think about motherhood and life? In a spirit of love and forgiveness rather than the endless register of resentment and greed?

WHAT IS REALLY GOING ON

Yet if the absence of serious discussion and the innate contradictions alone were enough to stop this new religion of social justice, it would hardly have got started. People looking for this movement to wind down because of its inherent contradictions will be waiting a long time. Firstly because they are ignoring the Marxist substructure of much of this movement, and the inherent willingness to rush towards contradiction rather than notice all these nightmarish crashes and wonder whether they aren't telling you something about your choice of journey.

But the other reason why contradiction is not enough is because nothing about the intersectional, social justice movement suggests that it is really interested in solving any of the problems that it claims to be interested in. The first clue lies in the partial, biased, unrepresentative and unfair depiction of our own societies. Few people think that a country cannot be improved on, but to present it as riddled with bigotry, hatred and oppression is at best a partial and at worst a nakedly hostile prism through which to view society. It is an analysis expressed not in the manner of a critic hoping to improve, but as an enemy eager to destroy. There are signs of this intention everywhere we look.

Consider the example of trans. There was a reason to linger over the difficult and poorly discussed issue of people who are born intersex. It was not for prurience but to make a point. As Eric Weinstein has observed, anyone genuinely interested in addressing the stigmatization and unhappiness felt by people who are in the wrong bodies would have started addressing the question of intersex first. They would have seen there the clearest hardware issue of all, an issue which has been woefully under-represented. It would have raised awareness of the situation of such people, to get them better recognition as well as a better understanding of how to deal with an issue which really needs medical and psychological support. Social justice campaigners might have done this.

But they didn't. They decided instead to push vigorously on trans: to pick up the hardest part of the whole question ('I am who I say I am and you can't prove otherwise') and run with it: 'Trans lives matter'; 'Some people are trans. Get over it'. Everywhere, with a wearying predictability, the people who always complain about every aspect of the patriarchal, hegemonic, cis-supremacist, homophobic, institutionally racist, sexist state, decided to run with the trans issue. They specifically claimed that yes, if a man said he was a woman and didn't do anything about it, then yes he was a woman and it was transphobic to suggest otherwise. The pattern is clear. Why in her first weeks in Congress did Alexandria Ocasio-Cortez do a fundraiser for the British trans-rights group 'Mermaids' which advocates introducing hormone therapy to children?[30] Why are these people willing to defend, organize and argue for the hardest possible part of the case?

In 2018 there was debate in the House of Commons about trans issues. During it the case of Karen White came up. This was a man who was a convicted rapist but who now identified as a woman. Although he had not had gender reassignment surgery he asked to be put in a women's prison, and (with his male body) proceeded to sexually assault four female inmates. During the debate one Liberal Democrat MP, Layla Moran, summed up the extreme of trans thinking perfectly. Asked whether she would be happy to share a changing room with somebody who had a male body, Moran replied, 'If that person was a trans woman, I absolutely would. I just do not see the issue. As for whether they have a beard [a matter that had also been raised] I dare say that some women have beards. There are all sorts of reasons why our bodies react differently to hormones. There are many forms of the human body. I see someone in their soul and as a person. I do not really care whether they have a male body.'[31]

No sensible person or movement hoping to pull together a coalition to create a viable rights movement to defend trans people would make such a claim. They would not routinely claim that trans people are simply trans when they say they are. They would not say that a bearded man is no problem for them in the changing room because 'I dare say that some women have beards'. And they would not claim to be able to see into someone's soul and there recognize whether that person is a man or a woman. These are deranged claims and – like so many claims in the trans debate – they go on to derange anyone who has to listen to them, let alone those pushed to go along with them or assume that they are true.

A movement that sought to advance trans claims would start with intersex and from there move with enormous care along the spectrum of trans assertions, analyzing them with scientific precision in the process. It would not go straight to the hardest part of the claim and insist it is true and that everyone else must believe it is true too. That is not what you do if you are trying to build a coalition or a movement. It is what you do if you do not want to create a consensus. It is what you do if you are seeking to cause division.

Once you notice this counter-intuitive play you can see it going on with each issue. For instance, a number of wage gaps exist. There is, for example, as Jordan Peterson has pointed out, a pay gap that exists between people who are agreeable and people who are disagreeable. But this is a gap that exists across both men and women. A disagreeable woman will have a pay advantage over an agreeable man. And vice versa. So if anyone is worried about pay gaps why would that one not be something to linger on? Why would there not be an endless and retributive campaign calling for agreeable people to be paid more in the workplace and for disagreeable people to step back? Because that wouldn't fit the aim, which is not to advance women's rights or women's pay situation, but to use women as a wedge to do something else.

With each of the issues highlighted in this book the aim of the social justice campaigners has consistently been to take each one – gay, women, race, trans – that they can present as a rights grievance and make their case at its most inflammatory. Their desire is not to heal but to divide, not to placate but to inflame, not to dampen but to burn. In this again the last part of a Marxist substructure can be glimpsed. If you cannot rule a society – or pretend to rule it, or try to rule it and collapse everything – then you can do something else. In a society that is alive to its faults, and though imperfect remains a better option than anything else on offer, you sow doubt, division, animosity and fear. Most effectively you can try to make people doubt absolutely everything. Make them doubt whether the society they live in is good at all. Make them doubt that people really are treated fairly. Make them doubt whether there are any such groupings as men or women. Make them doubt almost everything. And then present yourself as having the answers: the grand, overarching, interlocking set of answers that will bring everyone to some perfect place, the details of which will follow in the post.

Perhaps they will have their way. Perhaps the advocates of the new religion will use gays and women and those of a different skin colour and trans individuals as a set of battering rams to turn people against the society they have been brought up in. Perhaps they will succeed in turning everyone against the 'cis white male patriarchy' and they will do it before all of their interlocking 'oppressed, victim groups' have torn each other apart. It is possible. But anyone interested in preventing that nightmarish scenario should search for solutions.

SOLUTIONS

Many people will have already found their way to deal with the current of the times and developed more or less clever ways to navigate it. There are options open to people. Whilst writing this book I learned about the behaviour of a type of cuttlefish which hides its intentions, thus making the mating game more complex even than it already is. The cuttlefish is among the creatures most adept at sexual mimicry. The giant Australian cuttlefish, *Sepia apama*, has a tricky male-to-female operational sex ratio, able to reach as high as eleven males to each female. Since female cuttlefish reject 70 per cent of male advances the competition among the males is especially high, and made higher by the trend of consort guarding. Consort males achieve around 64 per cent of the matings. For this reason the other male cuttlefish have a range of strategies at their disposal to have any chance of impregnating a female, and one of them is to mimic the behaviour of female cuttlefish. Smaller male cuttlefish hide their sexually dimorphic fourth arm, develop the skin pattern of their intended mate and even move their arms to imitate the pose of an egg-laying female. The strategy has been shown to be enormously effective. In one observed case, out of five male cuttlefish who used this method only one was turned away. Another was caught in the act by the consort male cuttlefish. But the other three cuttlefish successfully had their way.[32]

The cuttlefish prompted in me a flash of recognition, specifically about the many men who are adopting similar tactics. The day after the inauguration of President Trump in January 2017 there were large demonstrations in Washington, DC, and other cities. This 'Women's March' focused on the president's past remarks about women and included large numbers of protestors who wore pink 'pussy hats'. Banners bore legends like 'Don't DICKtate to my pussy'. At one after-march party in Washington a journalist colleague noticed the behaviour of some of the men who were present. Amid the bands, beer and plastic cups the girls stood around talking excitedly about the Women's March and their role in it. The young men present all strongly stressed their support for the march and all explained that they were feminists too. One young man 'nodded' gravely' as one attractive young woman recited all the correct beliefs of a modern feminist. After she briefly left he turned to his friend and whispered 'Dude, this is awesome! All these drunk, emotional girls in one city!'[33] Whether the tactic worked in his case is not known. But he cannot be the only young man developing a cuttlefish strategy in order to get through the period in which he finds himself. Yet cuttlefish strategies, among others, are ways to survive in a horrible natural environment. A better ambition would be to try to change that environment.

ASK 'COMPARED TO WHAT'?

One way to start might be to ask more regularly and more assiduously, 'Compared to what?' When people attempt to sum up our societies today as monstrous, racist, sexist, homophobic, transphobic patriarchies the question needs to be asked. If this hasn't worked or isn't working, what is the system that has worked or does work? To ask this is not to say that elements of our society cannot be improved, or that we should not address injustice and unfairness when we see them. But to talk about our societies in the hostile tone of judge, juror and executioner demands some questions to be asked of the accuser.

Very often dissection of our societal fall relies on the presumption of a prelapsarian age: an age before the invention of the machine, steam or the marketplace. These presumptions lie very deep, starting with the idea that we are born in a state of virtue from which the world has unfairly ripped us. Jean-Jacques Rousseau famously embodied this thinking in passages like this from Book II of *Emile, or On Education* (published in English in 1763) in which he writes: 'The first movements of human nature are always right. There is no original perversity in the human heart. There is not a single vice to be found in it of which it cannot be said how and whence it entered. In relation to others, he must respond only to what nature asks of him, and then he will do nothing but good.'[34] People who believe this strain of thought must find a culprit for their own failings and the failings of every other person around them, since they were born in such a state of grace. Inevitably such thinking spills out into a belief that simpler, older or earlier societies somehow provide an example of something worth going back to.

So, apart from reasons of historical guilt, many Western people today find themselves imbibing the idea that 'primitive' societies had some special state of grace which we lack today – as though in a simpler time there would have been more female dominance, more peace and less homophobia, racism and transphobia. There are an awful lot of unsupported assumptions among these beliefs. It is true that it is hard to quantify how much homophobia or racism would have been evident in various tribes. And perhaps there would have been more harmony and trans rights than we would suspect. But the facts often suggest the contrary. In his book *War Before Civilisation: The Myth of the Peaceful Savage* L. H. Keeley goes through the percentages of male deaths in conflict among a range of South American and New Guinean tribes. The violent deaths range from almost 10 to 60 per cent of males. By contrast the percentage of males killed in violent conflict in the US and Europe in the twentieth century is a single-digit blip.[35] If there is evidence that past societies would have been infinitely more tolerant of sexual and biological differences than we are in the twenty-first-century West, then it is incumbent on those making these claims to provide it.

Of course it may be that it is not with any society in history but another society in the world today that the comparison is being made. There are people who act as apologists for the revolutionary regime in Tehran, who like to cite the levels of transsexualism in that country as a demonstration of the progressiveness of the regime. This of course requires the listener to be ignorant of the fact that this is a country where right up to the present in 2019 men found guilty of homosexual acts are publicly hanged – often from cranes so that the maximum number of people can see the killing. In which other countries today are human rights at a more advanced stage than in Britain and America? If they exist then there is no harm – and only gain for us all – in hearing about them. Perhaps one reason why people – especially neo-Marxists – are coy about the precise comparisons they are making is that the comparisons they would cite (Venezuela, Cuba, Russia) would reveal the deeper underbelly of their ideology and the true reasons for the negative accounting of the West.

But most often the question 'Compared to what?' will elicit only the fact that the utopia with which our society is being compared has not yet come about. If this is the case, and the monstrous claims about our societies are being made in comparison to a society that has not yet been created, then a certain amount of humility and a great deal of further questioning might be needed. Those who claim that our society is typified by bigotry but believe they know how to fix any and all societal ills better make sure that their route maps are well plotted. If they are not then there is reason for everyone else to be suspicious about a project whose earliest stages are being presented as rigorous science when they more closely resemble an advocacy of magic.

THE VICTIM IS NOT ALWAYS RIGHT, OR NICE, DESERVES NO PRAISE – AND MAY NOT BE A VICTIM

In his biography of Franklin D. Roosevelt (2000), H. W. Brands makes a passing point about the 32nd president's polio. Men of Roosevelt's generation, he writes, 'were expected to meet misfortune with a stiff upper lip. Fate was more capricious then. When everyone was a victim at one point or another, no one won sympathy by wearing victimhood as a badge.'[36] Such reflections suggest the possibility that the extraordinary number of victimhood claims of recent years may not in fact indicate what the intersectionalists and social justice proponents think that they do. Rather than demonstrating an excess of oppression in our societies, the abundance of such claims may in fact be revealing a great shortage of it. If people were so oppressed would they have the time or inclination to listen to every person who felt the need to publicize that a talk by a novelist at a literary festival had upset them, or that it was intolerable to be sold a burrito by someone of the wrong ethnicity?

Victimhood rather than stoicism or heroism has become something eagerly publicized, even sought after, in our culture. To be a victim is in some way to have won, or at least to have got a head start in the great oppression race of life. At the root of this curious development is one of the most important and mistaken judgements of the social justice movements: that oppressed people (or people who can claim to be oppressed) are in some way better than others, that there is some decency, purity or goodness which comes from being part of such a group. In fact, suffering in and of itself does not make someone a better person. A gay, female, black or trans person may be as dishonest, deceitful and rude as anybody else.

There is a suggestion in the social justice movement that when intersectionality has done its job and the matrix of competing hierarchies has finally been nixed, then an era of universal brotherhood will ensue. But the most likely explanation of human motivations in the future is that people will broadly go on behaving as they have done throughout history, that they will continue exhibiting the same impulses, frailties, passions and envy that have propelled our species up till now. For example, there is no reason to assume that if all social injustices were ironed out and every employer finally had the correct diversity of people in their companies (as broken down by gender, sexual orientation and race) that all the Chief People Officers would stand down from their roles. It seems at least possible that six-figure salaries will be as hard to come by on that happy day as they are now and that those who have managed to get them by presenting a hostile interpretation of society will not volunteer up their own salaries even if their work is done. More likely is that a salaried class know that this puzzle is unsolvable and that they have got themselves jobs for life. They will remain in those roles for as long as they can until such a time as it is recognized that their solution to society's ills offers no solution at all, but only an invitation to madness on a vast and costly scale both to the individual and to society as a whole.

CAN WE INCLINE TOWARDS GENEROSITY?

When explaining the use of 'KillAllMen' and 'white people' in a derogatory way, Ezra Klein said that when reading such words he felt 'inclined . . . towards generosity'. Hence he felt able to interpret 'KillAllMen' as meaning 'it would be nice if the world sucked less for women' and interpreted the use of 'CancelWhitePeople' as a criticism of 'the dominant power structure and culture'.[37] Why did he feel inclined towards generosity in such cases? It would seem – as we saw in the issue of 'the speaker not the speech' – that highly politicized people are willing to interpret even extreme remarks from their own political tribe in a generous and forgiving light while reading the remarks of those in any opposing camp in as negative and hostile a light as possible.

Can the spirit of generosity be extended any more widely? If people were able to feel some generosity in interpreting the remarks of others, even of those on an opposing side, then some lessening of the trench-digging might be possible. The problem is that social media does not encourage this. It encourages the precise opposite. Not being able to meet, and not having any need to meet, makes people double-down on positions (and attitudes) and ramp up their outrage. When someone is face to face with another person it is far harder to reduce them to one thing that they have said, or strip them of all characteristics except one.

On his travels in America in the 1830s, Alexis de Tocqueville noticed the significance of assembly in the United States – specifically that face-to-face meetings of the citizenry allowed them to remedy problems often before any other authority was needed. In *Democracy in America* he attributes a great power to this ability to assemble and observes that face-to-face contestation is not only the best way to get to a solution but that in such interactions 'opinions are deployed with the force and heat that written thought can never attain'.[38] Although everything in the development of the new media is pulling people away from face-to-face encounters, it remains the best available forum in which to build confidence in others. To incline towards generosity you have to have a baseline presumption that your generosity will not be abused, and the best if not the only way to work that out is by personal interaction. Without it life will increasingly resemble a catalogue of easily searchable and eminently revivable historic grudges. So an inclination towards generosity not just among allies, but towards ostensible opponents, may be one of the first steps out of the madness. I do not especially like (Dr) Michael Davidson's ideas about being gay, but if I decided that he and his 'Voices of the Silenced' should be viewed only in the most negative possible light then I would not merely have no need to listen to him. I would not want to live in the same society as him. Yet we do live in the same society, and we have to find some way to get along together. It is the only option we have because otherwise, if we have come to the conclusion that talking and listening respectfully are futile, the only tool left for us is violence.

RECOGNIZE WHERE WE MAY BE GOING

In 1967, just a year before his death, Martin Luther King Jr gave one of his greatest speeches in Atlanta, Georgia. Entitled 'Where do we go from here?' it included a remarkable plea. 'Let us be dissatisfied until that day when nobody will shout, "White Power!", when nobody will shout, "Black Power!", but everybody will talk about God's power and human power.'[39] Among the many depressing aspects of recent years, perhaps the most troubling is the ease with which race has returned as an issue – bandied about by people who either cannot possibly realize the danger of the game they are playing or who do know precisely what they are playing at, which is unforgivable. Some of the inevitable end-points have already emerged and should have presented the clearest possible warning signals.

For instance, who would have expected even a generation ago that it would be acceptable for a liberal magazine to pose the question, 'Are Jews white?' This wasn't *National Geographic* a century ago, but *The Atlantic* magazine in 2016.[40] The question arose because of the dispute over where Jews might come in the oppression hierarchy that is being assembled. Should Jews be regarded as being high up in the oppression stakes, or can they be seen as benefiting from some privileges of their own? Do they benefit from white privilege or not? Once such questions start to get asked is it surprising that some people will come up with ugly answers? At the University of Illinois in Urbana some leaflets turned up on campus in 2017 which offered their own answer. They presented a hierarchical pyramid, at the bottom of which were the '99 per cent' who were oppressed by the alleged top 1 per cent. But the leaflets asked whether the top 1 per cent oppressing everyone else were 'straight white men' or 'is the 1 per cent Jewish?' The authors seemed to know the answer, arguing that Jews were the primary holders of 'privilege', concluding that 'Ending white privilege starts with ending Jewish privilege.'[41] Are those who engage in endless assertions about 'privilege' absolutely sure that their movement and analysis will not stampede in directions like this? Are they certain that after not just releasing resentment but encouraging it, such a basic human sentiment will not run free? What are their crash barriers to prevent this? And if they haven't got any such plans, perhaps we could return to Martin Luther King's vision. Perhaps we could aim to take race out of every and any debate and discussion and turn our increasing colour obsession back into an aspiration for colour-blindness.

DEPOLITICIZE OUR LIVES

The aim of identity politics would appear to be to politicize absolutely everything. To turn every aspect of human interaction into a matter of politics. To interpret every action and relationship in our lives along lines which are alleged to have been carved out by political actions. The calls to spend our time working out our own place and the places of others in the oppression hierarchy are invitations not just to an era of navel-gazing, but to turn every human relationship into a political power calibration. The new metaphysics includes a call to find meaning in this game: to struggle, and fight and campaign and 'ally' ourselves with people in order to reach the promised land. In an era without purpose, and in a universe without clear meaning, this call to politicize everything and then fight for it has an undoubted attraction. It fills life with meaning, of a kind.

But of all the ways in which people can find meaning in their lives, politics – let alone politics on such a scale – is one of the unhappiest. Politics may be an important aspect of our lives, but as a source of personal meaning it is disastrous. Not just because the ambitions it strives after nearly always go unachieved, but because finding purpose in politics laces politics with a passion – including a rage – that perverts the whole enterprise. If two people are in disagreement about something important, they may disagree as amicably as they like if it is just a matter of getting to the truth or the most amenable option. But if one party finds their whole purpose in life to reside in some aspect of that disagreement, then the chances of amicability fade vast and the likelihood of reaching any truth recedes.

One of the ways to distance ourselves from the madnesses of our times is to retain an interest in politics but not to rely on it as a source of meaning. The call should be for people to simplify their lives and not to mislead themselves by devoting their lives to a theory that answers no questions, makes no predictions and is easily falsifiable. Meaning can be found in all sorts of places. For most individuals it is found in the love of the people and places around them: in friends, family and loved ones, in culture, place and wonder. A sense of purpose is found in working out what is meaningful in our lives and then orientating ourselves over time as closely as possible to those centres of meaning. Using ourselves up on identity politics, social justice (in this manifestation) and inter-sectionality is a waste of a life.

We may certainly aim to live in a society in which nobody should be held back from what they can do because of some personal characteristic allotted to them by chance. If somebody has the competency to do something, and the desire to do something, then nothing about their race, sex or sexual orientation should hold them back. But minimizing difference is not the same as pretending difference does not exist. To assume that sex, sexuality and skin colour mean nothing would be ridiculous. But to assume that they mean everything will be fatal.

ACKNOWLEDGEMENTS

This is my second book with Bloomsbury, and once again it has been an enormous pleasure to work with everybody there. I have particularly benefited from the support, advice and editorial guidance of Robin Baird-Smith, and also from Jamie Birkett among others in the London office. I would particularly like to thank my agent, Matthew Hamilton of The Hamilton Agency.

The title of this book comes from a work by the Scottish journalist Charles Mackay, *Extraordinary Popular Delusions and the Madness of Crowds*. I hope he would have allowed the theft, given the disappointing prevalence of the phenomenon he described 180 years ago.

Several books back I learned to be wary of acknowledging any, let alone all, of the people who had any input into my work. Not because I am not grateful to them, but because I am reluctant to compile a list of people who might subsequently be accused of being guilty parties. That is especially the case with this book. Nevertheless, I have been enormously grateful for the vast number of conversations I have had with people across four continents during the research and writing of this book. And I would like to thank very sincerely all of my wonderful family and friends.

Yet there is one person I will name, because as well as appearing several times in this book, a number of the ideas featured have been best honed by their testing on his extraordinary mind. Of all the people from whom I have benefited when discussing these subjects, no one has opened my mind more often than Eric Weinstein. I am happy to credit any of my better ideas and observations to him, while insisting that any of the worst are original.

Douglas Murray
July 2019

NOTES

INTRODUCTION

1 See Jean-Francois Lyotard (trans. Geoff Bennington and Brian Massumi), *The Postmodern Condition: A Report on Knowledge*, Manchester University Press, 1984, pp. xxiv and 37.

2 Jaron Lanier, *Ten Arguments for Deleting your Social Media Accounts Right Now*, Henry Holt, 2018, p. 26.

3 Coleman Hughes in conversation with Dave Rubin, The Rubin Report, YouTube, 12 October 2018.

4 'Hunger strikers died for gay rights, claims Sinn Fein senator Fintan Warfield', *Belfast Telegraph*, 15 August 2016.

5 See chart at https://twitter.com/EricRWeinstein/status/1066934424804057088

6 See Greg Lukianoff and Jonathan Haidt, *The Coddling of the American Mind: How Good Intentions and Bad Ideas are Setting up a Generation for Failure*, Allen Lane, 2018, pp. 5–7ff.

7 APA Guidelines for psychological practice with men and boys, August 2018: https://www.apa.org/about/policy/boys-men-practice-guidelines.pdf

8 See 'Views of racism as a major problem increase sharply, especially among Democrats', Samantha Neal, Pew Research Center, 29 August 2017.

9 Ekow N. Yankah, *The New York Times*, 11 November 2017.

10 Helen Pidd, 'Women shun cycling because of safety, not helmet hair', *The Guardian*, 13 June 2018.

11 Tim Hunt interview by Robin McKie, 'I've been hung out to dry', *The Observer*, 13 June 2015. What got him into trouble were these words: 'Let me tell you about my trouble with girls. Three things happen when they are in the lab. You fall in love with them, they fall in love with you, and when you criticise them, they cry.'

12 See the exchange between Senator Katy Gallagher and Senator Mitch Fifield in the Australian Senate on 11 February 2016.

13 See for instance this thread: https://twitter.com/HarryTheOwl/status/1088144870991114241

14 CNN interview with Rep Debbie Dingell, 17 November 2017.

15 Kenneth Minogue, *The Liberal Mind*, Liberty Fund, Indianapolis edn, 2000, p. 1.

CHAPTER 1: GAY

1 *Good Morning Britain*, ITV, 5 September 2017.
2 John Stuart Mill, *On Liberty*, Penguin, 2006, pp. 60–1.
3 'Nicky Morgan says homophobia may be sign of extremism', BBC News, 30 June 2015.
4 Robert Samuels, *Washington Post*, 29 August 2016.
5 'Desert Island Discs: Tom Daley felt "inferior" over sexuality', BBC News website, 30 September 2018.
6 'Made in Chelsea's Ollie Locke to become Ollie Locke-Locke', BBC News website, 1 October 2018.
7 *The New York Times* (International Edition), 16 October 2017, pp. 15–17.
8 See for instance Russell T. Davies, 'A Rose by any other name', *The Observer*, 2 September 2001.
9 See 'Generation Z – beyond binary: new insights into the next generation', Ipsos Mori, 6 July 2018.
10 These are: B. S. Mustanski, M. G. Dupree, C. M. Nievergelt et al., 'A genome-wide scan of male sexual orientation', *Human Genetics*, 116 (2005), pp. 272–8; R. Blanchard, J. M. Cantor, A. F. Bogaert et al., 'Interaction of fraternal birth order and handedness in the development of male homosexuality', *Hormones and Behavior*, 49 (2006), pp. 405–14; J. M. Bailey, M. P. Dunne and N. G. Martin, 'Genetic and environmental influences on sexual orientation and its correlates in an Australian twin sample', *Journal of Personality and Social Psychology*, 78 (2000), pp. 524–36.
11 Royal College of Psychiatrists' statement on sexual orientation, Position Statement PS02/2014, April 2014 (https://www.rcpsych.ac.uk/pdf/PS02_2014.pdf).
12 Ibid.
13 Website of the American Psychological Association, 'Sexual Orientation & Homosexuality' (http://www.apa.org/topics/lgbt/orientation.aspx) accessed August 2018.
14 Bruce Bawer, *A Place at the Table: The Gay Individual in American Society*, Touchstone, 1994, p. 82.
15 Seth Stephens-Davidowitz, *Everybody Lies: What the Internet Can Tell Us About Who We Really Are*, Bloomsbury, 2017, pp. 112–16.

16 'This is why straight men watch porn', *Pink News*, 19 March 2018.

17 'Majority in U.S. Now Say Gays and Lesbians Born, Not Made', *Gallup*, 20 May 2015.

18 See the discussion of this episode in Alice Dreger, *Galileo's Middle Finger: Heretics, Activists, and One Scholar's Search for Justice*, Penguin, 2016, pp. 182–3.

19 'Attitudes towards homosexuals and evolutionary theory', in *Ethology and Sociobiology*. There is a useful summary of the Gallup–Archer exchange by Jesse Bering in *Scientific American*, 9 March 2011.

20 Aristotle, *Nicomachean Ethics*, Book 7, chs 5–6. Incidentally among recent translations, the Cambridge University Press edition (2014) goes with 'sodomy' while the Oxford University Press edition (2009) goes with 'paederasty'.

21 See for instance 'What are the most cited publications in the social sciences (according to Google Scholar)?', Elliott Green, LSE blogs, 12 May 2016.

22 Michael Foucault, *The History of Sexuality, Volume 1 – The Will to Knowledge*, trans. Robert Hurley, Penguin, 1998, p. 43.

23 David Halperin, 'Historicising the sexual body: sexual preferences and erotic identities in the pseudo-Lucianic *Erotes*', in Domna C. Stanton (ed.), *Discourses of Sexuality: From Aristotle to AIDS*, University of Michigan Press, 1992, p. 261. See also Andrew Sullivan, *Virtually Normal: An Argument about Homosexuality*, Picador, 1996.

24 Foucault, *The History of Sexuality*, p. 156.

25 Hunter Madsen and Marshall Kirk, *After the Ball: How America Will Conquer its Fear and Hatred of Gays in the '90s*, Doubleday, 1989.

26 See Paul Berman, *A Tale of Two Utopias: The Political Journey of the Generation of 1968*, W. W. Norton & Company Ltd, 1996, pp. 154–5.

27 Bawer, *A Place at the Table*, p. 191.

28 Ibid., p. 193.

29 Ibid., pp. 220–1.

30 Andrew Sullivan, *Virtually Normal: An Argument about Homosexuality*, Picador, 1996, p. 204.

31 Berman, *A Tale of Two Utopias*, pp. 160–1.

32 @TheEllenShow, Twitter, 25 October 2017, 5.53 p.m.

33 *Daily Telegraph*, 14 February 2018.

34 Stop Funding Hate, Twitter, 16 February 2018.

35 'Children of same-sex couples happier and healthier than peers, research shows', *Washington Post*, 7 July 2014.

36 *Sunday Morning Live*, BBC1, 27 October 2010.

37 'Study identifies predictors of relationship dissolution among same-sex and heterosexual couples', The Williams Institute, UCLA School of Law, 1 March 2018.

38 *Pink News*, 25 March 2018.

39 Bawer, *A Place at the Table*, p. 188.

40 'Sir Ian McKellen: Brexit makes no sense if you're gay', *Daily Telegraph*, 10 June 2016.

41 Jim Downs, 'Peter Thiel shows us there's a difference between gay sex and gay', *Advocate*, 14 October 2016.

42 'Bret Easton Ellis goes on Twitter rampage after GLAAD media awards ban', *Entertainment Weekly*, 22 April 2013.

43 'How straight people should behave in gay bars', *Pink News*, 30 November 2018.

44 'In the reign of the magical gay elves', Bret Easton Ellis, *Out*, 13 May 2013.

45 Ovid, *Metamorphoses*, trans A D Melville, Oxford University Press, 1998, pp. 60–1.

46 Daniel Mendelsohn, *The Elusive Embrace: Desire and the Riddle of Identity*, Alfred A. Knopf, 1999, pp. 73–5.

INTERLUDE: THE MARXIST FOUNDATIONS

1 'The social and political views of American professors', a working paper by Neil Gross (Harvard) and Solon Simmons (George Mason), 24 September 2007.

2 See https://www.racialequitytools.org/resourcefiles/mcintosh.pdf

3 Ernesto Laclau and Chantal Mouffe, 'Socialist strategy: Where next?', *Marxism Today*, January 1981.

4 Ernesto Laclau and Chantal Mouffe, *Hegemony and Socialist Strategy* (second edition), Verso, 2001, p. 133.

5 Ibid., p. 141.

6 Ibid.

7 Ibid., pp. 159–60.

8 Laclau and Mouffe, 'Socialist strategy: Where next?'

9 Laclau and Mouffe, *Hegemony and Socialist Strategy*, p. 1.

10 'What happens to #MeToo when a feminist is the accused?', *The New York Times*, 13 August 2018.

11 Steven Pinker, *The Blank Slate: The Modern Denial of Human Nature*, Penguin, 2003, p. x.

12 Judith Butler, 'Further reflections on conversations of our time', *Diacritics*, vol. 27, no. 1, Spring 1997.

13 Consider, for instance, Sheldon Lee Glashow, 'The standard mode', *Inference: International Review of Science*, vol. 4, no. 1, Spring 2018.

14 https://www.skeptic.com/reading_room/conceptual-penis-social-contruct-sokal-style-hoax-on-gender-studies

15 'Hoaxers slip breastaurants and dog-park sex into journals', *The New York Times*, 4 October 2018.

16 'American Psychological Association guidelines for psychological practice with boys and men', APA, August 2018, p. 10.

CHAPTER 2: WOMEN

1 Steven Pinker, *The Blank Slate: The Modern Denial of Human Nature*, Penguin, 2003, pp. 346–50.

2 Ibid., p. 350.

3 AccessOnline.com video, 'Rosario Dawson talks grabbing Paul Rudd's "package" onstage at the 2011 Independent Spirit Awards', 27 February 2011.

4 *The Late Show* with Stephen Colbert, CBS, 20 March 2018.

5 *Huffington Post*, 11 May 2007.

6 RSA Conference, 28 February 2014.

7 Mayim Bialik, 'Being a feminist in Harvey Weinstein's world', *The New York Times*, 13 October 2017.

8 *The Late Late Show* with James Corden, CBS, 8 February 2016.

9 See 'Loud and proud! Brand releases sets of $9.99 plastic stick-on NIPPLES that are sold in two sizes – "cold" and "freezing"', *Mail Online* (*FeMail*), 4 April 2017.

10 'The hottest new trend is camel toe underwear and we're all over it', *Metro*, 24 February 2017.

11 *VICE News* interview with Dr Jordan Peterson, 7 February 2018.

12 Christine Lagarde, 'Ten years after Lehman – lessons learned and challenges ahead', IMF blog, 5 September 2018.

13 BBC *Question Time*, 19 March 2009.

14 'When women thrive' report, Mercer, October 2016.

15 'Wall Street rule for the MeToo era: avoid women at all costs', *Bloomberg*, 3 December 2018.

16 United States Office of Personnel Management, 'Government-wide Inclusive Diversity Strategic Plan', July 2016.

17 See https://implicit.harvard.edu/implicit.

18 See 'Can we really measure implicit bias? Maybe not', *Chronicle of Higher Education*, 5 January 2017; 'Unconscious bias: what is it and can it be eliminated?', *The Guardian*, 2 December 2018.

19 See, for instance, Odette Chalaby, 'Your company's plan to close the gender pay gap probably won't work', *Apolitical*, 22 May 2018.

20 'Smaller firms should publish gender pay gap, say MPs', *BBC News*, 2 August 2018.

21 Susan Faludi, *Backlash: The Undeclared War Against Women*, Vintage, 1992, pp. 16–17.

22 Marilyn French, *The War Against Women*, Hamish Hamilton, 1992, pp. 1–2.

23 Ibid., pp. 5–6.

24 Ibid., p. 7.

25 Ibid., p. 9.

26 Ibid., p. 14.

27 Ibid., pp. 121–55.

28 Ibid., pp. 159 ff.

29 Ibid., pp. 210–11. Incidentally the 'women as the embodiment of peace' theme has a significant lineage. See for instance Olive Schreiner's *Woman and Labour* (1911).

30 See, for instance, Christina Hoff Sommers, *Who Stole Feminism? How Women Have Betrayed Women*, Simon & Schuster, 1995, pp. 11–12.

31 Laurie Penny (@PennyRed) on Twitter, 6 February 2018: https://twitter.com/PennyRed/status/960777342275768320

32 Sama El-Wardany, 'What women mean when we say "men are trash"', *Huffington Post*, 2 May 2018.

33 Ezra Klein, 'The problem with Twitter, as shown by the Sarah Jeong fracas', *Vox*, 8 August 2018.

34 Georgia Aspinall, 'Here are the countries where it's still really difficult for women to vote', *Grazia*, 6 February 2018.

35 *GQ* magazine foreword by Dylan Jones, December 2018.

36 'APA issues first ever guidelines for practice with men and boys', American Psychological Association, January 2019.

37 'We are a nation of hidden feminists', Fawcett Society press release, 15 January 2016.

38 'Only 7 per cent of Britons consider themselves feminists' *The Telegraph*, 15 January 2016.

39 YouGov/*Huffington Post*, Omnibus Poll, conducted 11–12 April 2013.

40 'Men with muscles and money are more attractive to straight women and gay men – showing gender roles aren't progressing', *Newsweek*, 20 November 2017.

INTERLUDE: THE IMPACT OF TECH

1 James Thurber, *My Life and Hard Times* (1933), reprinted Prion Books Ltd, 2000, pp. 33–44.

2 See the case of the Covington Catholic High School boys in January 2019.

3 Jon Ronson, *So You've Been Publicly Shamed*, Riverhead Books, 2015.

4 Barrett Wilson (pseudonym), 'I was the mob until the mob came for me', *Quillette*, 14 July 2018.

5 Tess Townsend, 'Google is still mostly white and male', *Recode*, 29 June 2017.

6 Private account of discussions involving a major tech company in Brussels, 5 February 2019.

7 See 'Twitter "bans women against trans ideology", say feminists', BBC News, 30 May 2018.

8 Meghan Murphy, 'Twitter's trans-activist decree', *Quillette*, 28 November 2018.

9 'Twitter has banned misgendering or "deadnaming" transgender people', *The Verge*, 27 November 2018.

10 Jack Conte interviewed by Dave Rubin on 'The Rubin Report', YouTube, 31 July 2017.

11 Google video at https://developers.google.com/machine-learning/fairness-overview.

CHAPTER 3: RACE

1 Anne Helen Petersen, 'Ten long years of trying to make Armie Hammer happen', *Buzzfeed*, 26 November 2017.

2 '*Call Me By Your Name* star Armie Hammer leaves Twitter after "bitter" *Buzzfeed* article', *Pink News*, 28 November 2017.

3 Ashley Lee, 'Why Luca Guadagnino didn't include gay actors or explicit sex scenes in "Call Me By Your Name" (Q&A)', *The Hollywood Reporter*, 8 February 2017.

4 '"White privilege" lessons for lecturers', *The Sunday Times*, 11 March 2018.

5 See footage on YouTube at https://www.youtube.com/watch?v=LTnDpo QLNaY.

6 See 'Campus argument goes viral as Evergreen State is caught in racial turmoil', *Vice News*, 16 June 2017; https://www.youtube.com/watch?v= 2cMYfxOFBBM

7   See footage on YouTube at https://www.youtube.com/watch?v=BzrPMet GtJQ

8   See footage on YouTube at https://www.youtube.com/watch?v=RZtu DqbfO5w

9   See footage on YouTube at https://www.youtube.com/watch?v=Pf5fAi XYro8&t=1941s

10 Evergreen State College, Board of Trustees meeting, 12 July 2017, on YouTube at https://www.youtube.com/watch?v=yL54iN8dxuo

11 *Vice News*, 16 June 2017.

12 See full video at YouTube https://www.youtube.com/watch?v=hiMVx2 C5_Wg

13 See video on YouTube at https://www.youtube.com/watch?v=V6ZVEVufWFI

14 Nicholas A. Christakis, 'Teaching inclusion in a divided world', *The New York Times*, 22 June 2016.

15 'Identity politics: the new radicalism on campus?', panel at Rutgers University, published on YouTube, 13 October 2017; https://www.youtube. com/watch?v=2ijFQFiCgoE

16 Michael Harriot, '"Diversity of thought" is just a euphemism for "white supremacy"', *The Root*, 12 April 2018.

17 The letter of 17 April 2017 can be viewed here: http://archive.is/Dm2DN

18 Andrew Sullivan, 'We all live on campus now', *New York* magazine, 9 February 2018.

19 *National Geographic*, April 2018.

20 David Olusoga, 'National Geographic's righting of its racist wrongs is well meant but slow in coming', *The Guardian*, 1 April 2018.

21 Emily Lakdawalla, Twitter, 13 February 2018.

22 *The Root*, Twitter feed, 22 November 2018.

23 *Vice*, Twitter, 6 December 2018.

24 Mathieu Murphy-Perron, 'Let Nora Loreto have her say', *National Observer*, 11 April 2018.

25 *Vice* review of *Dumbo*, 13 June 2018. Incidentally the online version of this was changed after wide online ridicule.

26 Eliana Dockterman, 'Altered Carbon takes place in the future. But it's far from progressive', *Time*, 2 February 2018.

27 'Sierra Boggess pulls out of BBC West Side Story Prom over "whitewashing"', BBC News website, 25 April 2018.

28 Ritu Prasad, 'Serena Williams and the trope of the "angry black woman"', *BBC News* online, 11 September 2018.

29 Carys Afoko, 'Serena Williams's treatment shows how hard it is to be a black woman at work', *The Guardian*, 10 September 2018.

30   The video (one of a series) is available on YouTube, produced by Soyheat (posted 23 September 2016).

31   See Andy Ngo, 'Would you like some strife with your meal?', *Wall Street Journal*, 31 May 2018.

32   Robby Soave, 'White-owned restaurants shamed for serving ethnic food: it's cultural appropriation', *Reason*, 23 May 2017.

33   Dawn Butler Twitter, 18 August 2018.

34   'Teenager's prom dress sparks cultural appropriation debate', *Independent*, 30 April 2018.

35   Lovia Gyarke, 'Lionel Shriver shouldn't write about minorities', *New Republic* blog, September 2016.

36   Yassmin Abdel-Magied, 'As Lionel Shriver made light of identity, I had no choice but to walk out', *The Guardian*, 10 September 2016.

37   *The Atlantic*, 7 May 2018.

38   The original article is captured online here: http://eprints.lse.ac.uk/44655/1/__Libfile_repository_Content_LSE%20Review%20of%20Books_May%202012_week%204_blogs.lse.ac.uk-Intellectuals_versus_society_ignorance_and_wisdom.pdf

39   Aidan Byrne, 'Book Review: Intellectuals and Society by Thomas Sowell', LSE Review of Books, 26 May 2012.

40   *The View*, ABC, 15 June 2015.

41   MSNBC, 17 June 2015.

42   'Benedict Cumberbatch apologises after calling black actors "coloured"', *The Guardian*, 26 January 2015.

43   Sarah Jeong tweets from 23 December 2014; 25 November 2015; 31 December 2014; 18 November 2014; 1 April 2014.

44   Sarah Jeong tweets from 28 November 2014.

45   Sarah Jeong tweet from 24 July 2014.

46   Statement from *The New York Times*, 2 August 2018.

47   Quoted in Zack Beauchamp, 'In defence of Sarah Jeong', *Vox*, 3 August 2018.

48   Ezra Klein, 'The problem with Twitter, as shown by the Sarah Jeong fracas', *Vox*, 8 August 2018.

49   Ta-Nehisi Coates, *The Beautiful Struggle: A Memoir*, Spiegel & Grau, 2008, p. 6.

50   Ibid., p. 70.

51   Ibid., pp. 74–5.

52   Ibid., p. 168.

53   Ibid., p. 177.

54   Ta-Nehisi Coates, *Between the World and Me*, The Text Publishing Company, 2015, pp. 86–7.

55 Dr Cornel West on Facebook, captured at https://www.alternet.org/2017/12/cornel-west-ta-nehisi-coates-spat-last-thing-we-need-right-now/

56 For some chapter and verse examples of this see Kyle Smith, 'The hard untruths of Ta-Nehisi Coates, *Commentary*, October 2015.

57 'Leak: The Atlantic had a meeting about Kevin Williamson. It was a liberal self-reckoning', *Huffington Post*, 5 July 2018.

58 Reni Eddo-Lodge, *Why I'm no Longer Talking to White People about Race*, Bloomsbury, 2017, pp. 14–15.

59 Photo via Martin Daubney on Twitter, 21 January 2018.

60 This piece was later retitled 'How white women use strategic tears to silence women of colour', 7 May 2018.

61 See *The Tab*, n.d. 2016.

62 See 'Asian Americans suing Harvard say admissions files show discrimination', *The New York Times*, 4 April 2018.

63 See Malcolm W. Browne, 'What is intelligence, and who has it', *The New York Times*, 16 October 1994.

64 Steven J. Rosenthal review of *The Bell Curve* at https://msuweb.montclair.edu/~furrg/steverbc.html

65 Douglas Murray in conversation with Jordan Peterson, *UnHerd*, YouTube, 4 September 2018.

66 David Reich, 'How genetics is changing our understanding of race', *The New York Times*, 23 March 2018.

67 Pete Shanks, 'Race and IQ yet again', Center for Genetics and Society, 13 April 2018.

68 Sam Harris, 'Waking up' podcast, with Charles Murray, 23 April 2017.

69 Ezra Klein, 'Sam Harris, Charles Murray and the allure of race science', *Vox*, 27 March 2018.

70 Diana Soriano, 'White privilege lecture tells students white people are "dangerous" if they don't see race', *The College Fix*, 6 March 2019.

INTERLUDE: ON FORGIVENESS

1 Quinn Norton on Twitter, 27 July 2013.

2 Ibid., 4 September 2009.

3 Quinn Norton, 'The New York Times fired my Doppelganger', *The Atlantic*, 27 February 2018.

4 'Labour, Work, Action', in *The Portable Hannah Arendt*, Penguin, 2000, pp. 180–1.

5 W. H. Auden. 'In Memory of W. B. Yeats', in *The English Auden: Poems, Essays and Dramatic Writings 1927–1939*, ed. Edward Mendelson, Faber, 1986, pp. 242–3.

6 'Manchester University students paint over Rudyard Kipling mural', *The Guardian*, 19 July 2018.

7 See 'Toby Young quotes on breasts, eugenics, and working-class people', *The Guardian*, 3 January 2018.

8 Toby Young, 'Confessions of a porn addict', *The Spectator*, 10 November 2001.

9 *The Times*, 6 January 2018.

10 *The Evening Standard*, 5 January 2018.

11 See Toby Young, 'The public humiliation diet', *Quillette*, 23 July 2018.

12 'Conor Daly loses Lilly Diabetes sponsorship over remark his father made over 30 years ago', Associated Press, 25 August 2018.

13 Matthew 18:21–2.

14 'Lewis Hamilton apologises for "boys don't wear dresses" remark', BBC News, 26 December 2017.

15 *GQ*, August 2018.

CHAPTER 4: TRANS

1 'Moeder van Nathan spreekt: "Zijn dood doet me niks"', *Het Laatste Nieuws*, 2 October 2013.

2 'Mother of sex change Belgian: "I don't care about his euthanasia death"', *Daily Telegraph*, 2 October 2013.

3 For instance, see *The Sunday Times*, 25 November 2018, p. 23.

4 In relation to the public consultation on the Gender Recognition Act (2018).

5 See 'Schools tell pupils boys can have periods too in new guidelines on transgender issues', *Daily Mirror*, 18 December 2018.

6 https://www.congress.gov/bill/115th-congress/senate-bill/1006

7 Alice Dreger, *Galileo's Middle Finger: Heretics, Activists, and One Scholar's Search for Justice*, Penguin, 2016, p. 21.

8 Ibid., p. 20.

9 Ibid., p. 6.

10 'Masculine Women, Feminine Men', lyrics by Edgar Leslie, music by James V. Monaco, 1926./

11 Jan Morris, *Conundrum*, Faber and Faber, 2002, p. 1.

12 Ibid., p. 42.

13 Ibid., p. 119.

14 Ibid., p. 122.

15 Ibid., p. 123.

16 Ibid., p. 127.

17 Ibid., p. 134.

18 Ibid., p. 138.

19 Ibid., p. 128.

20 Ibid., p. 143.

21 Dreger, *Galileo's Middle Finger*, p. 63.

22 'Criticism of a gender theory, and a scientist under siege', *The New York Times*, 21 August 2007.

23 Dreger, *Galileo's Middle Finger*, p. 69.

24 Andrea Long Chu, 'My new vagina won't make me happy', *The New York Times*, 24 November 2018.

25 See Anne A. Lawrence, *Men Trapped in Men's Bodies: Narratives of Autogynephilic Transsexualism*, Springer, 2013.

26 *Time* magazine cover, 9 June 2014.

27 'Stonewall to start campaigning for trans equality', *The Guardian*, 16 February 2015.

28 *New York Post*, 16 July 2015.

29 'When women become men at Wellesley', *The New York Times*, 15 October 2014.

30 Julie Bindel, 'Gender benders, beware', *The Guardian*, 31 January 2004.

31 Suzanne Moore, 'Seeing red: the power of female anger', *The New Statesman*, 8 January 2013.

32 See Suzanne Moore, 'I don't care if you were born a woman or became one', *The Guardian*, 9 January 2013.

33 Julie Burchill, 'The lost joy of swearing', *The Spectator*, 3 November 2018.

34 Germaine Greer, *The Whole Woman*, Doubleday, 1999, p. 66.

35 Ibid., p. 74.

36 'Germaine Greer defends views on transgender issues amid calls for cancellation of feminism lecture', ABC News, 25 October 2015.

37 Ibid.

38 Eve Hodgson, 'Germaine Greer can no longer be called a feminist', *Varsity*, 26 October 2017.

39 'Woman billboard removed after transphobia row', BBC News website, 26 September 2018.

40 Debate between Kellie-Jay Keen-Minshull and Adrian Harrop, *Sky News*, 26 September 2018.

41 'Blogger accused of transphobia for erecting a billboard defining "woman" as "adult human female" is branded "disgraceful" by This Morning viewers – as she insists trans women do not fit the criteria', *Mail Online*, 28 September 2018.

42 Julie Bindel, 'Why woke keyboard warriors should respect their elders', *UnHerd*, 24 October 2018.

43 See 'April Ashley at 80', Homotopia festival. On YouTube at https://www. youtube.com/watch?v=wX-NhWb47sc

44 See video from 2 mins in here: https://vimeo.com/185149379

45 The case of 'Lactatia' Nemis Quinn Melancon Golden is described, among other places, in 'Nine-year-old drag queen horrifically abused after modelling for LBGT fashion company', *Pink News*, 9 January 2018.

46 'The school was already calling her "him"', *The Sunday Times*, 25 November 2018.

47 'Trans groups under fire for 700% rise in child referrals', *The Sunday Times*, 25 November 2018.

48 Ibid.

49 Michelle Forcier interview on NBC, 21 April 2015: https://www.nbcnews. com/nightly-news/video/one-doctor-explains-the-journey-for-kids-who-are-transitioning-431478851632?v=railb&

50 https://vimeo.com/185183788

51 May 2018.

52 Jesse Singal, 'When children say they're Trans', *The Atlantic*, July/August 2018.

53 Johanna Olson-Kennedy, MD, 'Mental health disparities among transgender youth: rethinking the role of professionals', *JAMA*, May 2016.

54 'Deciding when to treat a youth for gender re-assignment', Kids in the House (n.d.).

55 Singal, 'When children say they're Trans'.

56 Wylie C. Hembree, Peggy T. Cohen-Kettenis, Louis Gooren, Sabine E. Hannema, Walter J. Meyer, M. Hassan Murad, Stephen M. Rosenthal, Joshua D. Safer, Vin Tangpricha, Guy G. T'Sjoen, 'Endocrine treatment of gender-dysphoric/gender-incongruent persons: An Endocrine Society clinical practice guideline', *The Journal of Clinical Endocrinology & Metabolism*, vol. 102, no. 11, 1 November 2017.

57 Video at https://archive.org/details/olson-kennedy-breasts-go-and-get-them

58 For one such description see Susan Faludi, *In the Darkroom*, Metropolitan Books, 2016, p. 131.

59 See http://uspath2017.conferencespot.org/

60 Audio available here: https://vimeo.com/226658454

61 Many of the screen-grabs and other materials on this case can be found here: http://dirtywhiteboi67.blogspot.com/2015/08/ftm-top-surgery-for-sky-tragic-story-in.html

62 'GP convicted of running transgender clinic for children without licence', *The Telegraph*, 3 December 2018.

63 'Things not to say to a non-binary person', BBC Three, 27 June 2017.

CONCLUSION

1 Figures from the World Economic Forum, June 2018.

2 See 'Do trans kids stay trans when they grow up?', *Sexology Today* (www. sexologytoday.org), 11 January 2016.

3 *Advocate*, 16 November 2008.

4 Voddie Baucham, 'Gay is not the new black', The Gospel Coalition, 19 July 2012.

5 Open letter to *Hypatia*: https://archive.is/lUeR4#selection-131.725-131.731

6 'Philosopher's article on transracialism sparks controversy (Updated with response from author)', *Daily Nous*, 1 May 2017.

7 *The Real*, KPLR, 2 November 2015.

8 Patrick Strudwick, 'The newly appointed editor of *Gay Times* has been fired for posting dozens of offensive tweets', *Buzzfeed*, 16 November 2017.

9 '*Gay Times* fires "Jews are gross" editor who sent vile tweets', *Pink News*, 16 November 2017.

10 Statement from *Gay Times* on Twitter, 16 November 2017.

11 Josh Rivers interview with Lee Gray, 'The Gray Area', YouTube, 8 June 2018.

12 'Transgender women in sport: Are they really a 'threat' to female sport?', BBC Sport, 18 December 2018.

13 Stephie Haynes, 'Dr. Ramona Krutzik, M.D. discusses possible advantages Fallon Fox may have', *Bloody Elbow*, 20 March 2013.

14 Joe Rogan conversation with Maajid Nawaz and Sam Harris, *Joe Rogan Experience* 1107, YouTube, 18 April 2018.

15 'Business insider deletes opinion piece defending Scarlett Johansson's role as trans man in new film', *Pink News*, 9 July 2018.

16 'Trans activists call for boycott of film starring Matt Bomer as transgender sex worker', *Pink News*, 15 April 2018.

17 William A. Jacobson, 'Cornell Black Students group issues a 6-page list of demands', *Legal Insurrection* blog, 27 September 2017.

18 The BBC's *This Week*, 26 October 2017.

19 Laith Ashley interviewed on Channel 4 News, 13 April 2016.

20 'Vox writer navel-gazes his way into a hole over fat-shaming', *The Daily Caller*, 5 November 2018.

21 See for instance Marieka Klawitter, 'Meta-analysis of the effects of sexual orientation on earnings', 19 December 2014 (https://onlinelibrary.wiley. com/doi/abs/10.1111/irel.12075).

22 See United States Department of Labor, Bureau of Labor Statistics: https:// www.bls.gov/opub/ted/2017/median-weekly-earnings-767-for-women-937-for-men-in-third-quarter-2017.htm

23 Sky poll carried out on 14–16 February 2018. Results at: https://interactive. news.sky.com/100Women_Tabs_Feb2018.pdf

24 Camille Paglia, *Free Women, Free Men: Sex, Gender, Feminism*, Canongate, 2018, p. 133.

25 Ibid., pp. 131–2.

26 CNBC on Twitter, 24 January 2019.

27 'Here's how much you save when you don't have kids', CNBC, 17 August 2017.

28 *The Economist*, Twitter feed, 17 November 2018.

29 Wendell Berry, 'A Few Words for Motherhood' (1980), *The World-Ending Fire*, Penguin, 2018, pp. 174–5.

30 See Madeleine Kearns, 'The successful, dangerous child sex-change charity', *National Review* online, 23 January 2019.

31 House of Commons, Hansard, 21 November 2018.

32 See 'Transient sexual mimicry leads to fertilization', *Nature*, 20 January 2005.

33 Freddy Gray, 'Nigel Farage's groupies party in DC', *The Spectator*, 28 January 2017.

34 Jean-Jacques Rousseau, *Emile, or On Education*, trans. Allan Bloom, Basic Books, 1979, pp. 92–3.

35 L. H. Keeley, *War Before Civilisation: The Myth of the Peaceful Savage*, Oxford University Press, 1996, p. 90. See also the graph made out of this in Steven Pinker, *The Blank Slate: The Modern Denial of Human Nature*, Penguin, 2003, p. 57.

36 H. W. Brands, *Traitor to His Class: The Privileged Life and Radical Presidency of Franklin Delano Roosevelt*, Doubleday Books, 2008, p. 152.

37 Ezra Klein, 'The problem with Twitter, as shown by the Sarah Jeong fracas', *Vox*, 8 August 2018.

38 Alexis de Tocqueville, *Democracy in America*, trans. Harvey C. Mansfield and Delba Winthrop, University of Chicago Press, 2000, p. 181.

39 Martin Luther King Jr, 'Where do we go from here?', delivered at the 11th Annual SCLC Convention, Atlanta, Georgia, 16 August 1967.

40 Emma Green, 'Are Jews white?', *The Atlantic*, 5 December 2016.

41 'Anti-Semitic flyers attacking "Jewish privilege" appear to UIC', Campus Reform, 17 March 2017.

INDEX